America's Most Famous Catholic
(According to Himself)

CATHOLIC PRACTICE IN NORTH AMERICA

America's Most Famous Catholic (According to Himself)

STEPHEN COLBERT AND AMERICAN
RELIGION IN THE TWENTY-FIRST CENTURY

Stephanie N. Brehm

FORDHAM UNIVERSITY PRESS
New York 2019

Fordham University Press has no responsibility for the persistence or accuracy of URLs for external or third-party Internet websites referred to in this publication and does not guarantee that any content on such websites is, or will remain, accurate or appropriate.

Fordham University Press also publishes its books in a variety of electronic formats. Some content that appears in print may not be available in electronic books.

Visit us online at www.fordhampress.com.

Library of Congress Cataloging-in-Publication Data available online at https://catalog.loc.gov.

Printed in the United States of America

21 20 19   5 4 3 2 1

First edition

Contents

1. Colbert as Character   1

2. Colbert as Catholic Authority   23

3. Colbert as Catechist   48

4. Colbert as Catholic Comedian   76

5. Colbert Catholicism   99

6. Colbert as Culture Warrior   132

7. Colbert's Continued Presence   152

Appendix   165

Acknowledgments   173

Notes   175

Selected Bibliography   205

Index   219

America's Most Famous Catholic
(According to Himself)

1   Colbert as Character

Two hundred excited people fill the waiting area at the Colbert Report studio on November 18, 2014. Small bursts of laughter fill the crowded room as two large flat screens adorning the walls play segments from the Comedy Central program on repeat: a two-minute clip about Wheat Thins crackers, the Daft Punk band playing a set on the studio stage, The Colbert Report in Afghanistan and Iraq performing for U.S. troops. The walls are painted in red, white, and blue as the crowd gathers in anticipation around the entrance to the studio. The studio doors open, and the crowd rapidly moves to fill in available seats in the theater. A half-hour before the evening's taping, Stephen Colbert enters the room to raucous applause. Wearing a dark suit, the actor (not the character) addresses the audience: "Anyone have any questions for me?"

Just a few hours before, I had been standing in line, waiting with hundreds of others to enter the studio. I had interviewed other audience members, asking them where they were from, what they thought of Colbert, and personal questions about their religious and political identities. As I raise my hand eagerly in response to Colbert, those seated around me (whom I had recently interviewed) quickly interject. "Ask her," a few audience members exclaim while pointing at me. "She's researching you." Bemused, Colbert acknowledges my raised hand.

"Why did you choose for your character to be Catholic?" Colbert smiles at this question, an amused grin as though he had not encountered this question as part of his regular routine. How often do audience members reference his religious identity? I am not his usual fan.

Colbert gives a three-part response. First, he replies that when he started The Colbert Report, he was given some advice. "Johnny Carson told David Letterman who told Conan [O'Brien] who told me, doing a show this much, four days a week, is going to take everything you know. And I know a lot about being Catholic." A few gasps of recognition betray that the lineage of this advice impressed me and some of my fellow audience members. In the second *part of his response, Colbert emphasizes that he knew he could "play up the liberal/conservative" divide evident in American Catholicism. He could take on an exaggerated conservative persona to become "Captain Catholicism." As Colbert strikes a superhero pose, audience members chuckle. In the third part of his response, Colbert pauses and steps back, away from the audience. He stares off, almost in amazement of his situation, and laughs, "I mean, it's pretty neat. I get to interview priests. It's pretty fun."*

With its debut in 2005, *The Colbert Report* cast the actor Stephen Colbert as the boisterous satirical character STEPHEN COLBERT. Two personae, but one name and one body. To distinguish the two in text, I use Colbert for the actor and COLBERT in small caps for the character (while it seems like shouting, all caps is appropriate, as yelling is one of COLBERT's exaggerated traits). Both the actor and character are devout, vocal, and authoritative Catholics. Colbert's exaggeration of COLBERT's position and power led COLBERT to proclaim that he was "television's foremost Catholic."[1] His religion was so central to the show that religion blogs dubbed him "Colbert the Catechist." The Jesuit magazine *America* even went so far as to recommend that Catholic educators take notes on his entertaining and persuasive evangelizing style.[2] As *The Colbert Report* ended its series run in late 2014, *The National Catholic Reporter* named Stephen Colbert their "Runner-up to Person of the Year," second only to Pope Francis. For the editors and readers of the progressive *Reporter*, Stephen Colbert represents a powerful mouthpiece for their political, social, and religious perspectives. And yet, the question I am asked most often is, "Colbert's really a *practicing* Catholic? In real life?" That juxtaposition between Colbert's revered status as a celebrity Catholic and as a polemical satirist of institutions lies at the heart of this book.

America's Most Famous Catholic (According to Himself) investigates the ways in which Colbert challenges perceptions of Catholicism and Catholic mores through his comedy. Through his television program and digital media presence, Colbert is a twenty-first-century celebrity pundit who inhabits a realm of extreme political and social polarization. I examine how Catholicism shapes Colbert's life and world, and also how he and his persona influence Catholicism and American Catholic thought and practice. In addition, I analyze how Colbert and his character COLBERT nuance the polarized religious landscape, making space for Americans who currently define their religious lives through absence, ambivalence, and alternatives. COLBERT and Colbert reflect the complexity of contemporary American Catholicism as it is lived, both on- and off-screen.

Religion and the foibles of religious institutions have served as fodder for a number of comedians. In this, Colbert is not unique. What sets Colbert apart is that his critical observations are harder to ignore because he approaches religious material not from the predictable stance of the irreverent secular comedian but from his position as one of the faithful. He uses humor to engage in significant public criticism of religious institutions, policies, and doctrines. In the satirical tradition of Jonathan Swift and Mark Twain, COLBERT informs audiences on current events, politics, social issues, and religion while lampooning conservative political policy, biblical literalism, and religious hypocrisy. Stephen Colbert and his character dwell at the crossroads of religion and humor. This book is a case study of that intersection: humor as an arena for the expression of religious identities and relationships. Comedy becomes a site for critique and dialogue between lay religious practitioners and their larger institutional authoritative bodies. Religious worlds are not solely serious, and individuals, in particular comedians, negotiate their relationship to aspects of religion with humor.

This book is a digital media ethnography and rhetorical analysis of Stephen Colbert and his character STEPHEN COLBERT from 2005 to 2014. In this analysis of Stephen Colbert and *The Colbert Report*, I present a case study of one comedian and his comedic television program in order to delve more deeply into the historical contextualization of a specific form of religious identity, authority, and oratory: the satirical commentator. Colbert and COLBERT give voice to the multiplicity of lived Catholic experiences in America. The different personae provide insight into the mechanisms behind lived religion: the processes of meaning-making and identity creation.[3]

This work asks similar questions to those of other lived-religion research: How do individuals encounter, negotiate, and reconfigure their religious understanding, identities, and authority in relation to institutional hierarchies, official teachings, and scriptural texts, and how do people use those categories to create, construct, and curate their religious selves? Cultural context and historical milieu are essential to the study of lived religion and interpretations of comedy. Colbert performs his religious identity through his dual personae and embodies the ambiguous and complicated nature of Catholicism. Examining Colbert and COLBERT offers a rare window into the process of making religious worlds and constructing wildly divergent religious identities in response to the same religio-socio-political contexts. This book analyzes how Stephen Colbert and *The Colbert Report* present Catholic identity and contend with issues of authority in twenty-first-century America. I grapple with the intellectual problem of integrating media studies topics and methods with the lived-religion approach by exploring the religious identities and meaning-making processes of one humorous mass media phenomenon. Colbert's interpretation and commentary about religion are outside both the institution and the smaller communities: a window into American religions, in particular Catholicism, brought to you by comedic mass media.

Satirical Infotainment

Before diving into the larger themes of the book, a few words on this satirical television program. In 2005, Comedy Central created the *Daily Show* spin-off, *The Colbert Report*, with a pundit named STEPHEN COLBERT. *The Colbert Report* featured STEPHEN COLBERT as a "Republican superhero" and a caricatured version of conservative pundits specifically intended to parody Bill O'Reilly and *The O'Reilly Factor*.[4] Dressed impeccably in suits and ties, with his well-coiffed hair he gave the appearance of a news anchor. He called President George W. Bush his "hero" and considered them comrades in arms against the "fact-inista."[5] COLBERT informed audiences about current events regarding politics, social issues, and religion. Before guests went onstage at *The Colbert Report*, an out-of-character Colbert would tell them, "my character is an idiot. So, disabuse me of my ignorance."[6] The idiocy of COLBERT was one of his many exaggerated traits. He has been labeled as egomaniacal, megalomaniacal, intense, ultra-conservative, xenophobic, inaccurate, obtuse, and hyperbolic. Through this overdrawn personality, COLBERT entertained the American public.

The premiere episode of *The Colbert Report* drew 1.13 million viewers, 47 percent more than the average for that time slot in previous weeks. *The Colbert Report* ended on December 18, 2014, after nine years and 1,447 episodes. The final episode garnered 2.5 million live viewers—the highest viewership in the show's history. (It is unknown how many people recorded it or watched it later online.) Each episode aired twice a day on Comedy Central, and the show also captured significant viewership on various online and cable streaming platforms. Despite the official end of the show, *The Colbert Report* and Colbert continue to flourish in the world of social media. As of December 2018, @Stephenathome (Colbert's personal Twitter account) has 18.3 million followers. The show's website, ColbertNation.com, reported more than 3.3 million "likes" on Facebook in its last season.[7]

The Colbert Report and its star have made a significant impression on American popular culture. The series earned multiple Emmy Awards and Peabody Awards. Stephen Colbert was invited to perform at the White House Correspondents' Association Dinner in 2006. In 2010, he spoke before U.S. congressional committees and was awarded the first-ever "Golden Tweet Award" by Twitter for having the most re-tweeted tweet. Ben & Jerry's even honored the comedian with his own ice cream flavor, Americone Dream. *The Colbert Report* was more than a late-night cable show; it became a cultural phenomenon. Colbert's position as a major player in popular culture has only further solidified since he took the helm of *The Late Show* as the anointed successor to David Letterman, sans COLBERT.[8]

Colbert's on- and off-screen activities illustrate his infotaining style. "Infotainment" is a neologism that refers to the consolidation and genre-mixing of "information" and "entertainment" in mass media forms. Infotainment can present itself either in the type of news (celebrity, human interest) or in the presentation of news (sensationalism and ostentatious graphics). Arguably, this occurs primarily through television programming and began with the onset of cable channels and the Internet. Because individuals have so many channels and media platforms to choose from, the most entertaining are often the most successful at garnering high audience viewership numbers. News media increasingly "sell" and promote news headlines through entertaining means. At first, daytime television shows, like *The Oprah Winfrey Show*, and programs with overt political biases, like *Hannity & Colmes*, were the primary means of infotainment, but by the twenty-first century, comedy programs, such as Comedy Central's *The Daily Show* and *The Colbert Report*, were parodying those forms.

Media critics are split over the ethical and moral consequences of infotainment. Some media commentators critique infotainment for its lack of seriousness, charging that it places substantive journalism on the same level as sketch comedy. Others argue that with more entertaining presentation, more people will care about current events. Regardless of its moral value, infotainment, specifically in comedy programs, is how many Americans consume information. Ignoring infotainment blinds us to how Americans are experiencing their worlds. The informational aspect has made Colbert one of the nation's most effective civic educators, evidenced by an Annenberg study which concluded that audiences found Colbert's reporting more informative than traditional news sources. In particular, Bruce W. Hardy, senior researcher at the Annenberg Public Policy Center, claims that the actor did a "better job than other news sources at teaching people about campaign financing" through his on-air analysis of his own political action committee (PAC) in the 2012 election.[9] Colbert's influence in American society makes his Catholic pronouncements and performances all the more significant.

Colbert and Catholicism

In the United States, we usually use the word "Catholic" to refer to individuals who are or have been members of the Roman Catholic Church. Catholicism is the largest religious denomination in the United States, if all Protestant Christian denominations are counted separately. The Roman Catholic Church is a global religious institution led by the pope and other central administration in Vatican City, an enclave of Rome, Italy. American Catholic history typically begins with Spanish and French colonization, followed by the newly formed United States' establishing its first archdiocese in 1789. Nineteenth-century immigration from Germany, Ireland, Italy, and Poland led to an increase in the Catholic population in America. In addition, immigration contributed to a rise in anti-Catholicism. By the mid–twentieth century, the presidential election of Catholic John F. Kennedy, Vatican II changes, and changing American demographics, including increases in Hispanic Catholics, transformed American Catholicism. In turn, fluctuating populations changed Catholicism's place in the broader American imaginary. Since the late twentieth century, critics of the Catholic Church have noted in particular its doctrines on sexuality, its stance on female ordination, and its handling of the clerical sexual abuse crises. The story of Catholicism in the United States has been about a nebulous association of individuals encountering and engaging with the authoritative institutional Catholic Church.

Stephen Colbert stands in a historical lineage of public Catholics who have navigated the shifting tides of American Catholic authority. As Colbert joked during his keynote address at the 68th annual Alfred E. Smith Memorial Foundation Dinner (a dinner honoring the first Catholic nominee for the American presidency), on October 17, 2013, "I am proud to be America's most famous Catholic."[10] With this bold statement in a room full of cardinals, priests, politicians, actors, and other Catholic celebrities, Colbert references both his intense popularity and his embodiment of both American and Catholic identities. He is the latest incarnation of Catholic religious celebrities and mass-mediated broadcasters in the United States.

Colbert presents a version of American Catholicism, but not the sole version. Colbert illustrates and embodies certain complexities of Catholic identity and relationships between Catholic lay and institutional authority both in his individual presentation of his Catholic identity and through the complicated endeavor of being both a celebrity and a character inhabiting the same body with the same name. While there are multiple sides of Colbert, that does not mean he represents all of the complexity in contemporary American Catholicism. Instead, Colbert's racial and ethnic status as a middle-aged white man mirrors that of other dominant images of Catholic representation. In mass media, as in other public arenas, Catholicism, and particularly Catholic authority, is often depicted as white and male, especially in the fields of entertainment, television, and comedy.

Colbert uses satire and humor to question hypocrisies and incongruities that he sees in the Roman Catholic Church. He is a Catholic celebrity who can bridge between critical outsider and participating insider. The persona he cultivates employs satire and critical humor to navigate what it means to be an American Catholic and the relationship between lay and institutional authority. Some viewers describe this as "Colbert Catholic[ism]." Colbert Catholicism complicates the existing literature about "cafeteria," "cultural," and "thinking" Catholics, the liberal and conservative Catholic divide, and the trajectory of twentieth- and twenty-first-century changes in Catholic authority.

Longitudinal sociological studies of American Catholicism help situate Stephen Colbert's Catholic identity, both in and out of character. These scholars describe the historical use of the term "cafeteria Catholicism" as descriptive of Catholics who "selectively value" certain theologies and traditions.[11] Stephen Colbert is listed as a "cafeteria Catholic" by Conservapedia.com, an online wiki started in 2006 to combat perceived liberal media bias. The son of the late conservative Catholic political activist Phyllis Schlafly, Andrew Schlafly, created this website.[12] Conservatives call Colbert a "cafeteria Catholic" disparagingly to undermine his presentation of Catholicism.

The "selectivity" inherent in "cafeteria Catholicism" is part of a larger trend in American religious history, specifically the individualism and "seeking" that enraptured sociology of religion for the last few decades. Sociologists of religion show an increase in supposed religious choice and questioning of traditional authority among those in the "seeker" generation(s).[13] Catholicism is not solely a fundamentalist tradition and is, in fact, a "living theological tradition that blends faith and reason."[14] That blending is often illustrated by individuals who maintain their Catholic identities while still confronting specific Church teachings and practices on certain issues.[15] Examining both Stephen Colbert and the COLBERT persona can illuminate the complicated nature of contemporary American Catholicism.

Being Catholic facilitates both the actor and character in making humorous statements and interventions. Catholicism embodies a paradox: being one of the many religions in a pluralistic world and being arguably the most recognizable institutional church in the world. Catholicism is multifaceted. The multidimensional aspects of Catholicism arise because the religion is both political and institutional, "a contested set of practices, and an embodied and ethical orientation to the world."[16] Furthermore, Catholicism is a perpetually "crystalizing system of patterns" consistently rearranging structures, traditions, and authorizing agents.[17] Catholicism is supposed to be homogeneous, but in reality it is, and has always been, heterogeneous. Perceptions and realities of Catholicism are already paradoxes, so Colbert puts that paradox on stage through the dual personae of Colbert/COLBERT. Ethnographers and, I would argue, many media studies scholars often find it difficult to create a single, unified definition of Catholic practices, systems, and beliefs. To compare the various forms and intricacies leaves scholars feeling center-less and floating. Crafting a definitive version of Catholicism usually prescribes the institutional "authorized" or "sanctioned" form. If one is relying on institutional definitions and normative assumptions, then the "polyphony" of Catholic thought, practice, and identity is erased.[18] This leads to inquiries into authenticity and authority that Colbert's and COLBERT's commentaries and dual existence call into question.

Catholicism is both invisible and ubiquitous. It is the institutional organization, the individuals who constitute it, and an agent in and of itself. It looms large in the American imaginary initially as the embodiment of the "other" and then later at the core of American religiosity. Protestant Americans have historically been wary of Catholicism, but since the 1960s, perhaps in part because of Vatican II shifts, a Catholicism that emphasizes the authority of white males has become more integrated into many American understandings of religion. A quarter of the American population is Catholic, the largest "denomination," if one could call it such, because Catholicism is not one thing. It is many and multitudes, but those complexities are often hidden or dismissed in stereotyping and essentializing Catholicism. The perception of the Catholic Church assumes one authority, which in turn leads to lay and clerical conflicts.

Through the persona COLBERT, Colbert explores the paradox of Catholic multiplicity. He can do so as a lay person in ways that many mediated and televised Catholic clergy have been unable to do. Colbert speaks for, with, and to an audience grappling with seeing Catholicism as multifaceted. Colbert's Catholicism creates this contemporary paradox of being religious while also mocking certain aspects of religion primarily because Catholicism is often defined with and against the institution of the Catholic Church. There is a perception of a right answer, a *real* way of being religious. While that perception is false and there are millions of ways in which to be Catholic in the contemporary world, the perceptions and assumptions remain. To be Catholic is to constantly define and redefine oneself with and against the perception of a unified, authoritative, and institutional Church.

So, how does Colbert embody and interrogate Catholic identity and authority in twenty-first-century America? Stephen Colbert exemplifies this blending of faith and reason through his satirical character and his personal affirmation of Catholic identity. His satire challenges and criticizes aspects of Catholicism but still praises institutional authorities in the Catholic Church and has befriended Father Jim Martin and Cardinal Timothy Dolan. Colbert appears to transcend the liberal/conservative binary as a Catholic on a television faux-news show who comes to work with ashes on his forehead on Ash Wednesday but still mocks Pope Emeritus Benedict's expensive red shoes. Colbert walks a fine line between the progressivism of certain groups and the traditionalism of those he reflects with his over-exaggerated conservative persona. Colbert is neither fully reverent nor fully irreverent. He is a quintessential American Catholic.

The Context of Colbert

Of course, Colbert's quintessential Catholic identity arises in a specific context. Colbert and COLBERT illustrate a Catholic paradox in an era that questions truth and embraces digital media. In the porous boundaries of news, entertainment, and culture in the age of digital media, Colbert and COLBERT infotained audiences about current events. In their capacity as celebrities, they braided together consumerism, democracy, and individualism. COLBERT is an individual pundit who promotes his politically, socially, and religiously conservative brand. His influence is built upon the scores of viewers who watch his television shows or interact with him through digital mass media. Social scientist Mel van Elteren connects contemporary celebrity culture to cultural narcissism that began in the 1970s.[19] That cultural narcissism has only grown, van Elteren suggests, with the onslaught of new media technologies such as the Internet, cell phones, cable television, and social media. As literary and cultural critic William Deresiewicz describes, "[T]he camera has created a culture of celebrity; the computer is creating a culture of connectivity."[20] New technologies and celebrity culture are intertwined, influencing, reaching, and communicating with broader audiences.

Colbert and COLBERT are "transmediated" subjects, meaning that their storytelling occurs across various media outlets.[21] *The Colbert Report* was on cable television, but many Colbert fans experienced his material through Twitter, Facebook, websites, video streaming services, taped appearances at the White House Correspondents' Dinner, and presentations at U.S. congressional hearings. Beyond Colbert and COLBERT, *The Colbert Report* fans, otherwise known as the Colbert Nation, use transmediated culture to interact with the comedian. Fans wrote blog posts on Colbert-NewsHub.com and created nofactzone.net, a website dedicated to the inside scoop on *The Colbert Report*. The Colbert Nation attended Jon Stewart and Stephen Colbert's "Rally to Restore Sanity and/or Fear," a gathering at the National Mall in 2010 promoting reasoned discussion and debates in American politics. The Colbert Nation remixes his interviews, creates GIFs of video clips, makes cartoon drawings of Stephen Colbert, and circulates Colbert Internet memes. These fans live in a transmediated world that dissolves the line between cable television, social media, and face-to-face interactions while also blurring the conventional divisions between producer and consumer as they actively engage Colbert's work, remix it, and pass it on. Something fans create can be seen on television and something they see on television can become part of their interactive personal media world just as quickly. COLBERT's celebrity antics, and those of his fans, epitomize the twenty-first century's transmediated culture model. It is through transmediated mass media that Colbert presents his Catholic identity and comedic commentary about religion in America.

Everyday lived religion in America happens on television, on the Internet, and in mediated worlds. Religion and media scholars Stewart Hoover and Lynn Schofield Clark assert that "all contemporary institutional, social, and cultural trends take place in a media context."[22] In the twenty-first century, people increasingly practice their religion through digital media, use media to do "religious work," and employ media narratives as resources for constructing and negotiating their religious worlds. In fact, as Hoover explains, contemporary media practices and worlds "make it possible for new religious forms . . . to emerge."[23] Religious work is being made and remade by, and in conjunction with, new voices. Those voices have changed scale and speed with changing media technologies. Television, as a storytelling vehicle, has been a space of religious work for several decades. As religion and media scholar Diane Winston argues, we build our worlds through storytelling, and the sacred stories of our time are found on television and other mediated forms. Television, according to Winston, is "a latter-day version of Western traditions, such as hearing scriptures, 'reading' stained glass windows, or absorbing a Passion Play."[24] Television and religion scholar Elijah Siegler succinctly explains that television "complexif[ies]" our meaning-making because it can "communicate religious possibilities, explore religious issues, and ask religious questions."[25] Televisions themselves may not be inherently sacred, spiritual, or religious, but the medium helps audiences make and unmake their worlds. Television is the medium through which Colbert and COLBERT mold their religious identities and present them to audiences.

Comedic television programs influence and reflect society, as Colbert demonstrates. Comedy and humor are inextricably tied to identity and intersectionality and, thus, can read the conventions and customs of a society, what historian Joseph Boskin refers to as humor's ability to act as a "cultural index, a reflector of social change and conflict."[26] Comedy and humor are excellent indicators of cultural codes. Communications studies professor Arthur Asa Berger contends that language and actions of humor and comedy "can be 'used' to gain valuable insights into the ethos and worldview" of cultures.[27] What groups of people think, do, and subconsciously understand can be glimpsed in what makes them laugh. At times, comedy adheres to Freud's analysis of the joke; it addresses incongruities between belief and action.[28] When comedians oppose through humor, they often do so in confrontation with authority. *The Colbert Report* uses irony to present material in which the intended meaning opposes the expressions of the words utilized. As a comedian, Stephen Colbert uses humor to confront authoritative ideas or structures, including those close to his Catholic religion, the authority of the Catholic Church. In *The Colbert Report*, most of the humor regarding religion stems from the incongruities between what *is* and what *should be*.

Of course, just as culture and society are not singular, neither is comedy. Colbert uses humor to present his Catholic identity, to illustrate the complexities of life, and to confront authority. Humor helps break down barriers, claims identities, and affirms a sense of community. Humor also attacks, parodies, critiques, satirizes, and mocks. The topics comedians choose to satirize or joke about are often central to a culture or society. As Eric Idle, of the British comedy troupe Monty Python, concisely phrased it, "[I]f anything can survive the probe of humor it is clearly of value."[29] Politics, identity, and even religion are tested through humor.

The context for Colbert's humor is grounded in America's religiopolitical society. Political life in twenty-first-century America is hyperpolarized, a continuation of the culture wars. Political scientist Lawrence R. Jacobs claims that "the hyperpolarization of American politics has cascading consequences for the information system," and communications scholars Kathleen Hall Jamieson and Bruce W. Hardy note that partisan media polarize where individuals obtain information about politics. Polarized ways of gathering information then affect the nature of politics itself.[30] Stephen Colbert and his *Colbert Report* character reconceive the boundaries between liberal/conservative and traditional/progressive. Stephen Colbert and his humorous personae represent a multiplicity of American Catholic identities, political and religious, and illustrate the complicated relationships between lay and institutional Catholic authority.

Persona and Truthiness

Colbert infotained audiences through *The Colbert Report* persona on a variety of transmediated screens. That persona highlighted America's political culture wars with a rhetorical style that replicated and probed the twenty-first-century categories of liberal and conservative. He used the same rhetorical style when presenting his Catholic identity and satirizing certain incongruities in religious authenticity and authority. One of Colbert's neologisms encapsulates twenty-first-century sentiments of hyperpolarization and the questioning of authority and facts: "truthiness."

In the pilot episode of *The Colbert Report*, COLBERT began his segment "The Wørd" with a word he created, "truthiness." According to the American Dialect Society, which chose the word to be its 2005 Word of the Year, "truthiness" "refers to the quality of preferring concepts or facts one wishes to be true, rather than concepts or facts known to be true."[31] As COLBERT explained in the segment, "I don't trust books. They're all fact, no heart."[32] Colbert felt that the word "truth" was not "dumb enough," saying in a *New York Times* interview, "I wanted a silly word that would feel wrong in your mouth."[33] Truthiness is not the exact opposite of truth; instead, it is a comedic play on truth.

Truthiness epitomizes the satirical nature of *The Colbert Report*. According to communications scholars Jonathan Gray, Jeffrey P. Jones, and Ethan Thompson in *Satire TV*, Colbert's ironic humor is defined by his "double-layered" speech. Colbert's meanings demonstrate a critical edge that lies "below the surface, or between the lines."[34] The problem arises when we try to interpret what Stephen Colbert the actor means and how to classify these comical and satirical elements. Context usually helps

Truthiness

establish the meaning, but comedy complicates this. The ambiguous nature of the "double-voiced utterances of parodic performance," as television studies scholar Jeffrey P. Jones points out, allows for a great deal of latitude in audience interpretations.[35] Colbert lives in that blurry line between meanings. The ambiguity changes how audiences are meant to perceive the television program and the character. Audience members' preexisting political ideologies shape how they perceive Colbert and his humor. Both conservative and liberal audiences consider Colbert funny (at least they did in 2009), but "conservatives were more likely to report that Colbert only pretends to be joking and genuinely meant what he said," and conversely, liberal audiences "were more likely to report that Colbert used satire and was not serious when offering political statements."[36] Interpreting COLBERT as a "truthiness-teller" places him in category where he both means and does not mean what he says. The double-speak is tied up in how audiences read the character.

Truthiness parodies truth as *The Colbert Report* parodies a "straight news . . . program," according to communications and rhetoric scholar Amber Day, because audiences understand the television program to be a "comedic send-up of the format."[37] Parodic techniques, according to communications and rhetoric scholar Robert Hariman, combine "imitation and alteration," but what begins as a reversal of binaries through mimicry exposes the limits of those binaries.[38] Neither solely radical nor conservative, parody is both simultaneously. Audiences often view Colbert's show as double-speak because the character says one thing and means another. The dual persona of Colbert and COLBERT, but with the same embodiment and name, only furthers the double-speak confusion.

STEPHEN COLBERT parodies current media pundits by pontificating in an absurd and extreme manner. As part of his goal of "parody with a point," Colbert lambasts media pundits through satire.[39] Satire is an artistic form that "makes fun of human folly and vice by holding people accountable for their public actions."[40] The purpose of *The Colbert Report* is to be funny, as a senior producer at Comedy Central described the show, and to make humor about what the writers, directors, and hosts find "interesting or compelling," and all of it serves to make audiences laugh.[41] The jokes presented in this satirical format make fun of various aspects of society and culture, religion included. Satire can challenge inequality as well as contribute to it.

Colbert is not separate from the political and cultural world he mocks. The conservative COLBERT embraces the extremism of polarized politics and religious language. COLBERT assumes that America is a Christian nation, co-constitutively founded with Christian values imbued in the political realm and the democratizing of Christian denominations in the religious realm.[42] Colbert parses the nature of what is "religio-political" through the satirical quality he employs. COLBERT equates conservative Christianity with goodness, truth, real religion, and correct political leanings, but because it comes from the humorist Colbert's lips, those sentiments emphasize a doubleness, a playing with reality, a truthiness.

COLBERT performs truthiness by blatantly making up facts and using his hyperbolic punditry to highlight the forcefulness of believing something is true. As actor Stephen Colbert explained in a 2009 *Rolling Stone* article, the character COLBERT does this by arguing beyond reality: "Liberals will come on the show and say, 'Well conservatives want this to be a theocracy.' And I'll say, 'well, why not, the Founding Fathers were all fundamentalist Christians.' And they'll say, 'no they weren't.' I say, 'Yes, they were, and if I'm wrong, I will eat your encyclopedias.'"[43] Such hyperbolic language epitomizes the infotainment genre Colbert embraces with the term "truthiness."

Colbert performs his truthiness persona on multiple platforms. This, in addition to the fact that the character on *The Colbert Report* is also named STEPHEN COLBERT, creates confusion. In a January 2012 *New York Times* article, media critic Charles McGrath claimed that there were more Stephen Colberts than the actor and his character.[44] The other Colbert(s) ran for president in South Carolina, testified before Congress about illegal-immigrant farmworkers, and started a Super Political Action Committee (Super PAC) that collected real monetary donations. Acknowledging the confusion of such performances, Colbert opened his Knox College commencement address in 2006 with the following remarks:

> My name is Stephen Colbert, but I actually play someone on television named Stephen Colbert, who looks like me and talks like me, but who says things with a straight face he doesn't mean. . . . I'm not sure which one of us you invited to speak here today. So with your indulgence, I'm just going to talk and let you figure it out.[45]

As seen in this speech, the character COLBERT has moved from the television screen to real life. The conflation and co-constitutive nature of Colbert and COLBERT are integral to his impact. As he melds together comedy and real-world experience into a brand of "infotainment," Colbert also melds together his dual persona. Through the complexity and fluidity of his dual persona, Colbert emerges as a politically savvy and knowledgeable personality who has done far more than caricature conservative Republicans. He has become an American celebrity.

Ironically, Colbert's type of celebrity, that of media star, is considered more trustworthy than that of contemporary politicians or world leaders. This is because media celebrities' fame transcends personal integrity and public service.[46] A comedian who creates a word—"truthiness"—to describe the gut feeling of truth over fact can be perceived as more trustworthy than a politician because of his celebrity status. That celebrity status makes Colbert influential in American society, as well as a reflection of that society.

In his role as a celebrity fake news pundit, Colbert's religiously imbued commentary becomes bolded and pronounced. He punches up the infotainment with religious material, and his religious identity becomes part of his celebrity persona. As religion scholar Kathryn Lofton explains in *Consuming Religion*, the connection between celebrity and infotainment has only deepened since the 1980s. A celebrity's religious engagements and entanglements are fodder for information and entertainment. Considering the roles Colbert and COLBERT play in American political life, it makes sense that his celebrity affects his ability to be seen by some as a "meaningful religious authority."[47] Colbert's influence does not reach the levels of those of Beyoncé or Oprah, but audiences still consider, interpret, and contend with his religiously focused remarks.

Beyond commentary about religion, Colbert's celebrity status is imbued with sacrality. As religion scholar Gary Laderman remarks, celebrity culture has influenced American religious history in part because "technologically advanced forms of communication brought entertaining popular cultures into the private lives of listeners and viewers." There is a sacrality, Laderman notes, to celebrities in that their images could be used as alternatives to other forms of meaning-making and purpose. Celebrities have not replaced religion writ large, but there are religious aspects to celebrity culture that merge "entertainment and devotional rituals, commerce and sacred auras, in ways that transform public and popular figures as well as fans themselves."[48] Colbert's celebrity status is more tied to a particular religion, Catholicism, than to being sacred in and of himself. However, the COLBERT persona might disagree. That guy has a God complex.

Themes and Methodology

This interdisciplinary book employs religious studies, media studies, and American studies to engage questions of identity, representation, and authority. In terms of methodology, I utilize discourse analysis, textual analysis, historical contextualization, and media ethnography of a cultural product to narrate this story. I specifically analyze the connection between the text and the context by examining the content of *The Colbert Report* and the journalism and media surrounding the show in connection with broader aspects of American religious history. I explore both the content of *The Colbert Report* and the "religion around" Colbert and COLBERT.[49] My analysis of Stephen Colbert as a religious broadcaster relies on the reception studies of *The Colbert Report* by other scholars, especially those by Jill Dierberg and Lynn Schofield Clark.[50] Most academic studies of religion and media are sociological reception studies. In complementary contrast, this book fits into a more narrative style reminiscent of other American religious history and ethnographic scholarship.

My primary sources include a self-curated catalogue of 1,700 videos, transcriptions of more than 500 video clips, and hundreds of media and journalism reports. My research also includes interviews with Father James Martin, S.J., and Comedy Central writers and staff. Father James Martin, S.J., editor of *America* magazine, the "Chaplain of the Colbert Nation," and a frequent guest on the show, writes extensively about religion and humor.[51] In a project like this one, primary documents and secondary sources often merge, and sorting through the immense amount of materials is a never-ceasing task.

This media ethnography has two parts: in-person ethnography and digital ethnography. Before *The Colbert Report* ended in December 2014, I attended the show, where I engaged in participant-observation methodology as an audience member and stood in the stand-by line for four tapings, conducting field observations and interviewing audience members. I noted the interactions of audience members, stage managers, and actors. I also explored the sets, material culture, and performance materials associated with the show both in person and digitally in order to understand how the show is produced and how to interpret the nuances of that production. I conducted more than thirty in-person interviews with audience members at *The Colbert Report*.

I began my research at a serendipitous moment, although it did not feel so in the moment. My research was initially going to involve more in-person ethnographic work. However, in April 2014 CBS announced that Stephen Colbert would be the next host of *The Late Show*, replacing David Letterman. This project shifted significantly toward one of more digital ethnography and content analysis, with one site visit in November 2014. The content analysis began in earnest in October 2014, aided by the *Colbert Report*'s searchable website. I could type any phrase or word into the search feature and it would populate the page with all of the videos that mention or are connected to that phrase. These videos could then be sorted by "most popular" (meaning most viewed), "most recent" (describing when the video had been released), and "most relevant" (meaning that the search algorithm dictated the terms of pertinence). I did not assume that these groupings were correct, but it was a useful starting point for initial findings. By December 2014, the initial searches were complete and I was slowly watching individual videos through the website and transcribing them.

In mid-January 2015, I glanced at a Facebook post from *The Colbert Report*. Comedy Central would be removing *The Colbert Report* videos, in their entirety, from the website in ten days. In a panic, I worked with every librarian, media specialist, and computer-savvy friend I had to save 1,700 of the most useful videos to watch later for transcription. Over the next four months, I transcribed 581 clips from *The Colbert Report*. These transcriptions formed the basis of my work for this book, although I ended up incorporating journalistic and *Late Show with Stephen Colbert* videos as research progressed.

Digital media and the Internet have provided even more opportunities for greater media anthropology research, and I conducted virtual ethnographies of blogs, comment boards, and other Internet postings. When discussing the twenty-first century, I use the terms "digital age" and "media age" interchangeably because most media today can be accessed through online means, thus making them digital media. Even film and television are made digitally through digital projection and filming practices. In my media ethnography, I turned to documents found through social media and Internet sources to gain a fuller picture of the reach of *The Colbert Report*. Like other media scholars, I ground my abstractions in the particularities of a specific program that is "socio-historically dependent and embedded in complex social relations and negotiations."[52] Analysis of blog posts, video comments, and *The Colbert Report* content provides a map of the intersecting and often contradictory American religious landscapes in ways that surveys and sociological data cannot: through the humor and popular culture of a mass-mediated television program. This method enables me to consider the role of humor in perceptions and reflections of religion in the United States from a vantage point that does not deride humor as frivolous or irrelevant to American religious life.

This book is a case study of the intersection between lived religion and mass media through the work of Stephen Colbert. I move from an exploration of how Catholicism shapes Colbert toward a conversation about how Colbert shapes Catholicism. I provide the historical context for Colbert by examining how this contemporary character compares to his lineage of Catholic figures who present their views of Catholicism to Americans through radio, film, and television. In the twentieth century, Catholic figures consistently used mass media technologies to enact religious authority.

These mass-mediated figures informed national audiences about Catholic ideologies and politics; created an imagined, idealized Catholic life; and joined American and Catholic identities. While previous eras had media figures such as Father Charles Coughlin and Bishop Fulton Sheen who were official clergy members, Colbert is a lay Catholic. Colbert marks a significant shift because he is not a priest, does not portray a clergy member on *The Colbert Report*, and utilizes over-exaggerated, humorous segments to address issues of Catholic authority for twenty-first-century audiences. *The Colbert Report*'s famous religion segment, "Yahweh or No Way," serves as a lens through which to examine lay religious authority as COLBERT judges contemporary culture on God's behalf.

Further, I explore Colbert's role as a catechist. Colbert presents himself as a Catholic on- and off-screen with humor that combines catechetical knowledge and satirical comedy. On *The Colbert Report*, he uses his Catholic knowledge and identity as fodder for his television persona. He describes "Catholic Benders" and quizzes guests on the intricacies of Catholic theology. For example, in 2011, he challenged rock star Jack White to a "Catholic-Throwdown" in a segment extended for digital media viewers. In journalistic interviews, out-of-character Colbert describes his religious life and family history to mass audiences through print and digital media. Stephen Colbert is a contemporary paradox in mass media: a comedian who can truly mock and identify with his religion simultaneously. His relationships and interviews with contemporary Catholic authorities demonstrate how he reifies and critiques the institutional Catholic Church.

Catholic comedians control late-night comedy programs in the twenty-first century, from Jimmy Fallon to Conan O'Brien to Stephen Colbert. I consider Colbert as part of a distinct group of Catholic comedians in the twentieth and twenty-first centuries, many of whom mine their Catholicism for humorous material. A defining characteristic of Catholic humor is the comedians' relationships with the institutional Catholic Church and their own Catholic identity. Colbert is distinct from his contemporaneous comedians because he continually asserts that he is a "practicing" Catholic, and his mild critiques do not disturb America's institutional Catholic Church. I describe Catholic comedy using Don Novello, George Carlin, Louis C.K., and Jim Gaffigan as examples.

Additionally, I ask about the broader implications of this television show. What does COLBERT's and Colbert's religious humor reveal about the conflicts and tensions in contemporary American Catholic life? Colbert's lay catechist role (one who teaches people about Catholicism) makes him a type of Catholic who searches for his own individual interpretations of Catholic faith, not unlike other Catholics today. American Catholicism is not a unified entity, and the multiplicity of the Colbert(s) reflects the multiplicity and diversity in American Catholic identities. Colbert does not represent the vast groups of Catholics of differing ethnicities and socio-economic backgrounds, but he does illustrate an often ignored form of Catholic multiplicity: thinking Catholics, cultural Catholics, cafeteria Catholics, and lukewarm Catholics. Here, I put Colbert's theological musings in context with his comedy to define "Colbert Catholicism," a type of Catholicism that sees humor as beneficial to one's faith. Colbert Catholicism also uses humor and satire to grapple with twenty-first-century conflicts in the Catholic Church, specifically the priest sexual abuse scandals.

I also contend with Colbert, COLBERT, and the extreme polarization of the twenty-first century's culture wars. The turn of the twenty-first century and the first decades of this millennium are marked by the rise of cable news and celebrity pundits, fractures in religious identities on political fault lines, and the increasing number of religious "nones." Colbert's character is a right-wing political media star who plays up the divide of liberal and conservative for comedic effect, as evidenced by the 2010 "Rally to Restore Sanity and/or Fear," co-hosted with Jon Stewart. Colbert's culture wars rhetoric came to a head during a critical moment in the history of *The Colbert Report*. In 2014, an Asian American activist tweeted a response to what she felt was a racist tweet from the show. #CancelColbert became a media phenomenon that put Colbert and the COLBERT persona at the heart of the culture wars. However, Colbert's new position in the culture wars did not just perpetuate them but actually illustrated a reconfiguration of the alliances of left and right, conservative and liberal, in American religious life.

The final sections of this book look beyond *The Colbert Report* to Colbert's move to CBS's *The Late Show with Stephen Colbert* in 2015. Even in its earliest episodes, there have been moments on *The Late Show* where Colbert catechizes to broader American audiences than those of his cable show; moments when Vice President Joe Biden and Colbert describe how their faith helps them cope with tragedy; moments when Colbert pokes fun at Pope Francis's 2015 visit to America; and moments when Colbert sits behind a confessional, admitting his "sins" as jokes to the audience. Colbert still challenges other celebrities to "Catholic-offs," quizzing them on Catholic doctrine. The character COLBERT left the air in 2014, but "truthiness" has never been more relevant, especially evident in the 2016 election when false claims and "fake news" drew COLBERT back into the spotlight. The final chapter ponders Colbert's role in the 2016 election and the position of "America's Most Famous Catholic" in a post–*Colbert Report* world.

2   Colbert as Catholic Authority

Stephen Colbert stands in a long lineage of influential Catholic figures in American mass media and public life. In the early to mid–twentieth century, those who represented Catholicism on the air were primarily priests and nuns. In contrast, Colbert is a lay Catholic who uses his stage as a pulpit not merely to evangelize but also to be a lay Catholic enthralling the world with his interpretations and discussions of religion in the United States. He presents his own Catholic identity in the contemporary moment. His character, COLBERT, self-aggrandizes and considers himself a religious authority. Traditional religious authority includes decision makers who "maintain control" of religious "symbols, practices, texts, and doctrines" and have the ability to mark certain elements as "authentic."[1] In the contemporary moment, shifting dynamics of media create "new and emergent centers and sectors of authority, rooted in their ability to find audiences, to plausibly invigorate or invite practice, and to direct attention," according to religion and media scholar Stewart Hoover.[2] COLBERT is the ultimate Catholic and the one self-chosen to explain life "to heathens and the excommunicated," determining, authenticating, and presenting what is "religious" to his audiences.[3] COLBERT's rhetoric and interpretation of religious life situate him as a Catholic authority via mass media who "speaks for" a Judeo-Christian God. But, since COLBERT is a humorous character, Colbert's own influence becomes complicated. Colbert is not, strictly speaking, a religious authority, but his character assumes the role of Catholic authority on *The Colbert Report*. This is particularly the case during the recurring segment "Yahweh or No Way."

In "Yahweh or No Way" segments, COLBERT demonstrates his self-crafted Catholic authority, similar to that of other Catholic authorities who present their opinions, pronouncements, and judgments on American mass media. However, his are different because many of those twentieth-century figures were clerical, not lay Catholics like Colbert.

Historian Jay P. Dolan argues that as Catholics felt more comfortable in the United States in the twentieth century, "a public style of Catholicism began to emerge."[4] Catholicism developed in the public sphere at the same moment as the inventions of radio, film, and television. Through those media forms, influential figures presented and represented Catholicism to American audiences. Other scholars have discussed Protestant Christian uses of media innovations from radio preaching and phonograph recordings to televangelism and video games, but Catholics have also capitalized on new media forms to evangelize and enter into different conversations.[5] In the twentieth century, Catholic authorities in media were often priests, actors playing priests, or nuns. Examples include Mother Angelica, the founder of the cable Eternal Word Television Network (EWTN), and Bing Crosby playing Father Chuck O'Malley in the film *The Bells of St. Mary's*. Colbert breaks that lineage by portraying his lay Catholic identity.[6] And COLBERT breaks all molds by paradoxically presenting himself as the sole judge of what God wants, all the while advocating for traditional, institutional Catholic authorities to be male priests.

COLBERT's satirical and paradoxical presentation as a religious authority illustrates changes in religious authority that align with changes in mass-media technology. In particular, authority has shifted away from centrally located hierarchical and clerical institutions toward more individual and lay-focused varieties.[7] In the story of Catholics and mass media in the twentieth century, this lineage traces the narratives of broadcasters and entertainers who did not solely present the praise, worship, or prayer services to mass audiences. Instead, these stories consider the secular and religious as braiding religion into the quotidian.

Long before Colbert, a cadre of Catholic celebrities capitalized on contemporary innovations in technology. The ones discussed in this chapter were exemplars in their particular media forms. Father Charles Coughlin of Detroit transmitted vitriolic radio broadcasts to advocate political agendas in the 1930s. Radio, as a medium, reached a national audience and prompted a dialogue with the Catholic "other" now active in the American political realm. Bishop Fulton J. Sheen's 1950s television show combined the visual nature of film and the serialized, informative elements of radio. Sheen taught Catholic morality and catechism to Catholic and non-Catholic audiences and brought Catholicism into the mainstream.

COLBERT is also on television but has extended his reach into the digital world through YouTube clips, GIFs, images, and memes, soliciting active responses and engagement from his audience. Audiences interface with each mass media technology differently, and perceptions of audience interaction also change over time. For example, fans interact with COLBERT's Catholic, religious, or sociopolitical messages through digital media technologies, such as Twitter, Facebook, and other social media outlets. The Colbert Nation fandom of *The Colbert Report* creates a new arena for mass media interaction with Catholic celebrities and allows for a relationship between lay and institution that goes beyond the Catholic Church and into everyday mass-mediated life.

While Stephen Colbert and Fulton Sheen have both appeared on television, Colbert moves the narrative of Catholics as entertainment toward a discussion of a lay Catholic entertainer. His identity is Catholic, and he represents Catholicism as an individual, a lay catechist, and an influencer. Colbert can simultaneously be fully Catholic and fully enmeshed in the world. He does not pretend to be a priest on his own shows because his Catholicism is part of his identity, not the entire plot of the stories he tells. The character merges the threads of idealized and politicized Catholicism in his political satire.

When Colbert is at his most influential, he is a lay person with no official institutional authority. But his shift away from earlier instantiations of institutional authority is a measured and tempered one. As we have seen, Colbert often defers to institutional authority such as chaplain of the Colbert Nation, Father James Martin, S.J., or Cardinal Timothy Dolan of the New York Archdiocese. In the American public's perception, those changes in who speaks for the Catholic Church are complicated and often paradoxical. Colbert does not claim to take religious authority away from clergy; rather, he conducts dialogues with them. COLBERT, on the other hand, does not claim to supersede institutional authority but aggrandizes and equates his own authority with that of Catholic clergy, perhaps even with papal authority. COLBERT is not just an intermediary. He claims to be the only one who can make decisions and judgments on Yahweh's behalf. Colbert's humorous play on religious authority through COLBERT's antics highlights a shift in American perceptions of religious authority: It can be played with, satirized, and mocked through hyperbole. His efforts and influence should be included as part of understanding authority in contemporary American religious culture. From Coughlin to Sheen to Colbert, there is an element of leadership and authority in these mass-mediated voices.

While most religious authorities are often connected to religious institutions (rabbis, priests, imams, gurus, nuns, or monks), this chapter illustrates that lay and mass-mediated authorities are also religious leaders who model identity construction and religious practice.[8] Lay authorities decentralize institutional structures. Yet Stephen Colbert's popularity and influence demonstrate that the decentralization of authority does not mean that traditional institutional authorities disappear. Rather, religious authority vacillates between lay and clerical. The contemporary American context becomes one of competing, colliding, and collaborating religious authorities.

The concepts of modernity and authority contextualize this contemporary shift in the location of religious authority. Sociologist Anthony Giddens, in *Modernity and Self-Identity*, claims that in high modernity there are many "claimants to authority" but no "determinant authorities."[9] While earlier and smaller cultures usually had one religious authority, and earlier nonpluralistic cultures had orthodoxy in opposition to heresy, the contemporary "modern" era has no such singularity of voice. Giddens further argues that contemporary religious authority is in contrast with historical religious authority. Forms of traditional authority are now only one among many authoritative voices. Instead of being the authority because of hierarchy or organizational structure, religious expertise becomes the new authoritative stance. As sociologist Adam Seligman describes in *Modernity's Wager*, the individual's power of reason becomes the foundation for civic order and moral authority.[10] Thus, "modernity" encourages individuals to encounter numerous religious experts and decide for themselves.

Individual choices and "seeking" have been the key argument of sociology of religion for the last few decades.[11] Giddens's assumptions, along with the work of sociologists of religion, suggest that the "seeker generation" reflects both an increase in religious choice and a rise in skepticism about traditional religious authorities. Scholars originally assumed that the lack of deference to previously respected religious authority was a by-product of a decrease in religiosity more generally. As many scholars have noted, no such eradication of religion has occurred.[12] Thus, the changes in religious authority are more likely linked to the increased individualization of the seeker generations' religious choices. In the twenty-first century, those choices are made in media-rich contexts.

In the "media age," it is even more important for us to pay attention to non-institutional sources of political, social, and religious authority. Religion and media scholar Stewart Hoover and others argue that the age of digital media changes how people perceive the authorization of religions. The contemporary media moment expands who constitutes a key religious figure. The list no longer consists solely of the pope, the Dalai Lama, the late Billy Graham, Bishop Desmond Tutu, or the occasional charismatic local clergyperson. Instead of solely a top-down, orthodox authority associated with religious institutions, increasingly, people perceive that religious authority resides in a tension between individual sanctioning and communal co-creation. When examining the lived religious practices and experiences of American religious life, authoritative religious institutions and clergy are one part of the picture. And part of the creation and acquisition of religious authority comes from media, the public, and celebrated figures who are seen on screens (television, film, Internet media, social media) across the country.[13] The religious institutions, the Bible or other sacred texts, personal sense of right and wrong, or familial faith structures are shaped and formed, in part, through rhetoric and communication presented in mass-mediated forms. The digital media age may have brought the democratized nature of religious authority to the foreground, but it has not made religious authority an artifact of an earlier time.

Religious leaders are not the only authority in religious circles. Historian of religion Bruce Lincoln asserts that authority should be understood relationally, meaning that two realities which acknowledge the authority interact in ways that "make audiences act as if" the authority were manifest in that reality.[14] Thus, religious authority becomes a discursive performance that involves religious leaders' persuading audiences with claims. While usually associated with religious institutions, the media age changes who authoritatively controls religions and allows for mediated figures in the public imaginary to have authority, such as the character STEPHEN COLBERT on *The Colbert Report*.

In what religion and media scholar Lynn Schofield Clark has called a "remixing" of "consensus-based authority," Stephen Colbert, the character and the actor, has become an authoritative religious figure.[15] Colbert's consensus-based authority comes from his ability to publicly articulate and interpret perspectives concerning current events. Colbert does speak to American audiences through his television shows, social media, and Internet presence. However, not all audience members consider him implicitly authoritative on all matters because of his humorous and satirical presentations in popular culture venues (venues that are still considered antithetical to *serious* and *real* issues of the day). When compared with priests, rabbis, and imams, whose authority comes from texts, practices, traditions, and communities, Colbert's authority, crafted through humor and COLBERT's hyperbolic messages, appears trivial.

Regardless of the heft of Colbert's religious influence, his persona, COLBERT, does presume to be a Catholic religious authority, judging what is correct, right, and good in American religions. COLBERT presents those judgments on *The Colbert Report*, which situates the television program and its accompanying digital media communication in a lineage of Catholic mass-mediated religious authorities. Before diving into Colbert's segments, this chapter examines the context and content of two such authorities: Father Charles Coughlin and Bishop Fulton J. Sheen. While different, both Coughlin and Sheen illustrate elements of mass-mediated Catholic authority that Colbert performs decades later, including integrating conservative political rhetoric and Catholicism, hyper-American patriotism, and catechizing to broad audiences through mediated forms.

Vitriolic Clergy on the Radio

With every new technological advance, religious practitioners have sought to use those technologies to further their religious causes. As radios gained popularity in the 1920s, Americans began broadcasting religious materials and messages across the airwaves. As historian Tona Hangen asserts in *Redeeming the Dial*, radio technology "permitted some changes in the devotional practices of ordinary Americans."[16] For example, people in Chicago could hear a preacher in Boston without either party's ever visiting the other's state. Evangelizing over the airwaves brought more Christians into worship on Sundays, a change from the typical notion that radio services were in lieu of other church gatherings. In reality, Hangen claims, radio also encouraged a rethinking of what constitutes "church" and "where worship could take place."[17] Radio "shrunk distances" and collapsed "time and space with unseen power," analogous, for many, to religious experiences.[18] Further, radio presented new religious authorities, those not seen, but heard. Radio personalities garnered enormous followings and fans, and radio hours became must-hear moments that marked calendrical time across America. Radio, like other technologies, helped people recognize that religion and "secular" entertainment were not oppositional forces. In fact, entertaining and informative radio had lasting effects on how audiences considered religion's place in society.

One key example is the "Radio Priest," Father Charles Coughlin. From 1926 to 1939, Father Coughlin was a vitriolic, populist, conservative political radio pundit who was also a Catholic priest. This was a time of upheaval for Catholics in America as they moved from the ghettoization of the late nineteenth century toward a place in the American public sphere, epitomized by Al Smith's 1928 presidential campaign.[19] Father Coughlin conflated politics and religion, demonstrating a Catholic as a moral authority and religious leader across the airwaves and beyond the Catholic circles. Sociologist Donald Warren argues that Coughlin's blend of religion, politics, and entertainment was a predecessor to political talk radio and televangelism.[20] In the study of the polarizing American culture wars, we might place Coughlin at the beginning of the connection between Catholic conservative populism and vitriolic conservative radio. Conflating religion and politics, Father Coughlin's dramatic oratory exemplifies "infotainment"—the presentation of information in entertaining ways.[21]

Charles E. Coughlin was born in 1891 in Ontario, Canada. He attended Saint Michael's College in Toronto before being ordained in 1916 and joining the Congregation of St. Basil. As a result of changes in the order, he became a priest in the diocese of Detroit in 1923. In 1926, the bishop of Detroit, Michael J. Gallagher, asked him to create a new parish in the suburb of Royal Oak, a parish named for Therese of Lisieux, becoming the Church of the Little Flower. Coughlin searched for new ways to raise funds for his fledgling parish, as well as ways to present Catholicism to anti-Catholic neighbors, including the Ku Klux Klan (KKK), which had burned a cross on the church's yard.[22] He discovered one such way, which gave him his popular moniker, the "Radio Priest."

On October 17, 1926, Detroit's WJR station presented Father Coughlin's first broadcast. An "unimposing" presence, Coughlin wore glasses and his dark hair had a "slight wave at the top."[23] As Raymond Swing wrote in

Forerunners of American Fascism in 1935, Father Coughlin had a look that "goes with so many Irish priests."[24] But that stereotypical look did not extend to a stereotypical priestly timidity. His sermons included colloquial and "near-profane" language with an advertising tone. As Warren explains, Coughlin's style was more akin to that of "a superconfident salesman than a traditional preacher."[25] Writer Wallace Stegner described Coughlin's mellifluous voice as a "voice of such mellow richness, such manly, heartwarming confidential intimacy, such emotional and ingratiating charm, that anyone tuning past it almost automatically returned to hear it again."[26]

For more than thirteen years, Father Coughlin's voice carried the Roman Catholic Mass over the airways, often from his office, housed in the Church of the Little Flower with its "startlingly modern 150-foot 'Crucifixion Tower' and its unique, octagon-shaped shrine," constructed during the Great Depression.[27] Warren, in his book *Radio Priest*, claimed that the "silver tongued . . . golden voiced . . . Radio Messiah" was one of the "most persuasive mass media orators" who held significant political power throughout the United States.[28] Coughlin's stance against political elites resonated with the populist public, as well as the public's stance "against alien minorities [who] they thought were intent on betraying the nation."[29] Warren asserts that Coughlin invented a new kind of preaching dependent on the radio "microphone and transmitter."[30] But radio, despite the expectations of its medium, is never a passive entertainment. In response to Coughlin's broadcasts, tens of thousands of fans sent letters each week to his Shrine of the Little Flower, illustrating his acclaim and the flow of his ideas across the nation. At the height of his popularity, approximately 30 million listeners tuned in to his weekly radio broadcasts.[31]

Those listeners heard a variety of messages. Coughlin presented himself as a priest who championed the poor and criticized corporate culture and federal economic policies. Such rhetoric resonated with the "hopes and fears of lower-middle-class Americans," regardless of individual religious affiliations.[32] Initially, Coughlin's political commentary supported President Franklin D. Roosevelt, creating the slogan "Roosevelt or Ruin," and even solicited an invitation to speak at the 1932 Democratic National convention. Once Roosevelt was elected, however, their political stances diverged, and Coughlin became more critical of the president. He began setting up his own publications and organizations, including *Social Justice* and the National Union for Social Justice. Coughlin's political views included monetary reforms, nationalizing major industries (including the railroads), and labor rights.[33]

Father Coughlin chose the radio over the newspaper, in part, because he realized that Catholic newspapers were rare in Protestant homes, and scarcely "did a Protestant journal adorn a Catholic reading-table."[34] He wanted to convey Catholic ideas into non-Catholic arenas as a way to evangelize and to place Catholics prominently in the public sphere. However, Coughlin was not accepting of all religious minorities. By the late 1930s, his radio broadcasts and magazine articles were filled with anti-Semitic language, including a version of the well-circulated propaganda "The Protocols of the Elders of Zion."[35] He hated Marxism and communism, equating Judaism with those political ideologies, as evidenced by his description of Karl Marx as a "Hebrew."[36] Coughlin became a face of American fascism, aligning himself with Adolf Hitler and Benito Mussolini. While he rarely outrightly blamed Jews on religious grounds, his political and economic stances had religious underpinnings. Many in the Roman Catholic Church hierarchy, both in the Vatican and in the United States, disagreed with Father Coughlin, but his direct superior, Bishop Michael Gallagher of Detroit, advocated for him. The official cancellation of his radio program came not from Rome but from Washington, D.C., because of the beginning of World War II in Europe in 1939.

After his broadcast was canceled, Father Coughlin's political influence decreased. As his biographer Sheldon Marcus described him, Coughlin was simultaneously

> . . . the most revered, the most loved, the most hated and the most feared American of his time. He was Christ; he was Hitler; he was Savior; he was destroyer; he was patriot; he was demagogue—he was Father Coughlin.[37]

Father Coughlin died in 1979. Yet his "broadcast heirs" live on in the angry media personalities who utilize evolving technologies to project "populist sincerity and trustworthiness" and create arenas for "violence-provoking political expressions."[38] In the 1980s and 1990s, extreme right-wing organizations re-popularized Coughlin's rhetoric, often divorcing it from its Catholic heritage. Even searching for his materials on YouTube today presents some challenges for one's web browser history; I came across some of his speeches sponsored by white supremacy groups. Nevertheless, his "right-wing extremist" status as a "denizen of the lunatic fringe" creates a powerful image of Catholics in the pre–World War II era.[39]

Catholic authority in mass media took the form of a vitriolic priest in the era of radio. Warren claims that Coughlin was one of the first public figures to "obliterate the distinction between politics, religion, and mass media entertainment."[40] On *The Colbert Report*, Stephen Colbert portrays a conservative Catholic news pundit, and his vitriolic fervor and tone are as much a satire of contemporary Fox News and right-wing pundits as it is a mocking impression of Father Charles Coughlin, especially when it concerns the realms of politics as seen through the eyes of a Catholic.

Fulton Sheen Teaching Catholicism to an American Audience

On February 12, 1952, during prime time, the DuMont Television Network introduced a new television program, *Life Is Worth Living*, hosted by Bishop Fulton J. Sheen. The stage was set as a study, with bookshelves and a blackboard. A *Madonna and Child* statue he christened "Our Lady of Television"[41] was one of the few "explicitly religious" elements on stage, besides Bishop Sheen himself, dressed resplendently in a "princely cape."[42] Sheen's show mixed secular and religious materials, a divide that held little resonance in the Catholic imagination wherein every aspect of life was sacramental.[43] The program was a catechism for all ages, and the books and learning materials on set easily transported viewers into a classroom, including into the power-dynamics of classroom authority with Bishop Sheen demanding their full attention when discussing life's biggest questions.

This new program, which featured Sheen speaking extemporaneously, often directly into the camera, aired against two highly rated programs hosted by Milton Berle and Frank Sinatra. One would expect a priest to preside over a Mass or prayer and worship services, but Sheen introduced his interfaith audiences to a Catholic priest as a moral authority outside a formal church setting. This show became the longest-running religious program on prime-time television. At the height of its popularity in 1953–54, 10 million people watched *Life Is Worth Living* weekly.[44] Milton Berle, a losing competitor with Sheen for household television viewers, commented on their competition, "If I'm going to be eased off TV by anyone, it's better that I lose to the One for whom Bishop Sheen is speaking."[45] Running for approximately 125 episodes, *Life Is Worth Living* holds the honor of being the only religious program ever to be "commercially sponsored and to compete for ratings."[46]

Fulton Sheen was born Peter John Sheen in El Paso, Illinois, in 1895. He attended Catholic schools and continued his studies at St. Viator's College in Illinois, followed by St. Paul's Seminary in Minnesota. In 1919, Sheen was ordained and sent to Catholic University of America to earn a Doctor of Sacred Theology degree in philosophy. Further, he earned an *agrégé* in philosophy from the University of Louvain in Belgium in 1925. He became a pastor in the Peoria diocese in Illinois, then a moral theology professor at Catholic University. In 1950, Sheen became the national director for the Society for the Propagation of the Faith, "which served Catholic missions around the world."[47] His intellectualism and charisma led him to preach on the *Catholic Hour* radio broadcast in the 1930s and 1940s.

Time magazine, in its 1952 cover story on Sheen, claimed that his radio broadcasts made him "perhaps the most famous preacher in the U.S., certainly the best-known Roman Catholic priest."[48] Although radio was his initial foray into mass media, Sheen's celebrated status increased tenfold as he moved into television. He challenged expectations of religious authority as somber by displaying the human qualities of his personality. By 1956, Fulton Sheen was the third-most-admired man in America, only slightly behind President Dwight D. Eisenhower and British Prime Minister Winston Churchill and ahead of Pope Pius XII and American evangelical preacher Billy Graham, according to a Gallup poll.[49] As historian Anthony Burke Smith describes, Sheen served as a "moral guide" for Americans grappling with postwar life in the 1950s and the "moral anxiety" created by the influx of television technology into American homes.[50] Sheen filled an open role as a scholarly and moral authority with a "flair for the drama."[51] Displaying that drama and religion can not only co-exist but can often be mutually reinforcing, when Sheen received an Emmy Award in 1952 as Most Outstanding Personality, he thanked his writers, "Matthew, Mark, Luke, and John."[52]

Sheen created his role as moral guide by being an authoritative catechist. He taught Catholic morality to the world, regardless of creed. Sheen's show addressed a variety of issues in postwar life, including "Catholic devotionalism, family life, communism, and social justice."[53] Historian Mark S. Massa, S.J., asserts that Sheen's theological discussions were "essentially ecumenical and nondogmatic" as he mixed "serious scholastic philosophy" with jokes and humor.[54] For example, in a 1955 "How to Think" *Life Is Worth Living* episode (still circulating on the Internet through YouTube), Sheen begins with a letter sent by a small child asking if bishops are bald under their *zucchetto*. Sheen bows to the camera, removing his cap for everyone to see his full head of hair. As the program continues, however, audiences encounter the authoritative catechism of Sheen as he writes on the chalkboard (always with the heading of JMJ "Jesus, Mary, and Joseph," a familiar teaching model for anyone attending parochial schools in the 1940s and 1950s). His assertive hand gestures, louder proclamations, and direct eye contact with the camera engage viewers with his message:

> . . . Therefore to think well, one has to have principles that are independent of space and time by which one can live. We know these principles exist and we know there's such a thing as truth, simply because there's a *logos*, there's an intelligence behind the universe. One of the great thrills of thinking is to know all the sides, but also to know what is right and what is true.[55]

As scholar Christopher Owen Lynch describes it, Sheen's rhetorical persuasiveness focused on the "distinction between right and wrong" in order to teach audiences "timeless values" and be a source for answers to everyday life questions.[56] Sheen presented a Catholicism wherein Americans could discover their identities and joy in the private sphere. Although he rarely spoke about Catholic theology directly, his enactment of his pastoral and priestly persona represented the tension between the secular and the spiritual, what Lynch illustrates as a "roadway to unite heaven and earth" through the small screen.[57] Sheen described his work as teaching by "working out a Christian response to the challenge of our times."[58]

One of those challenges included bridging the "Catholic" and "American" divide. According to Lynch, Sheen constructed his television program as a way to alleviate tensions "between the Catholic subculture and the wider culture of an America heavily influenced by Protestantism."[59] Sheen's most ardent critic was the mainline Protestant magazine *Chris-*

tian Century. Even that magazine noted, however, that Sheen was "Catholicism's most gifted performer"—a jab, perhaps, but at the very least, Catholics were topics of Protestant magazines, not separated as in previous decades.[60]

The wildly popular, interdenominational reception of *Life Is Worth Living* illustrates that Sheen's packaging of "Catholic scholastic philosophy" served as an exploration of broader Judeo-Christian religious aspects during the 1950s.[61] Sheen did not deny his Catholicism but rather "resignified it" and, as Smith claims, turned the "minority faith of Catholicism into a means of making sense of the new social order of the postwar nation."[62] For Sheen, Catholicism and religion in general were paths that could lead to America's success. The Catholic Church was not, therefore, a political force to reckon with (at least overtly), but was a place for spirituality in a tri-faith American culture. In an episode entitled "Reparation," Sheen confirms the wider American religious understandings and pluralistic moments of the 1950s, ". . . Let Jews, Catholics, and Protestants from their pulpits, as men and women of God, all of us, make America free, make America at peace."[63]

Sheen brought Catholicism into the American mainstream, but he also highlighted the patriotic nature of American Catholics. For many American Catholics, his television program announced an acceptance of their religious identities as "safely 'American.'"[64] Sheen connected American ideology with Roman Catholicism through a common enemy: communism. His rhetoric propagated the notion that America is a nation chosen by God to fulfill a special destiny. Whereas Lyman Beecher, in his 1834 *Plea for the West*, equated America's chosen-ness with Protestantism, Sheen reversed that connection by making Catholics fully American. In a 1954 episode entitled "Signs of Our Time," Sheen listed moments of grace and blessing for the United States, from George Washington to Abraham Lincoln. With a fervent intensity, Sheen looked directly into the camera (and thereby into the eyes of the American people) and declared, "We have been blessed too in our Constitution," then yells emphatically, "which none of us want to change!"[65] The studio audience erupted in applause, sealing the patriotic catechism. Sheen's patriotism did not embrace secularism but rather imbued American identity with a Catholic morality and sensibility. No longer foreign, Catholics were Americans, who were sometimes critical of secular life, but who also emphasized tolerance.

The public perception of priests is that they are authoritative figures. That authority derives from a power dynamic wherein the priest is in a hierarchy above the lay people. By presenting himself as an authority on television, Sheen could have been seen as a stoic, static figure. What resonated with audiences, however, was how he used humor to balance his roles as both priest and celebrity. His humor, often described as corny and self-deprecating, such as "Long time no Sheen," illustrated Sheen's ability to laugh at himself.[66] The humor also offered insights into the life of Catholic priests, something that most non-Catholics, and even some Catholics, were not privy to in everyday life. For example, Sheen used humor to discuss life at the rectory; "We climb four flights of stairs for breakfast, lunch, and dinner. During Lent it is not worth it."[67]

Beyond American patriotism, Sheen also shares with Colbert an emphasis on humor, comedy, and laughter. In an episode entitled "Why Do People Laugh?," Sheen educates audiences with rationales for why humans alone laugh, stating "man alone has a soul, man alone has an intellect, man alone is able to grasp meaning, therefore man alone can laugh."[68] Sheen explains jokes, teaching and speaking without a script as he would any subject. He provides three reasons for human laughter. First, that humans can see meaning in words; second, that humans are introspective and able to laugh at themselves; and third, that humans comprise matter and spirit and that the two often collide in humorous incongruities.

Sheen provides examples throughout the episode of double-meaning puns. In one case, a little girl was asked, "What will you do when you get as big as your mother?" To which the little girl responded, "Diet." Sheen explained that while some people consider puns the lowest form of humor because they redirect your thinking, television's popular bishop disagreed. He then connected those more mundane puns to "the greatest pun in the history of the world [which] was used by the son of God himself."

> He saw a man fishing one day, his name was Simon, he changed his name. He changed his name to rock. Then a year and a half later, he met him and our Blessed Lord asked who he was and this man rock answered, "Thou art Christ the son of the living God," and our lord answered, "Blessed art thou, Simon . . ." it was his old name. "Thou art the rock upon which I will build my church." It was a pun on his name and if the Lord uses puns, we can get along with them, too.[69]

According to Sheen, all of these jokes, puns, and incongruities are linked to human souls and spirit. He connects a sense of humor to a sense of the mysteries of the world and turns scientists, poets, and humorists into theological examples. Sheen describes these three vocations and their divine senses of humor: The scientists see through things, the poets look out into the world and see things others do not, and the humorists "pierce our foibles, relieve tensions."[70] Bishop Sheen grounds his discussion of divine senses of humor with biblical examples. He presents his religious authority throughout his discussion of humor and laughter, what some might consider profane and secular concepts. Instead, Sheen's humor and comedy, while not the primary focus of his genre, are infotaining through narrative teaching style and homily-esque rhetoric.

Through his teachings about human and divine nature, often with humor and purpose, Bishop Sheen redefined Catholics as Americans. The visual aspect of the television medium brought a Catholic priest into the homes of millions of Americans weekly during the 1950s. Sheen complicated expectations about sacred and profane spaces, teaching and informing Catholic and non-Catholic audiences. Sheen's use of humor and puns in self-deprecating ways humanized his scholarly bishop persona, a theme history sees in the twenty-first century with the lay Catholic character STEPHEN COLBERT, who exploits the inverse of this dynamic to good effect. Rather than his being an authority who gains influence through humor, Colbert's humor is the source of his authority.

COLBERT: Religious Authority

Like Fulton Sheen, Stephen Colbert uses Catholic humor to inform and entertain a diverse audience via television. However, genre and positionality divide the two hosts. Bishop Sheen was an institutionally approved Catholic authority. Colbert, when portraying his character COLBERT, is a self-appointed lay Catholic authority, parodying the media personality and informative genre of Coughlin, Sheen, and political pundits like Bill O'Reilly and Sean Hannity. He fuses Catholic "infotainment" and American political rhetoric to satirize authorities, lay or clerical, who speak for God.

Neither Coughlin nor Sheen ever claimed to speak for God, as COLBERT unabashedly does. As a lay Catholic and political pundit, COLBERT demonstrates his bravado and self-aggrandizement when he asserts that he is America's most famous Catholic, who has appointed himself "God's mouthpiece on Earth" in the recurring segments "Yahweh or No Way."[71] Through self-authorization, COLBERT becomes an authority because he claims to be one. In a moment of truthiness, COLBERT might refer to his authority as the infallibility of STEPHEN COLBERT. COLBERT's statement summarizes his authoritative status succinctly: "Who better to figure out which is which than someone with a God complex?"[72]

Born in 1964, Stephen Colbert grew up in Charleston, South Carolina, the youngest of eleven children in a devout Catholic family. In a *CBS Sunday Morning* interview with comedian and journalist Mo Rocca in 2015, Stephen Colbert described his family as a "humor-ocracy."[73] Everyone was funny, and the way to have a voice was through your comedy. His father and his two brothers closest to him in age died in a plane crash in 1974 when Stephen was ten years old.[74] He pinpoints that as a turning point in his life that taught him about the concept of laughing through tears: "You cannot laugh and be afraid at the same time."[75] After earning his undergraduate degree in theater performance from Northwestern University, he joined Chicago's Second City improvisational theater troupe. Immersed in a network of sketch comedians, he met his future collaborators in projects such as *Strangers with Candy* and *The Dana Carvey Show*. Colbert's professional comedy career launched in 1997 when he joined *The Daily Show* as a caricature of a conservative news correspondent. He performed as a correspondent for the next eight seasons. When *The Colbert Report* spun-off from *The Daily Show* in 2005, many popular segments revolved around the intersection of COLBERT's boisterous character and religious authority, most often in "Yahweh or No Way."

A *Rolling Stone* magazine retrospective of *The Colbert Report* succinctly summarized the "Yahweh or No Way" segments:

> Declaring himself "America's most famous Catholic," Colbert the character has been a subversive way for Colbert the person to demonstrate his faith with more humanity and less dogma than is displayed by the Religious Right. (It's a toss-up between Stephen and Pope Francis for Best Catholic Rebrander of the 21st Century.) "Yahweh or No Way" was one-stop shopping for recent religious news, with the star divining God's stance on everything from Christian Mingle to the new English

translation of Catholic Mass introduced in 2011. No program has made deep-cut Bible passages so damn funny.[76]

Rolling Stone deftly highlights the complexity inherent in a *real-life* religious person's subverting public conceptions of religion while in character. With ample swagger and charismatic assurances, COLBERT establishes his authentic authority to bestow a religious decision, presuming to "speak for" a Judeo-Christian, monotheistic American God. He claims it is his "burden to determine whether divine messages are really from the Big Guy" and the authenticity of those messages.[77]

The hyperconservative persona conflates American patriotism and conservative Christian beliefs, as evinced by the opening credits of *The Colbert Report* wherein COLBERT descends through the "empyrean" while holding an American flag and standing proudly and stoically as words like "truth" and "honest" scroll in the background.[78] The *Colbert Report* set demonstrates the hyperpatriotism with its red, white, and blue background and its focus on the stars and stripes. As such, this character earnestly presents himself as an authoritative and authentic religious figure in America. It is not difficult to see the messianic quality of *The Colbert Report*, according to communications scholar Jeffrey P. Jones:

> The host is the source of truth, and because the host shares that truth with the viewers, he must suffer and endure attacks (as messengers of the truth) from those who don't want to hear it and for the sake of the audience who believes in it and him.[79]

The entire set intentionally presents the COLBERT persona as an icon, "to reflect this aspect of the character and his special religious relationship to his audience."[80] Colbert describes it in an interview with Nathan Rabin of *The A.V. Club*,

> Everything on the show has my name on it, every bit of the set. One of the things I said to the set designer . . . was, "one of your inspirations should be [Leonardo's painting] *The Last Supper*." All the architecture of that room points at Jesus' head, the entire room is a halo, and he doesn't have a halo. . . . [O]n the set, I'd like the lines of the set to converge on my head. . . . And so if you look at the design, it all does, it all points at my head. And even radial lines on the floor, and on my podium, and watermarks in the images behind me, and all the vertices,

are right behind my head. So there's a sort of sun-god burst quality about the set around me. . . . I said, "I don't want anything behind me [e.g., television sets behind news anchors' head], because I am the sun. It all comes from me. I'm not channeling anything. I *am* the source."[81]

The concerted use of patriotic aesthetics on set strategically evokes a mingling of religion and politics within the conservative narrative of America as a Christian nation. Wrapping himself in this patriotic aesthetic, COLBERT also suggests that he is the best kind of American, not just a Christian but a Catholic.

COLBERT is a Catholic capable of challenging deep polarizations in both American political life and American Catholic life. In the recurring *Colbert Report* segment "Yahweh or No Way," Colbert plays with the line between liberals and conservatives to challenge the polarization of religious, political, and media authorities in twenty-first-century American life. When the first "Yahweh or No Way" segment aired on January 8, 2009, COLBERT introduced the segment by asserting his religious authority and trivializing God's religious authority,

[A] lot of people claim to talk to God but God can't really be speaking to all these people, He's way too busy deciding high school basketball

The *Colbert Report* set in 2014

games. Go Cougars! Well, someone has got to speak for God and God told me it should be me. That's why I am introducing my brand new segment, Yahweh or No Way.[82]

"Yahweh or No Way" appeared intermittently fourteen times between January 2009 and December 2014, usually occurring after the first commercial break and before the guest interview on *The Colbert Report*. The segment uses clips from actual news shows and adds humorous commentary from character COLBERT. Frequently, COLBERT addresses an off-camera director/stage manager, "Jimmy," who edits in a video clip about the topic. COLBERT often improvises gestures and comments, for example singing along to the segment's theme song or dancing between questions. "Yahweh or No Way" presents current events in religion to religiously diverse audiences (similar to the popular "This Week in God" segment, which Colbert helmed when he was a correspondent on Jon Stewart's *The Daily Show*). More than in any other part of *The Colbert Report*, this segment illustrates COLBERT's self-proclaimed religious authority and claims of knowing the mind of God.

"Yahweh or No Way" begins with an opening joke that usually comes from a cliché about religion or God, such as "cleanliness is next to Godliness, which is why I sometimes pray to Mr. Clean."[83] This is followed by an introductory song and opening credits. The credits depict "Yahweh"

"Yahweh or No Way"

through medieval religious paintings, and "No way" with a still photo-graph from the movie *The Wizard of Oz*, depicting Dorothy, Toto, the Scarecrow, the Tinman, and the Lion addressing the Great and Powerful Oz in the Emerald City. The "No Way" visuals are meant to illustrate the difference between the real God and false gods (the Wizard). The rest of the segment presents a current event regarding religion, usually includ-ing a video clip or an image (real or digitally altered). COLBERT then com-ments on the event and decides if an object, action, or person is approved by God (Yahweh) or disapproved by God (No Way). Occasionally, COLBERT provides a less definitive response, such as "Maybeweh" or "I Don't Know Weh."[84]

By becoming an over-the-top religious authority figure on "Yahweh or No Way," Colbert challenges other religious authorities and questions their validity and authenticity. As the person self-authorized to speak for God, COLBERT proclaims which current events are legitimate, right, true, and good, and what God would want. Most of these current events defy mod-ern logic or rationality—finding an image of Christ in grilled cheese, while perhaps a common occurrence, is not considered direct communication with a deity. COLBERT does not decree that he is the only one to whom God speaks, but he does present himself as the only mass-mediated fig-ure who can decide the validity of the claims of others.

Like other religious authorities, COLBERT demonstrates his power to judge on God's behalf through sacred texts. In the "Yahweh or No Way" segments, he frequently establishes his faux authentic knowledge about religion with real and fake biblical references. More often than not, they are actual quotes from the King James or New Revised versions of the He-brew Bible and the New Testament. Other times, they are less authentic, like when a woman saw the image of Jesus in her sandwich. An image of the Holy Bible appears on the left corner of the screen. COLBERT, off-camera, recites the words as they appear in text on the screen: "This bread is my body. Cover it with Kraft American cheese, place it in the broiler for 10 minutes, and enjoy."[85]

The joke comes with a visual and auditory punchline that could be read multiple ways. On the one hand, it mocks the authority of those who read the Bible literally by changing the sacred text. On the other hand, it also mocks the woman in the clip who saw the face of Jesus in her cheesy toast, presenting her as someone who illogically searches for religious meaning

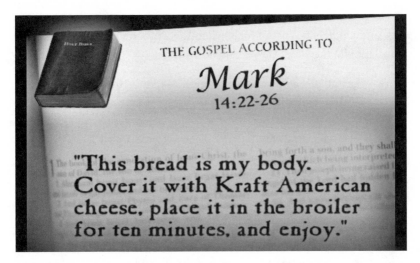

THE GOSPEL ACCORDING TO

Mark

14:22-26

"This bread is my body. Cover it with Kraft American cheese, place it in the broiler for ten minutes, and enjoy."

Faux Bible quote

in mundane places. Both interpretations of this joke evoke assumptions about religion that are present in the American cultural ethos. COLBERT's self-authorized biblical proof-texting comes across as mocking conservatives mainly through the exaggerated conservative persona he portrays. Regarding the political valence of humor, satire, and parody, political humor is not inevitably subversive or boosting of the status quo. Rather, in Colbert's case the political leanings aim leftward toward a more liberal approach because of the inherent critique embedded in an ultra-conservative-pundit parody.

Many of the "Yahweh or No Way" segments evaluate current events within the Catholic Church. COLBERT gives himself the power to judge these issues because, as he explained in November 2011, "I am basically the pope of basic cable, so when something happens in the Catholic Church everyone is waiting for my imprimatur."[86] At the bottom of the screen, a chyron reads "Yahweh or No Way" in medieval-style font with an image of an old man with a beard wearing a flowing white cloth, presumably depicting God. So COLBERT's claims to authority are reinforced in two ways. The first is through an image of God's seemingly approving COLBERT's judgments. And second, by using the same language as the institutional Catholic Church, COLBERT aligns his decisions with those of official clerical authorities.

However, sometimes COLBERT disagrees with Catholic Church teachings and judgments, for example when the Church changed the English translation of the ritual text during Mass in 2011.

> Yes, they changed the words to the Mass. . . . Listen up, Catholic Church. You do not mess with the liturgy. It is the infallible word of God, which was translated from the Latin, which was translated from the Greek, which was translated from the Aramaic, which of course was translated from the original English.[87]

The search for biblical primacy, together with an emphasis on traditional and familiar liturgy, demonstrates COLBERT's conservative Catholic leanings. He never wants changes in his Church, a misconception of the Roman Catholic Church as stagnant. But he also adds a conflation of Catholic traditions with American popular culture when he continues, "Besides, do you know how long it took me to memorize all these prayers? It was harder than memorizing 'We Didn't Start the Fire.'"[88] COLBERT then creates a mash-up of the *Our Father* prayer and Billy Joel's classic song:

> Our Father who art in heaven hallowed be thy name thy kingdom come thy will be done. Einstein, James Dean, Brooklyn's got a winning team, Davy Crockett, Peter Pan, Elvis Presley, Disneyland. Amen.[89]

As this hodgepodge prayer demonstrates, American and Catholic identities are not at odds but rather the mixing of religious and popular culture language contributes to the humor. While the combination of "sacred" and "secular" creates transgressive humor here, for COLBERT the two categories are co-constitutive to the point of inseparability. Interestingly, Billy Joel's method for coming up with the song included searching for forty years of headlines from 1949 to 1989, a time period that was one of upheaval and immense change in American Catholicism.[90] The connection becomes more than a list that most Americans of a certain age might know. Instead, it becomes a marker for the de-marginalization of Catholics in America. COLBERT's conservative fervor continues the rant, expanding to further changes in the liturgy.

> . . . The new Nicene Creed, the seventeen-hundred-year-old profession of what all Catholics must believe, has been tweaked. It now describes Jesus not as the, understandable, one in being with the Father, but as

consubstantial with the Father. Really? Consubstantial? What the hell does that mean? We're trying to get into heaven here, not take the SATs.[91]

In these moments, COLBERT catechizes about the Nicene Creed and judges the Catholic Church's decisions simultaneously. He both presents and yet confronts some aspects of Catholic doctrine and life that he disagrees with as a conservative traditionalist.

God is a Catholic deity in "Yahweh or No Way" segments as most of America's current political events are Catholic-flavored for COLBERT. In May 2011, after Navy SEALs killed Osama bin Laden, Colbert explains where the true credit for this global event lay. While Democrats give credit to President Barack Obama and Republicans give credit to former President George W. Bush, COLBERT agrees with Peruvian President Alan García, who gives credit to the late Pope John Paul II. According to COLBERT, this is the logical conclusion to the pope's beatification:

> The first step to sainthood is called beatification and John Paul was beatified the same day bin Laden was killed, which was also the same day that the Memphis Grizzlies won a second-round playoff game, so you could put J.P. down for two miracles. The point is, the Lord works miracles every day, you just gotta know how to spot 'em.[92]

By facetiously attributing this global political event to the Catholic Church, COLBERT further narratively links American politics and American Catholicism. Connecting God's will to geopolitical events illustrates the differing valences in the religious and political perspectives Colbert presents.

COLBERT's Catholic identity is both explicit and hidden. The judgments and pronouncements he makes in "Yahweh or No Way" can be read as religiously conservative rather than as specifically Catholic. However, these themes are of course interrelated, as COLBERT also judges what is really religious and really Catholic. Through his self-asserted religious authority, COLBERT defines what constitutes sacred and truthful religion in America. COLBERT draws on forceful rhetoric similar to that of Father Coughlin, while also managing to follow in Bishop Sheen's model of teaching Catholicism to broad audiences.

Colbert presents an angry commentator, infotaining the masses by playing a patriotic character who follows Catholic doctrine to the letter.

But Colbert is a comedian, which means that every comment has multiple valences. When COLBERT explains proper behavior in contemporary society, he is tongue-in-cheek when he instructs, "You should never attack someone based on sexual orientation and gender. You should attack them based on fear and anger."[93] Father Coughlin presents the hyper-real; Coughlin presents his persona in a way that plays up his real self. COLBERT, on the other hand, presents the hyper-unreal, an over-exaggeration that probes what is really real.

The persona Colbert portrays and the polysemic double-speak of that performance constitute the satirical challenging of religious authority. COLBERT conflates American patriotism and conservative Catholicism to a hyperbolic extent, while comedian Colbert lampoons political and media authorities who act precisely as COLBERT does, though the others act without Colbert's comic intent. By delegitimizing particular political and media authorities through his humorous parody of a conservative pundit, Colbert legitimizes his own authority as a truth-teller. The satire turns truthiness into truths. Colbert's humor debunks the notion of one capital "T"-True authority, but he does so by having his character become the ultimate authority in the recurring segment "Yahweh or No Way."

What differentiates Colbert from both Father Coughlin and Bishop Sheen is that his source of authority comes not from the priesthood but from his position as a lay Catholic entertainer. He debates with prominent Catholics, such as Garry Wills, Sister Simone Campbell, and William Donohue, but never claims to speak with official authority. For that he brings in the "Chaplain" and "Priest" of the Colbert Nation, Father James Martin, S.J. Colbert complicates the misconception that lay Catholics toe the institutional line through COLBERT's self-sanctioned authoritative position as a judge for Yahweh and by personifying the tension between lay and institutional authority with a humorously over-exaggerated character.

In American religious history, the discussions about broadcast or mass-mediated religion rely on assumptions about clergy-led worship. The most popular example is televangelism in the 1980s and 1990s. Televangelism's "electronic church" broadcast *real* religion to millions across the airwaves. Colbert is situated in a history of mass media and American religion that extends beyond the history of Evangelical televangelists and praise-and-worship media. The connections between lay and clerical, between "religious" and "secular," are connected rather than segmented.

Mass media is one site of the nuanced, messy, and incredibly powerful shifts in American religious authoritative bodies and structures.

Understanding Colbert as a religious commentator is controversial because he blends fiction, comedy, satire, and reality differently from what we normally consider religious. Yet, as his historical lineage suggests, this gives us the tools to question the connection between Catholic and American identities and to question the link between vitriolic political dialogue and religion. COLBERT constantly contests Catholicism. He is the authority of non-authority and the identity of multiple-identity. Stephen Colbert is part of a larger history of mass-mediated Catholics, both clerical and lay. Scholars and audiences do not often place Colbert as part of this tradition because he mocks, jokes, and satirizes. But Catholic comedians, including Colbert, grapple with issues of authority and presentation of identity in their humor. They are inherently part of the lineage of Catholic mass-mediated figures but disrupt the narrative in specific and humorous ways.

3   Colbert as Catechist

As discussed in the first chapter, in a question-and-answer session before the taping of his show on November 18, 2014, I asked the "out of character" Stephen Colbert why he decided his character would be Catholic. His answer had a three-part response. First, Colbert replied that when he started *The Colbert Report*, he was given some advice: "Johnny Carson told David Letterman who told Conan [O'Brien] who told me, doing a show this much, four days a week, is going to take everything you know. And I know a lot about being Catholic." Second, he said he could "play up the liberal/conservative" divide evident in Catholicism and take on an exaggerated conservative persona to become "Captain Catholicism." Third, he stepped back from the audience and stared off, almost in amazement of his situation, and chuckled, "I mean, it's pretty neat. I get to interview priests. It's pretty fun."[1]

The ways in which Colbert utilizes both infotainment and his dual persona are, perhaps, most evident in a key component of his on- and off-screen identity: his Catholicism. Colbert represents Catholicism to a broad audience of Catholics and non-Catholics alike. In doing so, he relies on his personae and infotainment to embody and teach a particular sort of contemporary American Catholicism to his audience, namely that it is possible to identify as Catholic while also critiquing the Church's institutions and doctrine.

As a self-identified Roman Catholic, both in the guise of his conservative talk show character and out of character as himself, Colbert provides insights into the anxieties, conflicts, and demands of American Catholic culture. During his nine years hosting *The Colbert Report*, in his more recent position as host of *The Late Show*, and as a contemporary celebrity speaking on policy issues to Congress or to college students, Colbert's self-identification as a Catholic gives him "insider" status that lends his critiques greater credibility and weight. It is a form of self-mocking, because he identifies as a Catholic, someone inside the fold of the faith tradition. Colbert satirizes conservative Catholicism, faulting its hypocritical and incongruous elements through his satire. He does so, though, without being offensive or vindictive, arguably staying within the bounds of basic decency. Colbert's humor may at times reinforce certain Catholic stereotypes, beliefs, and cultural assumptions. Yet it also skillfully embodies a tension held by many white middle-class Catholics in America: that religion can often be hypocritical, but that does not mean that religion itself is irrelevant to life or that it is not important to identity and community.

Colbert's Infotainment-Catechism

Colbert presents himself as someone who knows a lot about being Catholic. He is a lay Catholic who uses his performance stage to catechize. In contemporary American life, it is notable that a lay entertainer acts as catechist for Catholic and non-Catholic audiences because catechism often happens at local levels (teacher to student, parent to child, priest to parishioners), and Catholics usually catechize to other Catholics only. While we should not be surprised that Colbert catechizes because he taught Catholic "Sunday school," in the public sphere comedians are often less likely to be associated with teaching about religion.[2] Although Colbert's version is not the official, authorized catechism, his status as a self-identified Catholic and media catechist affords him a kind of authority that in some sense allows him to mock aspects of Catholicism in a familial, teasing way.

In November 2014, a small group of Colbert Nation members gathered on the corner of 54th Street and 10th Avenue in New York City in freezing temperatures, hoping to become audience members at a live taping of *The Colbert Report*. During the next four hours, 140 audience members slowly made their way into the red, white, and blue waiting room lined with Stephen Colbert cut-outs, posters from the show, and eagle statues from earlier episode tapings. Three big screens showed clips from *The Colbert Report* on a loop. The audience ranged in backgrounds, including a middle-aged Indian Hindu couple and their adult children, four Columbia University college freshmen from Long Island and Florida, and a

Catholic family from Connecticut.[3] Under his large, puffy coat, a non-practicing Muslim news reporter wore an American flag sweater, "for Colbert."[4] They had all won the lottery (a literal ticket lottery) and were eagerly anticipating meeting their favorite "truthiness" commentator. But what did they really know about him?

Many of his fans, particularly the Catholic ones, know that he is religious. In 2015, when transitioning between *The Colbert Report* and *The Late Show with Stephen Colbert*, Colbert appeared out of character in many Catholic and mainstream media outlets. When asked by Neil Strauss of *Rolling Stone* about his time as a Confraternity of Christian Doctrine (CCD) teacher, Colbert replied, "I teach the seven year olds. I'm the catechist for their first communion."[5] As Father James Martin, S.J., said in an interview, "[T]here's a great pride among young Catholics that [Colbert is] publicly Catholic."[6]

For those outside the Catholic Church, those who often think Colbert is only character COLBERT, those who have seen one or two episodes, or those who know of him only as a celebrity, it is easy to question the *realness* of Colbert. "Is he really Catholic, like in real life?" They know he is American; they know he is a satirical comedian. Some who know his background can tell you he is from South Carolina and that he performed improv at The Second City in Chicago. But, as one male audience member assured me, he is "as religious as he is Republican," implying that he is neither.

America's most famous Catholic? In reality, during *The Colbert Report*, the character COLBERT has so masked the *real* person that audiences easily assume that Colbert resides solely in the secular world. Some audience members I encountered could never imagine that anyone who mocks the institutions and corporatization of religion could in fact be a pious and reverent receiver of the sacraments. "But I didn't even know he was religious, is he Catholic?" A few audience members were shocked to learn that Colbert was a "practicing Catholic," and when pressed, they defined "practicing" as attending church, confessing to a priest, and receiving the Eucharist.[7] The point those fans miss is that humor about religion is not monolithic. Colbert's satirizing of hypocritical Catholic institutions does not reflect Colbert's disbelief in religion, any more than his mockery of Republicans indicates political apathy.

". . . I Know a Lot about Being Catholic"

Colbert's Catholicism comes off as a contest. In presenting his Catholic credentials to television audiences, Colbert equates Catholic family history and composition with authentic Catholic identity. He often does this by perpetuating the stereotype that Catholics have big families. He asks most Catholic guests how many siblings they have and usually challenges them to name all of their siblings faster than he can name his: "James, Edward, Mary, William, Margo, Thomas, Jay, Elizabeth, Paul, Peter, and Stephen." Counting siblings becomes a way for Colbert to classify himself as a Catholic, and also to brag about it. For Colbert, having a large, Mass-attending family indicates a strong Catholic religious identity.

Both in character and out of character, Stephen Colbert infotains as a catechist, teaching others about the principles of Catholicism in an engaging way. Usually, the catechism is presented in a book or text that summarizes Catholic doctrines and takes the form of a question-and-answer response. The catechism normally includes the text of the Lord's Prayer, instructions for how to pray the rosary, and lessons on creation, sins, and the institutional Church. In the lesson on the sacraments, for example, a twenty-first-century version of the catechism goes as follows:

Q. *What is a Sacrament?*
A. A Sacrament is an outward sign instituted by Christ to give grace.
Q. *How many Sacraments are there?*
A. There are seven Sacraments: Baptism, Confirmation, Holy Eucharist, Penance, Extreme Unction, Holy Orders, and Matrimony.
Q. *Whence have the Sacraments the power of giving grace?*
A. The Sacraments have the power of giving grace from the merits of Jesus Christ.

One might not expect a comedian to be an expert on religious doctrines or trivia, but Colbert proves such an assumption false in an extended clip of his 2011 interview with musician Jack White entitled, "2011–A Rock Odyssey featuring Jack White—Catholic Throwdown."

Colbert and COLBERT weave throughout this didactic interaction, infotaining audiences while quizzing White, a Grammy Award–winning musician most famous for his band, The White Stripes. White grew up in a

Catholic family, and his father and mother both worked for the Roman Catholic archdiocese of Detroit.[8] He was an altar boy as a child and later thought he would become a priest, having been accepted to a seminary in Wisconsin, but changed his mind at the "last second."[9] With such an illustrious Catholic background, Colbert and White were formidable opponents for a test of Catholic strengths. This catechism is not one compiled by the Catholic Church. They created their own question-and-answer catechism that kept the essence of form and content but played wildly with the actual responses.

During the "Catholic Throwdown," Colbert waffled in and out of character, moving with Jack White between sets. In some shots, they were set up in an interview style, two chairs facing each other with cameras set to film the two performers together and in close-ups individually. Then they moved into a studio control room with hundreds of lit buttons and volume knobs connoting a "behind the scenes" look. Eventually, Colbert and White transferred to a dressing room with lighted mirrors, hairbrushes, and makeup. In the last two sets, they stood up, as if in conversation at a cocktail party. They appeared to be in the corner of the room testing each other on their Catholic trivia and a camera happened to catch the action.[10] While many of COLBERT's interviews are improvised, this seemed not only unscripted, but as if the normally combative COLBERT were slowly moving out of character into Colbert, similarly competitive but with a playful edge.

COLBERT and White begin their modernized catechism conversation with White asking whether COLBERT's first name, STEPHEN, is spelled "properly, like St. Stephen." "Like St. Stephen," COLBERT responds, "the first martyr." From there, the two delve into a competitive demonstration of their knowledge of the saint's hagiography:

> White: Stoned by his peers, I believe.
> Colbert: In Antioch, yup, misunderstood, or properly understood and killed anyway.
> White: Aren't we all? Yup. I was named after John the Baptist.
> Colbert: I didn't ask that . . .
> White: I thought we were talking about each other's names.
> Colbert: No, we were not, we were talking about my name . . .
> White: Are you trying to out-Catholic me, right now?

Colbert: Yeah, I'm trying to out-Catholic you . . .
White: Let's do this.
Colbert: Throwdown.

Here is where we see COLBERT shining through, the self-obsessed egotist who affirms White's presumption that yes, Jack White, COLBERT is trying to "out-Catholic" you. Both are playing with a modernizing of rote answers, crafting criteria that would denote which of the men was more Catholic, more authentic, more real.

From there, White and COLBERT quickly hurl questions at each other about the lives of saints. "Who's the patron saint of the impossible?" White asks. "St. Jude," Colbert answers. White shakes his head, "St. Rita," he knowingly retorts. "Oh," Colbert exclaims, "Jude is hopeless causes, isn't that impossible also?" White acknowledges, "It's in the impossible realm, but . . . ." Changing the interrogation, Colbert pauses for a long time, thinking of tricky questions, then asks, "Who's the patron saint of clowns?" "Clowns"? White seems surprised when answering, "Uh, maybe St. Joseph?" Colbert smugly retorts, "St. Genesius." "Oh really," White says skeptically, "I don't think that's a real saint." White's calling into question the validity of Colbert's lesson illustrates the playfulness of the segment but also the authenticity of COLBERT's persona. Through the character, Colbert constantly mocks by presenting false information with gravitas. White picks at a special key that could unlock the mask of COLBERT, and, as such, Colbert abruptly deflects and begins a line of questioning about Catholic doctrines.

Colbert: Immaculate Conception.
White: Mary.
Colbert: of? . . . The Conception of whom? . . .
White: They conceived the idea.
Colbert: . . . Who was conceived immaculately?
White: Jesus.
Colbert: Bullshit! Mary.

As Colbert, screams "Mary," White incredulously asks, "Really?" then quickly realizes his mistake and, as if reciting a well-remembered song from childhood, "Mary was born with, Mary was conceived without sin."

Always a generous winner, COLBERT exclaims, "It's over, it's over, first one out of the gate." "You confused me," White says. To which Colbert responds, "Confused you what, with dogma? That's what 'Catholic Throwdown' is." Later on, Colbert is stumped with a question about the Feast of the Ascension, yelling, "God damn it, God damn it" after his incorrect answer. Colbert and White then look at each other and laugh hysterically, presumably at the correlation between the religious catechesis and the blasphemous language both have been using. They end that scene of the interview by shaking hands, making the sign of the cross, and then pointing their forefingers up toward heaven.

Throughout the "Catholic Throwdown," these two men embody the braiding of sacred and profane. They continually use foul language in ways many could consider blasphemous; at the very least, the juxtaposition between the religious content and the competitive intellectual dueling can be read as humorous. There is an incongruity between asking about the Immaculate Conception and ending the response with "God damn it."

The distinction between sacred and profane has been well researched and theorized in the field of religious studies. Stephen Colbert and the study of religion and humor serve as an excellent example of the blurred boundaries between these two categories. For the sake of brevity in this book, sacred is an object or concept that is "set apart" for a special purpose, one that usually possesses religious or consecrated functions, as defined by French sociologist Émile Durkheim.[11] This can be taken in two ways—as a noun, "the sacred," or as an adjective, "sacred." The former implies a *sui generis* understanding of the sacred as something wholly distinct from anything else with characteristics different from all other things in the universe. The adjectival form of "sacred" describes the humanly constructed specialness or set-apartness of an object or concept. "Profane" is often defined in reference to sacred or the sacred, but in various ways. Etymologically, "profane" refers to anything "outside the temple." Thus, one definition of "profane" refers to neutral objects or concepts "not related or devoted to what is sacred." These are excluded from the category of sacred but are not necessarily its opposite. Another definition concerns the desecration or pollution of the sacred, the profane as oppositional and contrasted with sacrality. The act of profaning concerns expressions of contempt for sacred objects or concepts, usually synonymous with pollution, blasphemy, irreverence, or sacrilege. Sociologists and scholars such as Freud, Weber, and Berger were some of the first scholars to recapitulate the sacred/profane distinction into a religious/secular discussion. Later scholars, such as Ann Taves, mark sacrality with new nomenclature, such as "special things."[12] In the instance of Colbert and White's "Catholic Throwdown," the comedian and the musician blend sacred content and profane language. They blur the lines between sacred and profane contexts by being lay catechists infotaining backstage in a theater. In the scene between White and Colbert, the incongruity comes from "secular" entertainers, a comedian and a musician, enacting a form of catechism for Catholic and non-Catholic audiences. This scene epitomizes infotainment, delivering religious information in entertaining ways.

The next scene in the "Catholic Throwdown" has the two men standing in front of a record or CD stand, similar to ones at a music store. Now the line of catechism questions moves toward discussions of the papacy, institutional intricacies of the Church, and material objects of the Mass. While lay catechists usually explain those materials when teaching the catechism, the entertaining banter between White and Colbert conceals a competitive nature one would not expect from people discussing religion. Furthermore, the competition seems to be about more than having the correct answer. It becomes about questioning Colbert's and White's authority, their authenticity, and their Catholic credentials. For example, Colbert asks White, "What was Saint Mary's mother's name?"

> White: . . . Which Saint Mary? . . . It's pretty ambiguous since there's about 65 Saint Mary's, Stephen.
> Colbert: Mary, mother of God . . . what's her mother's name?
> White: Virginia.
> Colbert: It's Elizabeth . . . immaculately conceived Mary. That's one you got wrong before. It's a really rough area for you.
> White: So you're trying to bring up the ones I got wrong . . . .
> Colbert: What was Mary's cousin's name?
> White: That would be, uh, Anaheim.
> Colbert: You know what, I steered you wrong.
> White: The cousin's name is Elizabeth. You were wrong, oooh. That's what I thought when you just said that, that her cousin's name was Elizabeth, so you were wrong.
> Colbert: I was totally wrong, but I shook ya, by saying you were wrong. I shook you. How strong could your faith be?

Of course, both Colbert and White give incorrect answers: Mary's mother's name is Anne. The true answer is less relevant than their competition. For Colbert and Jack White, Catholic faith can be demonstrated in jokingly competitive games, but not one that questions whether or not they are *really* Catholic. This game also pokes fun at Catholic one-upmanship, a test to see who is more Catholic, who is included and who is excluded. By performing these trivia contests, Colbert is also making a statement about the exclusionary dimensions of religions.

True Catholics, these men suggest, are educated and knowledgeable about their faith from a young age. When Colbert asks White about the title of the leader of the Jesuits and White does not answer correctly, Colbert asks if he was Jesuit-educated. "I'm Redemptorist-educated . . . yeah Holy Redeemer," says White. In this competition, Catholic schooling becomes a marker for Colbert and White that they have enough lay authority to perform this catechesis. Also, their Catholic primary education ties their identities together, even though they are from different regions and different backgrounds. Still, their language would be unfamiliar to non-Catholics. There is a reason this extended "Catholic Throwdown" was not included in its entirety on *The Colbert Report* and instead shown as a video clip on the website. The insider jokes, the distinction between Jesuit and Redemptorist, for example, might go over the heads of non-Catholic viewers.

After a jump in the footage, Colbert asks White about Christ's first miracle (turning water into wine), and White begins a diatribe about the purpose behind miracle narratives.

> White: Can I say this? Why is Jesus, all his miracles revolve around partying? Turning the water into wine, everyone's hanging out, he's making fishes and loaves for everybody. Is it, is it this important for us to learn about making sure everyone's fed and is drink, is drunk?
> Colbert: Absolutely, whatsoever you brew for the least of my brothers . . .
> White: That you brew for me.

That began a series of inquiry around biblical quotes. "What's the first verse of 'be not afraid'?" White asked Colbert. "Be not afraid," Colbert retorted. "That's the first line, what's the first verse," quipped White. As Colbert tries to answer, White begins singing it, "Be not afraid, I go before you," and Colbert pipes in as well, mirroring White's lyrics on a delay, as he does not seem to know the words. When they complete that song, Colbert begins singing others,

> Colbert: This is my body, given for your freedom, this is my blood, shed for all mankind. Do you know that one? . . . The king of glory comes, the nation rejoices, open the gates before him, lift up your voices. Who is this king of glory? How shall we call him? . . .

To which White responds, "See, this is some 1960s Catholic stuff." "No," Colbert corrects him, "1960s Catholic stuff is 'Our Father, Who Art in Heaven . . . ,'" singing a tune reminiscent of *Godspell* or *Hair*, a distinctly pop-musical and bright tone. Thus, it is not just Colbert and White's content and question-and-answer format of the catechesis that makes this Catholic, but also the connection to American Catholic culture. They perform and enact their faith by singing specific tunes that connect with their memories. The entertaining catechists demonstrate that they know a lot about Catholicism, but that it takes mental prodding to recall the ingrained religious culture.

Colbert and White present their Catholic identities as part and parcel of the Catholic teachings, doctrines, dogmas, and material culture that encapsulate their worlds. The "Catholic Throwdown" illustrates how experienced Catholics play with the intricacies of their faith. Some could say that they are not being true, pious Catholics by joking with each other, but that demonstrates a limited view of Catholicism, one that discounts real, non-institutional lay practices, including the joviality of religious identity and knowledge. As evidenced in this "Catholic Throwdown" and other *Colbert Report* segments, Colbert does know "a lot about being Catholic," and he puts that knowledge to use throughout his television programs. He is fully immersed in Catholic language and culture, and he builds that knowledge into his COLBERT brand.

"Captain Catholicism"

In February 2010, COLBERT interviewed historian Henry Louis Gates Jr., who had tested COLBERT's genetic and ancestral lineage to locate COLBERT's family history. First, Professor Gates informed COLBERT that he was "the whitest man [he] had ever tested," and that even then, his history could demonstrate surprises in his family background. Gates continued that COL-BERT was an avowed "Roman Catholic, super Irish," to which COLBERT asserted "I'm Captain Catholic!" However, Gates was not finished. COL-BERT may be Captain Catholicism, but his seventh great-grandfather was a Lutheran. "Exactly," COLBERT exclaimed, "he was a heretic!" COLBERT's own lineage shed light on the contrast between expectations and reality of religious identity. The Catholic heritage may not be "pure" under con-servative COLBERT's strict standards, but his personal Catholicism remains undeterred by heretical relatives.[13] In a segment with Martha Stewart later that year, Colbert declared that if you are once a Catholic, you are still a Catholic, to which the queen of home lifestyle responds, "You're always a Catholic."[14] Catholic credentials, for Colbert, are interconnected with per-sonal identity.

One may always be a Catholic, but presenting that identity on national television is another matter. Not many pundits or comedy show hosts are as dedicated to representing their Catholicism as COLBERT.

For example, COLBERT came on-screen Ash Wednesday in 2011 wearing ashes on his forehead, indicating that he had participated in Mass that day before the 6:30 P.M. taping of his show. On this segment, COLBERT dis-cussed what he was giving up for Lent, asserting, "But as America's most famous Catholic, I need to set a good example," which that year meant giving up Catholicism for Lent. Instead he tried other religions, such as Islam and Judaism, only to backslide the week before Easter. In a segment entitled "Catholic Bender," COLBERT returned to the show having binged on his preferred religion:

Colbert on Ash Wednesday

Well, long story short, I went on a Catholic bender and . . . I don't remember a lot of the weekend, . . . I tell ya folks, I got totally pious-faced. I did every Station of the Cross. I don't even remember how many sacraments I did. For all I know, I'm celibate now. I vaguely remember doing a Hail Mary and an Our Father at the same time. That's right, the Catholic speedball. People told me I was stumbling through the streets of Manhattan in a chasuble and a mitre, begging for quarters to buy votive candles. And at one point, I genuflected all over the back of a cab. When I came to, I was in a monastery next to an abbot, whose name I couldn't remember, illuminating a manuscript . . . . God, anyway, I thought I could kick it, but I guess I just have to accept that I am a functional Roman Catholic.[15]

As Colbert described in answering my question before a November 2014 taping of *The Colbert Report*, in order to play up the liberal/conservative divide in Catholicism, he created an exaggerated hyperconservative persona who mocks political and mediated authorities, and the character is in turn satirized through Colbert's portrayal. Through the COLBERT persona, Colbert embodies multiple ideologies and conceptions simultaneously that in turn lead to multiple interpretations of Colbert/COLBERT. The weaving of the persona's and the real person's opinions and comments scrambles who and what might be considered authoritative, both in American society and American religions, including Catholicism. This blending of progressive and conservative viewpoints in Colbert's dual personality reflects the adversarial, at times uncomfortable, political combinations within the Catholic Church. More broadly, this dual personality becomes a stand-in for the divisive political culture of the United States more generally.

Colbert's comedy derides the deep polarization between conservative and liberal segments of American Catholic culture. By doing so, he also calls into question the idea of a politically, socially, and culturally homogeneous Catholicism. One could argue that Catholicism addresses incongruities with more vigor (than, say, certain types of Protestantism) because it grapples with supposedly unchanging institutional theologies and doctrines. Jay P. Dolan argues that religions cannot escape history and that the "historical conditioning of religion means that religion can and indeed does change."[16] He also argues that prior to the Second Vatican Council, the Roman Catholic Church was perceived as ahistorical. While scholars agree that religions are not outside history or context, the perception that religions are ahistorical is still at play in the public imagining of religions. Those myths are incorrect, but persistent. On the one hand, the hierarchy of the Catholic Church makes infallible dogmatic pronouncements. On the other hand, lay devotional practices abound, with home shrines and individual Marian apparitions. The range of Catholicism extends beyond a binary, as those who define Catholicism for themselves or others are influenced through their contexts. There are myriad contextual factors, including region, nationality, language, ethnicity, gender, and race. This heterogeneity in Catholic culture becomes lost when Catholic people are segmented into liberal/conservative or progressive/traditional categories. Instead of ignoring the culture wars bifurcation, Colbert plays with it, blending its boundaries.

The actor and the character differ on their opinions of Catholic hierarchy and practices, but they are both Catholic. By being both a character and a *real* person simultaneously, Colbert/COLBERT embodies the contradictions and heterogeneity in the Catholic Church. Of course, the heterogeneity Colbert mocks is still a whitewashed Roman Catholicism. It ignores racial, ethnic, and gender diversity. As a heterosexual white male, Colbert does not embody African American, Latino, queer, homosexual, or female Catholic identities. Captain Catholicism, then, focuses on the political heterogeneity, not racial, ethnic, social, or economic heterogeneity, of American Catholic culture.

Of the conservative sources of authority and punditry that Colbert mocks, Roman Catholicism is just one example. In satirizing the intermingling of religion and politics in twenty-first-century American life, Colbert actually conflates conservative politics and conservative Roman Catholicism. For COLBERT, Paul Ryan—congressman, vice presidential candidate in 2012, and speaker of the House in 2016—exemplifies the intersection of Catholic identity and American politics, as described in *The Colbert Report*'s 2012 segment "Paul Ryan's Christian Budget Cuts":

> But folks, don't talk to me about separation of church and state. This is a Christian nation, our money says "In God We Trust," our Declaration of Independence name checks the Creator, and when Congress passes a law, it is nothing short of a miracle. So we have to be guided by Christian principles, and yet, President Obama is attacking the sa-

cred and deeply Christian Republican house budget written by my fellow Catholic, Congressman and Reagan-hair re-enactor, Paul Ryan. Just because the Republicans' plan gets 62% of its cuts, $3.3 trillion, from low-income programs while preserving tax cuts for the wealthy, Obama blasted Ryan.[17]

Colbert then plays a news clip showing President Obama describing Paul Ryan's budget plan as "thinly veiled social Darwinism." To which, an incensed COLBERT retorts, "How dare you, sir. These are Republicans. It is thinly veiled social creationism . . . and no one legislates in a more Christian way than Congressman Paul Ryan." The program then cuts to a clip of Ryan on the Christian Broadcasting Network, evangelical Christian preacher and 1988 presidential candidate Pat Robertson's television channel. In the clip, Ryan claims that "a person's faith is central to how they conduct themselves, in public and in private . . . . [T]he preferential option for the poor, which is one of the primary tenets of Catholic social teaching [which] means don't keep people poor, don't make people dependent on government so that they stay stuck in their station in life." COLBERT validates Ryan's conservative stance, stating, "Yes, helping the poor keeps them stuck in poverty. As Jesus said, 'Tough love thy neighbor as thyself, get your own loaves and fishes.'"

Throughout this segment, Colbert infotains audiences, apprising them of contemporary religion and politics through the use of entertaining humor. This segment exemplifies the co-constitutive, and often hypocritical, nature of religion and politics in twentieth- and twenty-first-century life. Colbert uses satire to interrogate what he perceives as hypocrisy between Catholic and conservative beliefs. He uses fake biblical quotes to criticize proof-texting from Catholic scriptures and doctrines to support a political perspective. Colbert also highlights the subtext of religio-political authorities who use hyperbole to emphasize extremism in media. He mocks the clichéd conservative Christian political message that the members of the Republican Party are the only God-fearing Americans. In using clips of Ryan from the Christian Broadcasting Network, Colbert strategically connects conservative evangelicalism to conservative Catholicism. This intermingling has historical roots, arguably from the 1970s Moral Majority rhetoric and post–*Roe v. Wade*, as conservative evangelical Christians and conservative Catholics joined forces to combat abortion rulings in the Supreme Court, the Equal Rights Amendment, and other perceived changes in societal values. Religion scholar Hillary Kaell discusses the connection between conservative Catholics and evangelical Christians, arguing that "in the 1970s, an explosion of vibrant non-denominational evangelicalism and Pentecostalism began to dominate Christian politics and pop culture in unprecedented ways. U.S. Catholics have navigated the post–Vatican II world in this cultural and political context, absorbing, rejecting, and adapting the diffuse evangelicalism around them." She connects this to Catholic Bible study groups that based their meetings and readings on an "evangelical template."[18] Scholars of Protestant American history recently described the late-twentieth- and early-twenty-first-century conflation of conservative Christianities, including American Catholicism.

Often, COLBERT's humor about Catholicism concerns the institution and its leaders, especially the pope and the Vatican. In some moments, the pope becomes the butt of the joke. At other times the pope and Catholic doctrine are repeated verbatim as a way to align COLBERT with conservative Catholicism. COLBERT loves Pope Benedict XVI but is "no fan of Pope Francis."[19] According to COLBERT, "that's the spare Pope, the real Pope's Benedict. This new Pope is just kind of a fake Pope."[20] COLBERT finds Pope Benedict's extravagant clothing and conservative dogmatic stances to be representative of the "true" Church. He does not appreciate Pope Francis's welcoming attitude. In 2013, he derides Pope Francis for saying that "even atheists can go to heaven." "Great idea, Frank," COLBERT retorts in an accusatory tone; "first dogs, now atheists. What's next, Presbyterians? . . . The only good thing about atheists' getting into heaven is that I'll be able to walk up to them and say, 'I told you so.' That's my idea of paradise."[21] COLBERT becomes Captain Catholicism by showcasing his affinity for the ultra-conservative pope emeritus.

Similarly, COLBERT disapproves of this "new guy" and his message of "hope and change." By correlating Pope Francis's election to the rhetoric of President Obama's 2008 campaign of "hope," Colbert does two things. First, he reinforces the connection between Catholicism and American politics. Second, he mocks 2008 Republican vice presidential candidate Sarah Palin's own mocking of Obama, with her folksy phrasing of "hope-y, change-y" liberalism. Colbert flaunts his character's Tea Party and Republican demagoguery when COLBERT claims that American Catholicism is conservative and traditional. For COLBERT, the new pope may not be aligning with what the former considers Catholic values: "What does he mean he wants the Church to be poor? That's not the Catholic Church I signed up for."[22] By having COLBERT associate himself with ultra-conservatism, Colbert's satire oversaturates the categories of liberal/conservative, blending the binary divisions into more fluid categories.

The jokes COLBERT makes are still in line with the conservative Catholic persona portrayed on the show. One example addresses an important issue for Catholic clergy: celibacy. In May 2009, a popular Latin American priest, Father Alberto R. Cutié, was caught "canoodling" with a bikini-clad woman on the beach. To which COLBERT first responds with a biblical allusion: "Apparently, he missed the part in the Bible about sparing the rod."

Captain Catholicism COLBERT then throws to a clip of Father Cutié on *Good Morning America* questioning whether celibacy for Catholic priests should be optional. While COLBERT acknowledges that many Catholics and non-Catholics ask similar questions, COLBERT ultimately affirms that priests should be celibate, "Don't you think Jesus is tempted by bikini-clad women? The guy spends half of his time carrying people on the beach." "Sorry, Father," COLBERT retorts, "but Catholics with options are called Protestants."[23] By highlighting the rigidity of certain Catholic doctrines and the lived responses that negotiate the institution, Colbert presents internal contradictions and diversity. Colbert both illustrates and employs the fact that the Catholic Church is not a monolith of singularly minded individuals, as it is often stereotyped in the media and public culture.

"It's Pretty Neat, I Get to Interview Priests . . ."

Colbert represents American Catholic culture as being inextricably tied to the Roman Catholic Church's hierarchy and institutional clergy. As Colbert has said, he really enjoys interviewing priests. Colbert reveres priests and as such is part of priest "fan culture." Fandom usually implies a relationship that is between a human and a fictional or fantastical subject, often a character portrayed in mass media. Colbert's fandom inverts that definition in some ways. First, being a "fan of priests" is actually more akin to lived religion than media fandom. Priests in local parishes have legions of "fans" even when they are not on television or on the radio. Priests' roles are often all-encompassing in a community. Catholic priests have many roles in their communities, as pastors, nonprofit managers, counselors, advisors, preachers, and prayer leaders. As such, there are charismatic and beloved priests who reach heights of popularity outside of a mediated medium. When it comes to priests, Catholics have mixed opinions; some adore priests, others find them terrifying. Colbert points to the authoritative role of clergy in the Catholic Church as a fan, one who has positive experiences with priests. Colbert satirizes and mocks not individual priests themselves but rather the system and institution of the Catholic Church. Priests are persons and friends; the institutional Catholic Church is full of incongruity, and therefore Colbert straddles the line by mocking the Church while still being a fan of specific priests.

The most popular clergy person on *The Colbert Report* (by sheer number of visits to the show), is Father James Martin, S.J. Father Jim Martin, as Colbert often refers to him, is a Jesuit priest, editor-at-large of the national Catholic weekly *America* magazine, and an author of many books, including *My Life with the Saints*; *A Jesuit Guide to (Almost) Everything*; and *Between Heaven and Mirth: Why Joy, Humor, and Laughter Are at the Heart of the Spiritual Life*. He did not attend Catholic elementary, high school, or college, somewhat anomalous for a life-long Catholic growing up in the 1960s. A native of Philadelphia, Martin graduated from the University of Pennsylvania's Wharton School of Business and worked in corporate finance at General Electric for six years, until he "saw the light," as he joked on *The Colbert Report*.[24] Those years made him "pretty miserable," and he realized he was in the "wrong place." A documentary about Thomas Merton, and Martin's reading of Merton's autobiographical *The Seven Storey Mountain*, began Martin's interest in religious orders. His local priest encouraged him to contact the Jesuits, and "everything sort of clicked."[25] He entered the Society of Jesus in 1988 and was ordained to the priesthood in 1999.

So, how does a Jesuit priest become the "Chaplain of the Colbert Nation"? By writing an op-ed, of course. In 2007, Martin wrote a piece about Mother Teresa's *Dark Night of the Soul*, in which she discusses her feelings of God's absence from her prayers. Some of the *Colbert Report* producers saw the *New York Times* article and invited Martin to the show. As Martin explains, he was "delighted to go" for a few reasons: "Number one, I was a fan of the show, . . . number two, you know, it's right down the street, and number three, um, . . . I knew it would help [*America*] magazine."[26] Martin and Colbert have a reciprocal fandom in which they are both aware and appreciative of the other's work and message. Reciprocal relationships between fans and the subject of their fandom usually have the valence of producer versus consumer. Producers think about and incorporate the thoughts and actions of their productions' fans into the productions themselves.[27] The valence is slightly different when one thinks about the relationship between Martin and Colbert not because both are Catholics, but rather because of the authority structure of the Catholic Church, to which both men align their beliefs. To an extent, Martin could be seen as the "producer" and Colbert the "consumer." In the realm of television, however, the roles are reversed. The two catechists, Colbert and Martin, hit it off both on- and off-camera as Martin considers them friends. Martin returned eight times to *The Colbert Report* as a guest, specifically on Catholic segments, a role he sees as a "great opportunity to evangelize."[28]

Not simply to evangelize, Father James Martin also infotains. As "Chaplain of the Colbert Nation," Martin teaches the catechism of the Catholic Church, but he does so while elucidating the incongruities in interpretations of Catholicism. When Martin first appeared on *The Colbert Report*, it was to address the same topic as his 2007 article about Mother Teresa's "recently disclosed letters" in which she doubted God's existence. After showing highlights of atheist Christopher Hitchens's excitement at what Hitchens considered to be proof of the non-existence of God, COLBERT brought on Martin to "help us cope with the news that Mother Teresa was in fact not a good person."[29] Father Jim Martin assured viewers that Mother Teresa was probably not in Hell for doubting her faith, that even saints could have times when they perceive God's absence. Martin nuanced the conversation from polarized atheist/believer rhetoric, to a more complicated story about Mother Teresa and her work in Calcutta. COLBERT performed the act of polarized idiot and Martin then taught COLBERT and the audience about the nuances of religious doubt and sainthood.

Martin also corrects how people in the American media, such as Glenn Beck, understand social justice. According to his website, Glenn Beck began his professional career as a talk radio host, winning the 2008 Marconi Award for Network/Syndicated Personality of the Year from the National Association of Broadcasters. From 2006 to 2008, he hosted a nightly television show on CNN Headline News. Beck then moved to his "self-titled topical talk show," which aired on Fox News from 2008 to 2011. As of 2018, *The Glenn Beck Program* can be heard on the radio and seen on a streaming site, TheBlaze TV. Beck has also published novels and nonfiction, seven of which were #1 *New York Times* bestsellers. His life narrative tells of a conversion away from drugs and alcohol in his thirties and into Mormonism.

On March 18, 2010, COLBERT addressed the topic of social and economic justice. He showed a clip of Glenn Beck telling listeners that "If you have a priest that is pushing social justice, go find another parish. Go alert your bishop and tell them, excuse me are you down with this whole social justice thing?"[30] COLBERT determined that Beck is not attacking Catholicism but rather correcting a long-overdue issue: "For over 100 years," the host complained, "popes have declared a doctrine of social justice, including support of labor movements and the distribution of wealth in capitalist societies." Not only was the Roman Catholic Church hierarchy active in social movements, but lay leaders were also involved in "temperance movements, immigration protection and rural settlement programs, urban welfare and settlement house work and women's voluntary associations," one exemplar being Dorothy Day of the Catholic Worker movement.[31] Conservative COLBERT aligns himself with Beck and merges his religious and political leanings when he says that his "personal relationship with Jesus" tells him that Jesus wants him to acquire wealth. Which, of course, is why Christ's symbol is a plus sign.[32]

The Colbert Report then showed a clip of Father James Martin arguing with "the gospel according to Glenn." On *ABC News*, Martin railed against Beck's indictment of Catholic doctrines, stating,

> I don't think it's as much an attack on my faith as it is someone who seems not to know what he's talking about. The ultimate defense, I think, comes from a bishop in Brazil who said when I feed the poor they call me a saint, when I ask why they're poor they call me a communist.

COLBERT then introduced Martin as his guest and allowed Father Jim to teach the audience a Catholic interpretation of social justice: "Social justice addresses the things that keep people poor and it's in addition to charity, which is, you know, helping the poor, but social justice asks you, why are these people poor?" Father Martin's discussion of the causes of poverty connects to a Catholic phrase, "option for the poor," first used by

"Plus" sign

Father Pedro Arrupe, Superior General of the Society of Jesus (Jesuits), in 1968 in a letter to the Jesuits of Latin America. In later years, the Catholic Bishops of Latin America (CELAM) and several popes, in particular Pope John Paul II, further defined the concept.[33] COLBERT rebuts this argument with conservative rhetoric, reasoning that "our capitalist society says everybody's got a chance, you dig down, you do what you have to do, and you got a chance to make it. Or don't you believe in capitalism?" Martin and COLBERT then spar for a few minutes, with Martin claiming that capitalism does not provide for the poor and COLBERT asking what is "in it" for him—why should he help the poor? "Other than eternal salvation?" Martin retorts.[34]

As Martin presents Catholic teachings, COLBERT argues slightly, but not vehemently. COLBERT gives Father Jim plenty of space to present his argument without much interruption. The contradictory nature of the conservative persona still respects the clergy's authority, but with an interesting twist. It is still Colbert's stage, and at the close of their discussion, COLBERT says, "Father, this interview has ended, go in peace to love and serve the Lord," in a cadence and rhetoric familiar to those who have experienced the end of a Catholic Mass. Both men then proclaim, "Thanks be to God."[35] This presents official Catholic authority figures as willing to joke around with traditional and liturgical elements of the institutional Catholic Church and in some ways make clergy and Church hierarchy more approachable, more human. Colbert uses Father Jim Martin's presence on *The Colbert Report* to demonstrate COLBERT's equating of himself with religious authorities, while still giving clergy a space to deliver Catholic messages and correct presumptions about religion. Colbert's rhetorical strategy sets up his persona as an ignorant adversary of Father Martin's in order to advance an agenda of critiquing and dismantling bombastically rigid Catholics. COLBERT fits the mold of such a Catholic identity.

Father Martin also teaches Colbert's American audiences about the Catholic Church's institutional intricacies. For example, when Pope Benedict resigned in February 2013, COLBERT brought Martin on the show to explain what would happen next:

> Martin: There will be a conclave, an election, where the cardinals will gather and elect a new pope . . . . He's going to resign on February 28th, and ah, there will be no pope, there will be what's called a vacant seat, *sede vacante*. And someone will take over in his place, you know, temporarily.
>
> COLBERT: Who takes over? . . . Who's mini-pope for a while?
>
> Martin: It's the person known as the *camerlengo*, or the chamberlain, [who] will take over for a bit.[36]

Father Martin explains to COLBERT and the American people, many of whom are unaware of canon law, about ballot procedures in the College of Cardinals. The conversation quickly turns, however, to COLBERT's narcissistic bid for papal nomination.

> COLBERT: Speaking of which, why not me? Could I be pope? Is it possible?
>
> [*crowd chants "Ste-phen"*]
>
> Martin: What would you choose as your name? What would your name be, you suppose?
>
> COLBERT: I'm a big fan of Urban.
>
> Martin: Hmm, that's good.
>
> COLBERT: I would be Urban the third.
>
> [COLBERT *holds his arms raised like during mass when the priest says "and also with you"*]
>
> Martin: Not sub-Urban the first? . . .

Colbert then breaks character, as evinced by a lack of eyebrow raising and smacking the desk in a playful, not forceful, way. He laughs at the corny joke Father Martin just used. "Very nice, Father," Colbert smirks, and calls Martin "Father Chuckles." The two men both enjoy their respective places, infotaining audiences with facts about the Catholic Church (Martin) and truthiness on how Catholicism feels (COLBERT). COLBERT represents feelings because the character describes truthiness as knowing in your gut, in your feeling, rather than through facts. Juxtaposing Martin and COLBERT highlights that the former knows actualities and realities and the latter chooses to believe things based upon how he feels.

The connection between Martin and Colbert becomes more obvious in Martin's 2011 book, *Between Heaven and Mirth: Why Joy, Humor, and Laughter Are at the Heart of the Spiritual Life*. As Martin writes in the book's Introduction, joy and laughter are spiritual virtues that are "lacking in religious institutions" and in our ideas about what constitutes religion.[37] Martin succinctly summarizes his own thesis about the value of laughter by quoting the Jesuit priest Pierre Teilhard de Chardin, who proclaims, "Joy is the most infallible sign of the presence of God."[38] Martin claims that joy, humor, and laughter are interrelated but that American Catholicism considers those virtues secondary to suffering. Martin's intervention appears to mirror Colbert's: to bring the funny into relation with the real and the true by catechizing to the masses.

Colbert shares a similar outlook on the need for humor in institutions, be they religious, political, or social. Martin, however, believes "there's good humor and there's bad humor, there's humor that builds up, there's humor that tears down."[39] Colbert, on the other hand, does not seem to draw such a sharp line. Colbert, whether in or out of character, questions the relevancy, purpose, and efficacy of political and religious institutions. He charges groups with hypocrisy, and American audiences often look to Colbert to be their truth-teller, their harbor of truthfulness in a world where reality and truthiness can be confusing. Colbert mocks those who are perceived as hypocritical in their belief and action, even crossing "over the line" of propriety. At the 2013 Alfred E. Smith Memorial Foundation dinner (a fundraiser for Catholic Charities), Colbert was asked to roast honoree Timothy Cardinal Dolan. Dolan was in full regalia in his black cassock and his cap. Colbert joked, "In that cape and red sash, you look like a matador who's really let himself go. Did you not see the invite? It said white-tie, not Flamboyant Zorro."[40] Perhaps because Martin is part of the institution, as a member of the Society of Jesus, he marks a distinction between good and bad humor, taboo and safe, sacred and secular. But Colbert, as a lay Catholic, holds those tensions in a looser relation. Colbert plays with them, demonstrating a way in which to be Catholic in America today: religious, yet not always serious.

Colbert, COLBERT, Father Martin, and Cardinal Dolan are all Catholic authorities representing different roles in twenty-first-century America. Dolan is the archbishop of New York, appointed by Pope Benedict XVI in 2009. He is from St. Louis, Missouri, and attended Cardinal Glennon College and completed his "priestly formation" at Pontifical North American College in Rome and Pontifical University of St. Thomas. Ordained in 1976, Dolan also has a doctorate in American church history from the Catholic University of America. Before moving to the archdiocese of New York, he also served as archbishop of Milwaukee. In 2010, Dolan became the president of the U.S. Conference of Catholic Bishops.[41]

Aside from several appearances on *The Colbert Report*, Colbert publicly encountered Cardinal Dolan again at a debate at Fordham University on September 14, 2012. Father James Martin moderated the event, entitled "The Cardinal and Colbert," before more than 3,000 faculty, staff, and students of the Jesuit university in the Bronx. The event was, in part, about evangelizing through entertainment, featuring "two charismatic Catholics who loom large in the American Catholic imaginary engag[ing] in lively intellectual debate about their faith, humor, and joy."[42]

Without knowing these two figures, an easy assumption to make would be that Colbert, as a comedian, would have disdain for the institutions he was critiquing, and because Cardinal Dolan embodies that institution, the two men would not get along. Further, as Cardinal Dolan is part of the spiritual hierarchy of the Catholic Church, another assumption would be that he would not care about Stephen Colbert at all. In reality, the two men were engaged and excited to discuss the issues of joy and spirituality at that event. In fact, when Colbert approached Cardinal Dolan to shake his hand, "the cardinal took Mr. Colbert's hand and kissed it."[43] This astounding reversal of authority, and reciprocal fandom, marks a significant moment in American Catholicism, a cardinal of the Catholic Church showing deference to the influence and power of a mass-mediated entertainer. The cardinal said to Colbert, "You're a Catholic and a comedian,

Fordham event (Illustration by Tim Luecke)

Stephen, and you're darn good at both."[44] Cardinal Dolan acknowledged Colbert's popularity, celebrity, and infotaining qualities and what his presentation of Catholicism both in and out of character means in American religious life.

Interestingly, there was a "media embargo" on the event, in part so that Colbert could speak freely without having to associate entirely with his COLBERT character. Despite the embargo, an official hashtag (#dolancolbert) and subsequent unofficial ones (such as #dolbert) allowed audience members to live-tweet the conversation. They tweeted some of the one-liners of the event, like Colbert's saying, "Humor fosters human relations" and

"Colbert: I love my church, warts and all."[45] Fordham students, such as Rachel Roman, also wrote about their experiences for articles in web magazines like *Busted Halo*, a media site with publishing, radio, TV, film, and digital media presences. A ministry of the Paulist Fathers, "Busted Halo is a unique media resource that utilizes a relevant and accessible voice to help people understand the Catholic faith, put it into practice in their everyday lives, and share it with others."[46] Roman described the pre-dawn wake-up call required to get a seat in the auditorium. Surprisingly, Roman knew little about Cardinal Dolan (although she did admit that she should have paid more attention at her high school senior Mass, which was "held in St. Patrick's Cathedral and presided over by Cardinal Dolan"). She described shock at seeing a "friendly, funny, and dare [I] say, jolly man" instead of an imposing image she initially associated with the rank of cardinal. Stephen Colbert, on the other hand, she knew quite well from his television shows. Roman admired his speaking out of character and openly discussing "his deeply rooted Catholic faith."[47]

In the comments section of the article on *Busted Halo*, Carl Sobrado, who according to his profile is a middle-aged Hawaiian man and self-describes as "a nurse and a Catholic Christian, and that's how I want my life to be defined," said that he related to Colbert's speaking "from the heart," especially as Colbert is one of his favorite comedians.[48] Sobrado further commented that he was "finishing up" his Catholic confirmation the following year and that "like Mr. Colbert," he was "accepting the entire legacy of the Catholic Church . . . the good and the bad."[49] Colbert's ability to mock Catholic institutions and incongruities while maintaining and presenting his Catholic identity can be summarized in a quote attributed to him from the Fordham debate. "Are there flaws in the Church? Absolutely," Colbert reportedly stated. "But is there great beauty in the Church? Absolutely . . . . The real reason I remain a Catholic is what the Church gives me, which is love."[50]

Of course, Colbert's language comes off as apologetic for the institutional Catholic Church. As discussed in later chapters, Colbert's reverence and praise for Catholic institutions and clergy ignore traumatic problems, such as the clerical sexual abuse scandal. The persona COLBERT mocks bombastic conservative lay Catholics much more than he mocks clergy. In fact, Father Jim Martin and Cardinal Dolan appear to get a free pass from Colbert. On *The Colbert Report,* COLBERT is more likely to confront atheists than he is to confront priests.

Even when being interviewed by priests, Colbert comes off as an obedient and reverent Catholic. That is especially interesting, as the priests often do not know which Colbert they will be interviewing. One such interview occurred on the Canadian Salt and Light Catholic Media Foundation television show *The Witness.* Salt and Light proclaims its mission to be:

> [sharing] the joys and hopes of the Gospel through television, radio, print, and online media. Our work unites people together through prayer, celebration, reflection, education, authentic dialogue and enquiry, thought-provoking reporting and stories of faith and action. We also challenge believers to grow in the knowledge of the faith and the Catholic tradition in its many expressions. We strive to offer an invitation to all peoples, especially those on the peripheries of faith and the Church, to draw closer to the Lord and experience the community of the Church.[51]

Father Thomas Rosica, the CEO of the media foundation and the host of *The Witness,* interviewed Stephen Colbert and uploaded the interview to YouTube as well as to other Internet outlets. In the forty-five-minute interview, Father Rosica asked, "Now, which Stephen Colbert is sitting in the chair here? Is this STEPHEN COLBERT of *The Colbert Report,* or is this a new Stephen Colbert? Are you born again?" "Wow," Colbert responded with a chuckle of surprise, "that's ambitious . . . . That's a good question." Father Rosica then called the interview the "presentation of Stephen Colbert to the world . . . born-again Stephen." The *real* Stephen Colbert, not the character. Colbert hesitated to agree with Rosica that he was "born again" and used the phrase "out of his cocoon" before agreeing to say that he was "born again" and shedding his old skin, the COLBERT character on *The Colbert Report.*[52] One reason Colbert hesitated might be the fact that both character and actor are Catholic and born again would imply the latter's becoming a Christian rather than his already being part of the family of Christ. Another reason is the evangelical Christian language implied by one's being "born again." On the other hand, being born again also implies an inauthentic self that is transforming into its authentic,

Christian self, this reading of "born again" becoming clearer when taking into account that both the character COLBERT and the actor Colbert play with notions of authenticity. As Colbert says, both he and his character are Catholics, "but he [COLBERT] just feels like a victim about it all the time," whereas Colbert (the person) "wears [his Catholicism] on his sleeve" happily, as Father Rosica points out.[53]

Later in the interview, Father Rosica asks a question about the television host character, and Colbert transforms into COLBERT, talking more rapidly, interrupting Rosica, and challenging the authority structure of the interviewer/interviewee. COLBERT argues with Rosica about Catholic knowledge: "just because you got the dog collar on doesn't mean you know more about the Catholic Church than I do, d'you understand me? Are we clear on that?" As the interview continues, Rosica tells Colbert that the whole Salt and Light staff was excited about the interview, saying it would be bigger than "three popes." The Salt and Light staff's response indicates that in this case, Colbert's popularity surpasses the institutional authority's popularity. Colbert described his character as a fool. "We are all fools for Christ," Rosica interjected. "Yeah, yeah," Colbert replied, "willing to be wrong in society or wrong according to our time, but right according to our conscience, which is guided by the Holy Spirit."

Rosica continued the interview by talking about how Colbert addresses religion on *The Colbert Report*:

> You're Catholic, everyone knows you're Catholic, you were able to make fun of the Catholic Church. I mean, I watch some of those episodes and just burst out laughing, and you got away with it . . . . [Y]ou had a way of doing it where you didn't cross a line, but you made us laugh at ourselves.

A relieved Colbert laughs when responding, "I'm so glad . . . I would sometimes scoot around my priest at the end of Mass," avoiding possible awkward conversations if his jokes about the Catholic Church had been perceived as blasphemous rather than as funny.[54]

As Father Rosica's experience of *The Colbert Report* indicates, Colbert's satirical critiques and joking break down expectations of the Catholic Church as solely a rigid and traditional organization. Catholic culture does not always reflect a somber, serious, suffering religion; Catholics can laugh at themselves, and quite often at others. Colbert presents this ability to

laugh with a priest about incongruities in the Catholic Church as historically anomalous, contending that a self-reflective humor about one's religion is "a fairly modern behavior; it's not a hundred-year-old behavior; this
is a modern behavior; this is, I hope, the right relationship to have with
your faith, which is to love it but not to exclude it from your intellect."
Both the character COLBERT and the actor Colbert engage in their Catholicism in different ways, but both perform as Catholic insiders who know a
lot about their faith tradition.

Being Catholic, according to Colbert, is engrained, examined, and promoted. Colbert knows a lot about being Catholic. He crafts COLBERT to
be "Captain Catholicism," satirizes the liberal/conservative sociopolitical-
religious divide in the Catholic Church, and cozies up to Catholic priests,
all while mocking aspects of the institutional Catholic Church. Colbert is
not the first celebrity to infotain about his or her religion. However, the
way Colbert grapples with issues within the Catholic Church illustrates
the multiplicity of lay beliefs and practices, showing that the Catholic community is not uniform and quite often takes its religion with a little bit of
humor.

4 Colbert as Catholic Comedian

Comedians often find humor in their personal identities. Anecdotes, family stories, and life narratives are woven into many forms of comedy, from stage to screen to podcast. Audiences understand that the comedian is performing and that the scripted, practiced aspects of comedy may not be the *real* thoughts of the comedian. But when a comedian uses his or her own name, one can assume that the comedian's personal identity is at least tangentially connected to the material being presented. And that identity incorporates the comedian's religious understandings, including beliefs, practices, rituals, connections to heritage and family, and conceptions of religious authority. Currently, identity-related humor focuses on race, ethnicity, and gender. But why not include religion? In discussing any religious comedy, the primary connection is to identity, and within that, to do so usually with marginalized identity and stereotypes. In the United States, religious comedy has been equated almost entirely with Jewish comedy. In academic research, Catholic comedy and how comedians grapple with identity and religious authority have hardly been examined.

I define Catholic humor, for this chapter and these comedians in particular, as connected to their experiences with the institutional Catholic Church. These comedians create a constellation of the tensions showing how American Catholics have dealt with religious authority. In the 1970s, satirists and stand-up comics like Don Novello and George Carlin dealt with the religious authority of the Catholic Church by mocking and parodying it. Decades later, in the twenty-first century, comedians still grapple with the institutional Catholic Church in their humor. Louis C.K., Jim Gaffigan, and Stephen Colbert all explore themes of religious authority in their comedy, but in various modes. These contemporary comedians present the variety among Catholic tensions: Catholic Church–sanctioning, truth-telling against hypocritical authorities, and catharsis. The conflicts

Novello, Carlin, C.K., Gaffigan, and Colbert have with religious authority stem from their Catholic identities.

Often, religious identity is a key aspect to how a person presents himor herself, but rarely do scholars explore how comedians or humorous content connects to religious understanding. Those who research religion and humor are usually in fields of literature or psychology, and they rarely look at comedians' lived religious lives. The field of religious studies is essential for those examining religious identity and authority in humor and comedy. This chapter explores how Catholic comedians grapple with institutional Catholic Church authority and their presentations of religious identity.

In addition to religion, other identity markers categorize an individual or group as marginalized. "Marginalized," in this context, means "a process by which a group or individual is denied access" to political, economic, and/or social power in any society.[1] The group or individual may not be in the minority, in numerical terms, but could perceive itself to be on the periphery or outside of a particular society. Marginalized groups in this sense are technically those with smaller numbers of people in a certain community, nation, or geographic region. Specifically with regard to humor, marginalized groups trade on concepts of authentic identity in three ways. First, jokes may be made about that group. Humor scholar Christie Davies describes jokes about Polish Americans, an oft-marginalized group in the United States in the first half of the twentieth century.[2] The Tony Award–winning musical *Avenue Q* points that out eloquently in the song "Everyone's a Little Bit Racist," "I bet you tell Polack jokes, right? . . . Well, sure I do. Those stupid Polacks!"[3] Second, a group might make jokes about its own members. Jeff Foxworthy's "redneck" humor fits this category: "You might be a redneck if," as he jokes, ". . . the stock market crashes and it doesn't affect you one bit."[4] Finally, marginalized groups make jokes about nonmarginalized groups.

These categories are not discrete: One joke, comedy set, or television program might include jokes about others, oneself, and the stereotypes connected to one's group. This typology of marginalized groups humor also correlates to certain theories of humor: superiority theory, incongruity theory, and relief theory. Superiority theory is the feeling of supremacy over another through humor. Incongruity theory, promulgated by Sigmund Freud specifically about religion's connection to humor, is about ambiguity, illogical reality, and appropriateness between belief and action.[5] Freud is also associated with relief theory (as is cultural theorist and philosopher Mikhail Bakhtin), viewing humor as a way to "release or save energy" and relieve tension.[6] Performances of African American humor might simultaneously address racism, mock the KKK, and parody the minstrel stereotype.[7] All three types of humor trade in stereotypes.

Stereotyping marks marginalized-group humor because it is a way to discern authenticity of identity, asking the question who is part of, or is not part of, the group. According to the *Encyclopedia of Humor Studies*,

> the presence of stereotyping can be detected if the ethnic group that is the butt of the stupidity joke is replaced by a different ethnic group and the joke fails to make any sense. If the joke fails to make sense, it is not applicable to all groups and thus connected to a stereotype of a particular group.[8]

These stereotypes are culturally and contextually specific. For example, African Americans go to see Tyler Perry's *Madea* films more than any other group does.[9] A marginalized-group member might laugh at a joke because of self-recognition, but simultaneously, a group member could disapprove of the joke because it maintains and perpetuates stereotypes about their group. The comedian is not speaking to or for the whole group but is addressing multiple audiences and identities. Comedy provides insights into how groups and societies operate, as it acts as "social thermometers that measure, record, and indicate" parts of the world around them.[10] Thus, humor illustrates the complexities of the world in ways other forms might miss or avoid. It also becomes a space for marginalized groups to have a voice.

Through humor, marginalized groups are able to criticize cultures, institutions, systems, and societal issues, both within their own group and within larger society. Marginalized groups have "a unique perspective" on many aspects of society, including what they view as "the dominant or majority culture."[11] Their humor also provides glimpses into the "borderlands" in which these marginalized groups exist.[12] Cultural values and stereotypes are affirmed and interrogated, often simultaneously. Some leaders of institutional humor outlets observe this, such as Deborah Liebling, previously the senior vice president of programming and development for Comedy Central, who acknowledges: "Comedy has always pushed the envelope or it's not really effective . . . . That is what comedy is . . . saying the things that are taboo."[13] Pushing the envelope and destabilizing prohibitions, according to scholar Joanne Gilbert, is part of the work of comics' "performing" marginality, "emphasizing and capitalizing on their marginality or 'difference' from the mainstream," which in turn holds a mirror up to society.[14] Gilbert affirms that being a woman, rather than the material used in her comedy, makes one a marginalized female comic.[15] These comics can criticize both their placement and the stereotypes of their grouping.

While religious identity, on the whole, has been understudied in humor studies, the one exception is Jewish humor, which colloquially stands in for "religious" humor. Jewish humor is not just about Judaism as a religion but arguably also about Jewish identity as an ethnicity. As such, the "otherness" of Jews becomes both a religious and an ethnic impetus for a particular type of humor. Jewish comedy is a trope in and of itself. Woody Allen, Mel Brooks, Sid Caesar, Joan Rivers, Lenny Bruce, and Sarah Silverman are just a few examples of brilliant Jewish comedians. Jon Stewart, Colbert's boss and frequent collaborator, exemplified aspects of Jewish humor on *The Colbert Report*'s sister show, *The Daily Show*. The tradition of Jewish humor has roots in the Torah and Midrash, and even during the Holy Roman Empire, with theological satire becoming a form of opposition to Christianization.[16] But, as many argue, the modern story begins in earnest in the United States with the wave of immigration from eastern Europe between the 1880s and 1920s.[17] Jewish humor illustrates the "process of acculturation" and the "double consciousness" of Jewish immigrant life in the early twentieth century.[18] As a group, Jews tried to assimilate into American culture and still hold on to aspects of their distinctive community. Throughout the eras of vaudeville, radio, stand-up comedy, film, television, and digital media, many famous comedians have identified as Jewish. One *Psychology Today* book review in 2002 estimates that "while Jews make up only about 3 percent of the U.S. population, 80 percent of professional comics are Jewish."[19] That statistic may be changing, or at least expanding to include other religious groups (including Catholics). However, there is no denying the breadth of scholarship on Jewish humor, most of which asks the question What is Jewish humor?

The idea of an authentic and cohesive Jewish humor is, perhaps, itself a myth that is truer than true, but one that lives on. Some scholars place the initial research at the feet of Sigmund Freud, who in 1905 wrote *Jokes and Their Relation to the Unconscious* and attributed "self-deprecating" humor to Jewish identity.[20] Jews were unique, according to Freud, because they mocked themselves rather than others. Almost a century later, humor scholar Christie Davies objected to Freud's analysis of Jewish humor's uniqueness of "self-deprecation," but nonetheless, Jewish humor is marked indelibly by the idea of self-mockery because of Jews' often religious and social marginalization.[21] Authentic Jewish humor, according to anthropologist Elliott Oring, relates to a "conceptualization of Jewish history" as one of "suffering, rejection, and despair."[22] For Oring, what makes Jewish humor distinct is that Jews should not be laughing after all of this suffering, and the fact that Jews are comedians "signal[s] the existence of a special relationship between the Jews and humor," a relationship forged out of despair.[23] Jews have transcended, been defensive of, or been pathological about their suffering, a range of affective responses that manifested in their collective humor. In part, many scholars agree that the socioeconomic conditions surrounding certain Jewish comedians made for a presumption of a unique category of Jewish humor. Those conditions still have some underlying themes, such as "anti-authoritarian[ism], mocking [both] religious and secular life."[24]

The history of Jews in America enabled Jewish comedians to embrace their position as "marginalized," especially in relation to white, Protestant Christianity during the twentieth century. The influx of Jewish immigrants changed American culture, especially in New York. After moving out of New York City's Lower East Side, some Jews sought leisure and entertainment in the Catskills' "Borscht Belt," where from the 1920s to the 1980s Jewish comedians became legends. In literary circles, authors such as Philip Roth have epitomized Jewish wit. Comic Jews in Hollywood are popular to the point of being a cliché. Jewish comedians are differentiated by their religious identities.

Catholic Comedy

Do Catholics have a distinctive humor because they are defined as a marginalized group? Not in the same way as Jews are known for having a distinctive humor, but yes, there is humor about and by Catholics that we could define as Catholic humor. In the nineteenth and early twentieth centuries, and even today, stereotyping jokes made at the expense of a Catholic's religious identity might also reference socioeconomic, ethnic, or racial stereotypes. In that way, humor pointed at Catholic stereotypes could be considered intersectional. While many twenty-first-century Catholics are not marginalized politically or economically based on their religious creed, there is a historical genealogy and lineage of Catholic comedy that connects it to marginalized and ethnic humor. Just as Jewish humor is varied and diverse, so is Catholic humor; whereas Jewish humor is inextricably tied to a conception of a singular, eastern European Jewish ethnicity, Catholic humor often has an additional ethnic modifier: Irish Catholic, Italian Catholic, Polish Catholic, Mexican Catholic. As Davies explains, "It would be futile to try to make a rigorous distinction between ethnic jokes about the religion of a particular people and jokes about religion per se."[25] Catholic humor in the contemporary United States illustrates the tangled nature of religious identity, which connects to ethnicity as well as other cultural markers.

While some Catholics have been on the margins of society, others have not. Colbert and twentieth- and twenty-first-century Catholic comedians have come at a time when they, usually heterosexual white males, are not considered on the periphery of American society. Catholics have emerged from the anti-Catholicism of the nineteenth and early twentieth centuries. Of course, this applies only to white, male, and heterosexual Catholics, especially in the comedy world, where ". . . women (and men) assume humor to be a male prerogative."[26] In addition, being Catholic does not prevent Latinx, African American, and other "non-white" racial and ethnic groups from being marginalized economically, politically, or socially. While this work does not fully address the issues of race and ethnicity here, certain racial and ethnic groups of Catholics have "become white." Catholic comedy is imbued with the same racial and ethnic hegemonic practices that produce marginalization in America. Simultaneously, comedy, as a category, questions and challenges the conditions of that marginalization. Catholic humor presents a complex picture of a group of people who identify in some way with a religion that can be heterogeneously classified.

Arguably, the most popular and well-established Catholic comedians are, in fact, not heterogeneous. They are often white, heterosexual males who come across as palatable to certain American audiences, especially audiences for prime-time television or comedy specials. Catholic comedy differs from Jewish comedy not just because it is a form of comedy with a relatively new genre-identity but because white, heterosexual male comedians who are Catholic are acceptable and nonthreatening to many white, heterosexual Christian audiences. Their Catholicism is a part of their complicated intersectionality, not always the distinguishing feature unless the comedian presents it as such. Catholic humor has not always been identified as "Catholic humor" because it has the ability to fade into the background.

The category of Catholic humor is rarely referenced in scholarly or popular sources. In the January 2004 edition of the journal *U.S. Catholic*, Tara Dix compiled a small segment entitled "Catholic Humor Painfully Un-Funny." She questions why Catholic jokes are so rare and do not produce "hysterical religious humor." She found some of the worst jokes, including this gem:

> A boy asks, "What is the difference between the Jesuit and Dominican orders?" The priest replies, "Well, they were both founded by Spaniards, and they were both founded to combat heresy—the Dominicans to fight the Albigensians, and the Jesuits to fight the Protestants." "So, what is the difference?" the boy asks again. "Well," says the priest, "have you met any Albigensians lately?"[27]

After a few more insider-focused generic jokes found in church bulletins, she noted that there were enough "dirty jokes to fill St. Patrick's Cathedral."[28] But she was not looking for dirty, blasphemous humor. Instead, Dix pleaded with fellow Catholics to come up with some "good, clean Catholic jokes that don't conjure images of Far Side–esque nerds cracking jokes about the real meaning of $E = mc^2$ at a physics convention."[29] As Dix points out, good Catholic comedy was hard to find. Searching for Catholic comedy in academic scholarship also proves to be a rather futile endeavor, as analyses of Dante Alighieri's *The Divine Comedy* and James Joyce novels are the closest one can find.

Academic and Catholic journals have largely ignored on-the-ground examples of Catholic comedy. Catholic material culture is littered with nun china dolls, joke priest vestments, and nunzillas (mechanical nun dolls that have light-up red eyes and make Godzilla sounds). There is a Catholic fake news website, à la *The Onion*, called *Eye of the Tiber*. Created in 2012, this website reports Catholic news "as it happens, when it happens, and before it happens."[30] Its story headlines range from the liturgical ("'Our Father' Ringtone Conveniently Goes Off During 'Our Father,' Keeping Everyone in Key") to the papal ("'In Short, Don't Be Hypocritical Little SOB's,' Francis Says in First Encyclical") to the political ("Rubio and Other Christian Birthers Demand to See Trump's Baptismal Certificate"). *Eye of the Tiber*'s self-description is littered with satirical witticisms,

> . . . Eye of the Tiber has become a leading source for Catholic satire to the astute, and legitimate Catholic news to the obtuse. We are proud to have recently been nominated for *Best Catholic News Satire*, narrowly losing out to the *National Catholic Reporter*, proving, thus, that, more trusted Catholic news sources aside, Eye of the Tiber is your most trusted Catholic news source.[31]

The appearance of a Catholic-specific faux news source that mimics a nominally secular faux news source, *The Onion*, illustrates a shift from seeing Catholics as separated by their individual, usually Euro-centric, ethnicities, to now a comedy audience connected by a common religion, regardless of the actual diversity and complexity in that grouping.

The present moment in Catholic comedy, according to *Eye of the Tiber* creator SC Naoum, might be an opportunity for the institutional Catholic Church and its constituents.[32] Naoum hopes that the Catholic Church will have "an honest dialogue with itself about important issues."[33]

> The death of satire, of humor, of art is when it's overly-sanitized or edgeless. Satire is an amazing weapon for revealing hypocrisy even within the Church, but when it's written without an edge, it's simply a dull blade. And that's one of the problems in the Church today. Too many Catholics feel like Catholic websites, channels and stations should be a safe zone: safe from everyone and everything they disagree with, when, in fact, it should be the opposite. It should be the first place we go to discuss and debate uncomfortable topics like the SSPX [Society of St. Pius X], Vatican II or whatever Pope Francis says on a plane.[34]

Catholic humor draws both new lines and new colors within preexisting lines of comedy. While some comedians hope to drag Catholics into conversations about the Church's place in contemporary society or the hypocrisies of institutional policy, others see Catholic comedy as a tool for evangelization and commitment to community.

According to *National Catholic Register* reporter Stephen Beale, the institutional hierarchy has also amplified Catholic comedy in the twenty-first century, specifically from the top because Pope Francis blends "humor with his characteristic humility."[35] When Pope Francis visited the United States in September 2015, the Pontifical Mission Societies created Joke-WiththePope.org as a charitable fundraiser. Comedians were invited to submit their best, and cleanest, jokes. Individuals in more than forty-seven countries submitted jokes. Jimmy Fallon submitted a joke about Donald Trump in the confessional. Bill Murray submitted a joke while wearing a shirt that read, "Funliness is next to Goodliness." Lino Rulli, host of the radio show *The Catholic Guy*, submitted a joke about Catholics' being the only ones who think they are in Heaven. Non-celebrities submitted hundreds of jokes, as well.

In a turn of events that belongs in the interfaith comedy record book, the winner of the contest, and the new "Honorary Comedic Advisor to the Pope," is Rabbi Bob Alper, the "world's only practicing clergyman doing stand-up comedy . . . intentionally."[36] Ironically, it took Jewish humor–personified to win a joke contest for the ultimate Catholic. In many ways, this demonstrates how religious humor has now broadened to include Catholic comedy and Jewish comedy. On the landscape of religious humor, comedy about, by, and for Catholics has begun to rival Jewish comedy. Jewish comedians, however, are still winning joke contests.

While Catholic comedy comes in many forms, we, instead of looking solely for comedy about Catholicism, need to pay attention to Catholic comedians. This allows us to include not just the moments when a comedian or entertainer addresses religious material but also when they do not. It is not just about the idea of "clean" and moral material, although those are a part of the conversation. Rather, Catholic comedy focuses on comedians' religious identity and how they present their humor to audiences.

Catholic comedy is multifaceted, and Catholic comedians discuss everything from the Virgin Mary to the daily stock market. Religious identity connects many comedians under the umbrella of Catholic comedy, but more explicitly, the comedians examined here are also connected by another thread. Catholic comedy explores the tensions of everyday lived religious experiences with a highly authoritarian religious institution in the Catholic Church. While many comedians claim that their purpose is to probe and challenge authority, Catholic comedians have a specific religious authority to confront. Comedians vary in how they encounter the Catholic Church, and the Church authorities respond in fluctuating degrees with explicit or implicit sanctioning or disapproval. Two comedians popular in the late twentieth century (Don Novello and George Carlin) and three in the twenty-first century (Louis C.K., Jim Gaffigan, and Stephen Colbert) illustrate the various ways in which American white, male, heterosexual comedians grapple with the religious authority of the Catholic Church and how the Church responds to their humor.

Don Novello Parodies Religious Authority

Catholic humor, like the comedians who create it, is not singular. Some comedians use their knowledge of Catholicism for parody purposes. Don Novello, for example, "satirized, skewered, and stood up to authority" with the character Father Guido Sarducci, a fictional Catholic priest.[37] Novello was born in 1943 in Ashtabula, Ohio, to an Irish mother and an Italian father.[38] Raised Catholic, Novello attended the University of Dayton in the 1960s. After graduation, he became an advertising copywriter in Chicago. In the 1970s, Novello moved into comedy and humor writing, creating the character of Lazlo Toth, a pseudonymous persona that wrote ridiculing letters to famous people, particularly politicians and corporations. As he later published in his book *The Lazlo Letters: The Amazing, Real-life Actual Correspondence of Lazlo Toth, American!*, Novello wrote letters to unsuspecting politicians who corresponded with the often misinformed and imperceptive Toth.[39] The name "Lazlo Toth" was not a pure invention but actually comes from an individual who took a hammer to Michelangelo's *Pietà* in 1972, "while declaring, 'I am Jesus Christ,' . . . [while] he wore a tuxedo."[40] Novello chose to use that name because the real Toth was "attacking the establishment," a purpose Novello mimicked with his right-wing American parody persona. Novello sees his role as comedian as a way to play with authority but "apolitically-political" in a way of questioning authority, "no matter who or what it is."[41] Truly, the authority could be anyone, including his sister-in-law, Antonia Novello, U.S. Surgeon General from 1990 to 1993. Popular magazines joked that Novello now had to take seriously the Surgeon General's advice on cigarettes, to which Novello responded, "I'm switching to menthols."[42]

Contemporary actors, such as Sacha Baron Cohen and Stephen Colbert, modeled their interactions with unwary conversation partners after Novello's humorous charade. In an interview in the *New York Times Magazine*, Colbert described how Novello's "ultrapatriotic correspondence" to corporations and politicians that concluded with the sign-off "Stand by our President" influenced *The Colbert Report*.[43]

Novello introduced what is arguably his most famous character, Father Sarducci, in 1972. He found a monsignor's outfit, "big floppy black hat, white clerical collar, and a long, red-trimmed black coat with cape" at a St. Vincent de Paul thrift shop.[44] The persona, with sunglasses, mustache, cigarette, and thick Italian accent, made Novello popular in San Francisco nightclubs and later on *The Smothers Brothers Show* and *Saturday Night Live*, where Novello also worked as a comedy writer.

The costume gave Novello a way to authoritatively discuss the Watergate scandal. Religious authority gave Novello proximate authority to that in the political realm. Even though he was parodying the priesthood on *Saturday Night Live*, Novello never "got a mean letter from the Church," chastising him for his parody.[45] Novello used his personal knowledge of catechism to criticize "the bullshit of [the hypocrisies], not Jesus."[46] However, when Father Sarducci visited the Vatican in 1981, the Swiss Guards arrested him for taking photos in a prohibited area and charged Novello with "impersonating a priest," charges that were later dropped.[47] Father Guido Sarducci appeared on *Saturday Night Live* after the death of Pope John Paul II and the election of Pope Benedict XVI. Novello also performed as Father Sarducci on *The Colbert Report* and at Jon Stewart and Stephen Colbert's "Rally to Restore Sanity and/or Fear" in 2010. Novello, in particular as the character Father Sarducci, parodied, mimicked, and challenged religious authority. Primarily, Novello saw his role as one of questioning power, not the religious doctrines associated with it. He also focused more on political and social authority but used religious authority to get his message across.

George Carlin Confronts Moral and Catholic Authority

Beyond Novello, the 1970s and the latter third of the twentieth century had another iconic Catholic comedian who confronted the religious authority of the Catholic Church, but through different means and to different ends. George Denis Patrick Carlin, born in New York City on May 12, 1937, was a provocative American stand-up comedian and social critic, an influential show business figure of the twentieth century. Carlin's humor focused on three main subject areas: everyday experiences of life; the English language and its peculiarities; and the big, unanswerable questions and issues that have plagued humans since time immemorial. Of the last group, religion and its hypocrisy were a major component. Historically, Carlin stands in a lineage of influential comedians, in particular "the martyred Lenny Bruce," whose influence helped Carlin remake comedy "for the rock 'n' roll crowd."[48] A comedian for the countercultural Baby Boomers, Carlin had fourteen comedy specials for HBO, performed on and guest-hosted *The Tonight Show*, was the inaugural host on *NBC's Saturday Night* (now *Saturday Night Live*) in 1975, played a priest in the 1999 film *Dogma*, wrote bestselling books such as *When Will Jesus Bring the Pork Chops* in 2004, and was posthumously awarded the Mark Twain Prize for American Humor in 2008.

One of Carlin's most famous routines, "Seven Words You Can Never Say on Television," was "more than mere titillation," according to biographer James Sullivan.[49] The routine exemplified Carlin's belief in "the power of reason" that ignited national debate as those seven words, "*shit, piss, fuck, cunt, cocksucker, motherfucker,* and *tits,*" were adjudicated by the Supreme Court in 1978. In the end, the *F.C.C. v. Pacifica Foundation* case affirmed the Federal Communications Commission's power to regulate, and arguably censor, "indecent material."[50] But Carlin continued to confront authorities regarding issues of indecency, morality, blasphemy, and freedom of speech.

Similar to other comedians, Carlin used his Catholic formative experiences in his comedy. At his first communion, he claimed that he was "disenchanted to find that he felt nothing . . . no transcendence, no oneness with God, no miraculous visitation." He describes that realization as a moment in which he discovered that church people were "clinging to beliefs they couldn't prove." Carlin's questioning of the Catholic Church's beliefs and practices, ironically enough, began at the Corpus Christi Grammar School on West 121st Street in New York, where his teachers were Dominican sisters of Sinsinawa, Wisconsin. According to a Carlin biographer, this Catholic school was progressive, "paradoxically instill[ing] in the young student just the inquisitive tools he needed to reject the religious education he was in line to receive." His home parish encouraged liberal thinking, perhaps because writer and activist Thomas Merton had been a parishioner.[51] As Carlin explained in his routine "I Used to be Irish Catholic," by the eighth grade, he and many of his classmates had lost their faith as the sisters "made questioners out of us and they really didn't have any answers."[52]

Questioning and confronting authority figures continued after school. A prime example is from Carlin's days working at a radio station in Boston. Nightly on this station, Richard Cardinal Cushing "led the rosary for fifteen minutes, just before NBC's *News on the Hour*." One night, Cardinal Cushing was behind schedule and Carlin was the only person at the station. "At 6:59 the cardinal was just midway through the Fifth Sorrowful Mystery of the Rosary," and Carlin panicked, not knowing what to do. At the stroke of seven o'clock, however, Carlin was sure of his next action. He "pulled the cardinal's feed and cut to the broadcast: 'The NBC News, brought to you by Alka-Seltzer.'" The studio phone rang: "I want to talk to the young man who took off the Holy Word of Gawd [sic]," yelled Cardinal Cushing in a booming Boston accent.[53] As Carlin remembers it, he did something he would never do again by hiding "behind the government" and telling the cardinal that the Federal Communications Commission enforced the schedule.[54] While this initial incident with the Catholic Church authorities might seem out of character for Carlin, it also illustrates the complexity of authority. Young Carlin confronted one form of authority and showed deference to another. Later, he would be embroiled with both authoritative entities.

As his comedy prowess increased, Carlin became more brazen, and so did his satire of Catholic doctrine. He focused on incongruity between belief and action when he hosted *Saturday Night Live*. At the series premiere on October 11, 1975, Carlin crafted one of his monologues around the "questioning of God and religion." In the monologue entitled "Religious Life," Carlin opined about society, "We're so egotistical about God," he joked, ". . . that we face our dashboard Jesuses toward us, rather than on the road ahead watching out for traffic, as they should be."[55] At the end of the program, "the NBC switchboard was lighting up with complaints," with one caller claiming to complain, "on behalf of Cardinal Cooke, archbishop of New York."[56] However, the *Saturday Night Live* producers, Dick Ebersol and Lorne Michaels, discovered by the following Monday morning that the call had been a hoax. Carlin's provocations on *Saturday Night Live*, unlike when he took the cardinal's rosary recitation off the air decades earlier, did not seem to cause the same level of outrage from the Catholic Church authorities.

Carlin also jabbed at American legal interpretations of religious morality and blasphemy through his "seven dirty words" act. Groups such as Morality in Media filed complaints about the act, and, as mentioned earlier, the case against the radio station went all the way to the Supreme Court. Unlike his mentor Lenny Bruce, however, Carlin was not the defendant in the case, a distinction that did not quash the fears of his Irish Catholic mother, Mary Carlin. What did help her come to terms with her son's supposed blasphemy and indecency came from a surprising source. On a walk one day, Mary stopped to speak with a couple of nuns from George's Corpus Christi Grammar School. The sisters commented on how they had watched George on television and marveled at how wonderful George's career was progressing. Mary Carlin lamented to the sisters about George's "awful language." One of the Sinsinawa Dominican sisters said to Mary, "No, no, no, you don't understand, he's using it for other purposes."[57] He is "doing a social service by underscoring the harmlessness of mere words."[58] As George Carlin expressed in a comedy special, "From that day on, she was okay with it because the Church had approved it."[59]

Overall, Carlin confronted the Catholic Church, but he claimed in interviews that he did not intend to educate or "open people's eyes" to make a difference in the world. He affected people's worldview only by accident and not through intention: "I *always* do it for *me*."[60] As he was eulogized at his Mark Twain Prize for American Humor celebration, "He's a moralist, as stern as the nuns in his catechism class."[61] Carlin's religious identity played a vital role in his challenging of authoritative Catholic voices.[62] He was a Catholic comedian not because he fervently advocated that identity but because his stand-up acts were influenced by his education and

Catholic knowledge. Carlin's challenges illustrate one form of Catholic comedy.

Louis C.K.'s Catharsis

Moving from the comedians popular beginning in the 1970s to comedians rising to fame in the early twenty-first century, we see even more stark comparisons between those who are sanctioned by the Catholic Church and those who forcefully confront the religious authorities to grapple with their darker moments. Some Catholic comedians use their performance platforms as a form of catharsis. Elements of Catholicism may have traumatized them, and their humor becomes as much a way of relief as a critique of an institution. Louis C.K. illustrates both individual and collective forms of catharsis in his Catholic comedy routines.

Louis Székely (pronounced see-kay) was born on September 12, 1967, to an Irish Catholic mother and a half-Mexican Catholic, half-Hungarian Jewish father. C.K. moved from Mexico to Boston as a young child. Although C.K. claimed that his mother did not care much about religion, she "made the decision" to give him and his three sisters a "Catholic upbringing" so that they would have a religious context. C.K. participated in after-school catechism classes until his first communion. In an interview with National Public Radio's *Fresh Air* host Terry Gross, C.K. noted that he appreciated his mother's giving him a Catholic "touchstone" and helping him "understand what religion is."[63] While C.K. no longer considers himself a practicing Catholic, the formation he received from Catholic religious authorities stuck with him.

Louis C.K. is a prominent comedian, actor, writer, producer, and director and has developed and starred in two television programs, *Lucky Louie* (2006–7) and the semi-autobiographical, Emmy Award–winning *Louie* (2010–15). One episode of *Louie*, entitled "God," examines C.K.'s Catholic education through darkly comedic catharsis.[64] In the episode, a flashback to C.K.'s childhood depicts a group of Catholic schoolchildren listening to a schoolteacher-nun struggle to "convey the enormity of Jesus' sacrifice." The group enters a church where they meet a medical doctor who "describes Jesus' crucifixion in gruesomely graphic physical terms." C.K. fixates on Christ's suffering in the whippings and in being nailed to the cross. Young Louie is instructed to drive nails into one of his classmates who is portraying a "pint-sized faux messiah."[65] Louie refuses and the intensity of the scene horrifies and traumatizes, connecting to young Louie's belief that his sin drove the nails into Jesus's body. He returns later to "free Jesus" by breaking into the church and removing the spikes from the plaster figure's wrists and feet.[66] The scene ends with young Louie's mother having a frank conversation with her son about her uncertainty of God's existence. The terror and anxiety of the earlier scene still lingers in this nominally humorous television series. C.K.'s cathartic humor blames the Catholic Church and religious authorities for traumatizing him. He confronts that authority by purging himself of the trauma he experienced at the hands of religious authority figures. Catholic Church religious authorities mark Louis C.K. as he cannot escape his own religious background and history.

In November 2017, five women accused Louis C.K. of sexual misconduct in the *New York Times*. C.K. admitted that he masturbated in front of female colleagues and fellow comedians without their consent or coerced them into watching him. Hypocritically, C.K. rose to prominence through his stand-up in which he candidly addresses his "flaws and sexual hang-ups," often miming masturbation in his act.[67] Additionally, until 2017, C.K. was viewed as a public champion of female comics. While I cannot psychoanalyze C.K., nor in anyway connect his misconduct with his Catholicism, it is ironic that while he condemns the Catholic Church for its hypocrisies and seeks catharsis from his Catholic childhood, he later traumatizes and harasses others.

Jim Gaffigan's Sanctioned Comedy

On an entirely opposite side of the Catholic comedy spectrum lies Jim Gaffigan. Unlike those searching for catharsis or confronting authority with their comedy, Gaffigan presents himself as an authentic practicing Catholic, who happens also to be a comedian. Jim Gaffigan, born July 7, 1966, grew up in the Midwest, primarily in Indiana. He is a stand-up comedian, actor, and author. Known for his deadpan wit, Gaffigan presents observational comedy that focuses on his Midwestern family, fatherhood, and food. From comedy specials, memoirs, and his own fictionalized account of his life on *The Jim Gaffigan Show*, Gaffigan is noted as a "clean" comic, one who uses little profanity in his act.[68] A far cry from Carlin and

Louis C.K., Gaffigan rarely bends the boundaries of blasphemy or indecency. In fact, Gaffigan has become something of the institutional Catholic Church's resident comic.

Journalist Michelle Boorstein agrees, arguing in 2013 that Gaffigan
embodied the "new evangelization" campaign of the Roman Catholic
Church. She described the campaign as a "subtle" evangelization, "highlighting Catholics who are just living out Catholic teachings and are happy
as a result."[69] Gaffigan self-describes as an ill-informed Catholic comedian,
"not hypercritical." He is perplexed by his status as a Catholic comedian
because his is not the humor of "somebody who went through seminary";
rather, its "roots are in the cultural Catholicism of America."[70]

> I don't know much about the Bible myself. I haven't read it 'cuz I don't
> have to 'cuz I'm Catholic. . . . Not a lot of Catholics have read the Bi-
> ble. It's a different perspective on rules for Catholics. . . . My wife, my
> wife's really Catholic . . . She brings me to church every Sunday. If
> you've never been to a Catholic Mass, that is the longest experience of
> your life. Makes you look forward to going to the D.M.V. At times it
> seems like they're dragging church out on purpose. . . . Let's wrap it up,
> I've got some sinnin' to do.[71]

Gaffigan's stand-up comedy highlights the quotidian aspects of lay Catholic practices. He weaves together daydreaming during Mass, family and
marriage, and cultural Catholic *laissez-faire* attitudes throughout his comedy. Gaffigan is the first to admit, however, that being a Catholic is not
necessarily a marginalized position in the United States: "Maybe it's not
cool to be Catholic, but it's nothing compared to what the early Christians
had to deal with . . . we're not being thrown to lions. Not yet."[72] Gaffigan
highlights a Catholic identity as the American everyman, "a devout member of mainstream American life."[73] Still, the *National Catholic Reporter*
identified *The Jim Gaffigan Show* as an example of comedy's pushing back
"against the increasing effort in contemporary society to marginalize
Christianity in general and Catholicism in particular."[74]

Catholic institutions celebrate Gaffigan's identity as a Catholic comedian. Gaffigan and his wife, Jeanne Gaffigan, jointly delivered the commencement address at Catholic University of America in May 2016.
Throughout the speech, they referenced their Catholic education (she received a "liberal" liberal arts degree from a Jesuit school) and their Cath-

olic faith. Gaffigan described how after reaching initial career success, he began to "question everything."

> Beliefs I had doubted, I opened my mind to. Maybe marriage wasn't giving up freedom. Maybe faith in something wasn't naïve. Maybe putting others first wasn't weakness.[75]

Unlike Catholic comedians who question, Gaffigan's inquisitive nature turned him toward the Catholic Church and its beliefs and practices. He described how his wife was a positive Catholic influence on his life and how she guided him through those questioning moments. In fact, until he met Jeanne, he considered himself an atheist.

> Before I met Jeannie I had lived across the street from a Catholic church for 15 years. I didn't notice it. I never went in it once. Because of Jeannie that same church became the place I was married, the same church my five children were baptized in and the church where once a week I'm reminded to keep focused on priorities. God, family, then work.[76]

To which Jeanne replied, "I can't take all the credit. My mother has been saying perpetual novenas for 15 years." Their Catholic identity colors all aspects of their lives, and not just because they were speaking to graduates of a Catholic college. These themes of family and God have become cornerstones of Gaffigan's work and self-presentation.

And the Catholic Church officially sanctions the bland Gaffigans. "I'm going to be doing stand-up comedy for Pope Francis," Gaffigan told Conan O'Brien in September 2015, ". . . and over a million people outside in Philadelphia . . . it's weird, felt like they asked me 'cuz I was the only comedian that admitted they believed in God or something."[77] O'Brien, another famous comedian who is also Catholic, remarked on the fact that Gaffigan was the only comedian asked to join the performance lineup.

> Conan: "Catholic event? I've heard nothing, my phone hasn't rung once. I'm like a super, Irish Catholic. I'm not there."
> Gaffigan: "How many kids do you have?"
> Conan: "Two."
> Gaffigan: "Yeah."[78]

O'Brien's feigned shock at not being asked to perform for the pope appeared to take Gaffigan off guard. The latter had a moment of awareness;

he had initially thought that he was chosen to perform because he was one of two "Catholic" comedians, the other being Stephen Colbert. On the *Conan* program, you can almost see Gaffigan scrolling through a Rolodex in his head, imagining all of his comedy brethren who are also part of the Catholic body of Christ. Although there are dozens of prominent Catholic comedians, Gaffigan, safe and bland, with his pro-institutional church and "clean" comic identity, won the coveted position.

On September 26, 2015, Gaffigan performed stand-up comedy at the Festival of Families in Philadelphia. Actor Mark Wahlberg hosted as more than 1 million visitors watched Aretha Franklin, Andrea Bocelli, and Sister Sledge perform. Initially, Gaffigan was confused by the invitation. He thought it would be interesting to be in "close proximity" to the pope but afterward realized he would not just be in the audience but would be performing for the pope.[79] The archbishop of Philadelphia, Charles J. Chaput, requested Gaffigan. (Archbishop Chaput has a reputation for promoting ultra-orthodox Catholic ideals, as well as for defending priests involved in the clerical sexual abuse scandals.)[80] This invitation surprised Gaffigan, who had never envisioned clergy listening to his comedy and perhaps does not agree wholeheartedly with Archbishop Chaput's conservative orthodoxy. But clergy did listen as more than a million people gathered for the pope's visit in Philadelphia as Gaffigan performed his sixteen-minute set. He billed himself as an opening act for Pope Francis:

> Do me a favor in the audience. I know when I'm done, you're going to be tempted to leave. . . . But stick around, we've got some amazing people coming up. There's a guy coming up. Seventy-eight years old. Used to be the bouncer of a dance club. He's going to talk for a little bit.[81]

The Gaffigans' social media are full of pictures from their family's trip to see the pope and from Jim's performance.

None of this is to say that Gaffigan agrees with everything the institutional Roman Catholic Church does or says. On *The Jim Gaffigan Show*, one character is an out gay man. Before his stand-up performance in Philadelphia in 2015 for the pope, Gaffigan presented a short piece on *CBS Sunday Morning* describing the pope. In his brief segment, Gaffigan presented a version of Catholicism that incorporates modern American understandings about religious belief and practices.

It's not easy being Catholic today in America. It's a little like being a Cubs fan for the last hundred years. Love the team, not crazy about some of the management we've had.[82]

This euphemistic language is uncharacteristic for Gaffigan, who usually presents a united front with the Roman Catholic institution. Nevertheless, his small moment of weak critique ends there, abruptly moving into a conversation about Pope Francis's humility.

Gaffigan himself is rather humble about his own knowledge and presentation of Catholicism. Gaffigan considers himself a "practicing Catholic" who needs a "lot of practice" and would not consider himself a Catholic role model.[83] Journalist Ruth Graham at *Slate* magazine calls Gaffigan "America's top Christian comedian" and adds that Stephen Colbert was "his main competitor for that title."[84] However, Gaffigan does not want to be a spokesperson. He reserves that title for another comedian, one with intellectual and theological prowess. Gaffigan claims, "I couldn't quote Thomas Aquinas, you know; I'm not Colbert."[85]

Multiple Colbert(s) in Tension with Catholic Authority

As Catholics in Media Associates' John Kelly highlights, Colbert's comedy offers a satirical and "even sometimes a critical" look into his own church in a way that comes across as "lighthearted" and "respectful."[86] Kelly even notes that there is an evangelizing component. Colbert can "change some people's perceptions of Catholics."[87] Colbert's Catholic comedy, as evidenced by Gaffigan's incisive comment, can be seen as intellectual, grappling with theological and sociological issues. But his alter-ego, COLBERT, self-describes as "America's best-known Catholic." Colbert and COLBERT both perform Catholic comedy by highlighting different valences. Colbert, the entertainer, is expected to be a satirical truth-teller, but when it comes to Catholic religious authorities, Colbert and COLBERT both toe the institutional line and never provide the harsh criticism or questioning of Catholic authority that Louis C.K. or George Carlin presents to audiences.

The satirist and his prolific character are intertwined. Audiences, fellow comics, and even Stephen Colbert himself find it difficult to separate them. The parodic mask of COLBERT raises questions about the role of authenticity. What Catholic identity are the Colbert(s) portraying? COLBERT, for example, equates conservative religion and conservative politics, conservative Catholicism with right-wing conservative evangelical Christianity. Colbert, on the other hand, claims that religion and politics should not be so friendly. The satirical persona's fake authenticity, symbolized in "truthiness," disrupts perceptions of authentic religious identity in Catholic comedy.

Just because he plays the wise fool with intense bravado, does that make COLBERT/Colbert's message compelling? Religion scholar Terry Lindvall compares Colbert's rhetoric with Jesus's rhetoric:

> As with the parables of Jesus, one is not quite sure what [Colbert] is really saying in his monologues, interviews, and skits, but one has a notion that it strikes deeply into the heart, while jogging the lungs with unexpected laughter.[88]

It is through the double-speak of satire that Colbert's Catholic comedy emerges. Columnist Matt Emerson argues that Colbert is a "covert Roman Catholic catechist," emerging as a hidden apologetic within the "hostile territory" of American modernity, maneuvering with his "razor-sharp satire."[89] As Father Jim Martin observes, Colbert's "holier-than-thou persona subverts and reaffirms his orthodoxy."[90] Colbert's Catholic comedy vacillates between silliness and influence. If, as Colbert defines it, satire is "parody with a point," then his Catholic satirical comedy is parody with a specific Catholic point to make: One does not always confront authority.[91]

Like those of other Catholic comedians, Colbert's Catholic formation comes from education and childhood. However, whereas some, such as Louis C.K. and George Carlin, overtly despise the authoritarian nature of the Catholic Church, and others, such as Gaffigan, seem comfortable being the pope's chosen comedian, Colbert comes out somewhere in the middle. He is not an unhappy Catholic; in fact, Catholic pride is one node shared by both COLBERT and Colbert. Colbert does not want to offend the Church authorities, even going so far as calling some of them his friends. But he also has a reputation as a truth-teller. The truths Colbert tells, more often than not, ridicule aspects and uses of Catholicism he finds absurd— for example, when an ad for Antonio Federrici ice cream was banned for featuring a pregnant nun with text that read, "immaculately conceived ice cream is our religion."[92] Colbert's response married his knowledge of Catholicism and silly witticisms.

Evidently the ice cream is so divine that it impregnated the nun. Well, let's not jump to conclusions; after all she is pounding down on an entire tub of gelato. She might just be fat. It's not like she has to keep her figure up for a guy. On the other hand, if this ice cream is trying to stir up sales [with] the image of a pregnant nun, this could be the most sacrilegious frozen dessert since the twelve-pack of aposticles. The Judas-sicle looks like refreshing lemon but is actually banana. What a betrayal.[93]

As illustrated, Colbert comes off not as uninformed and indiscriminately following Catholic teachings, but rather as the smartest Catholic in the room. Colbert invites Catholic apologists and clergy on *The Colbert Report*. He hosts Catholic-insider debates about women priests and Catholic social justice movements with Catholic religious authorities, but by being considered an evangelist by *America* magazine and hosting the Catholic social functions, Colbert seems friendly with clergy. He does not seem to truly confront their religious authority.

Both on *The Colbert Report* and in other media arenas, Colbert tackles topics of religion with "unmitigated bravado and cheek, mainly because Colbert knows of which he speaks."[94] Colbert infotains using Catholic humor. He "lectures on saints and sacraments" and "promotes the moral reform of his own church as much as puncturing the image of Christians as dour and dismal pious people."[95] In an interview with Stanford University psychologist Philip Zimbardo about the relationship between God and evil, Zimbardo punctuated his argument with a "condescending gibe" about Colbert's receiving his religious education simply at Sunday school, not with critical thought.[96] Colbert responded quickly with a reversal, "I *teach* Sunday school, *motherfucker!*"[97] That quip can be read multiple ways: that Colbert is an intelligent and critical Catholic who can simplify complex theology for young people, or that Colbert is not a scholar and thus is spoon-feeding a simplified version of the faith. Either way audiences read that statement, one aspect rings clearly. Colbert is on the side of those who embrace Catholicism and Catholic Church authority.

Occasionally, Colbert's point does have an edge. On an episode of *The Colbert Report*, COLBERT pontificated next to a picture of the pope, "Catholicism is clearly superior . . . . Don't believe me? Name a Protestant denomination that can afford a $660 million sexual abuse settlement." As discussed in later chapters, this is one of the few moments when Colbert actively disrupts the institutional Catholic Church's authoritative hold. Blogger Diane Houdek noted that that joke was not as funny as it was "powerful."[98] But what exactly is powerful about it? Compared with Carlin or C.K., or even Novello, who portrayed a priest, Colbert begins to look like a slightly more nuanced Gaffigan.

Colbert's Catholic comedy, while certainly not the only type of Catholic comedy, holds a particular place in American life. He is known as a Catholic and a comedian, but he is not as hostile to the institutional Catholic Church or his own Catholic identity as Carlin or Louis C.K. The American Catholic Church is a diverse group of individuals and communities that do not all think the same. There are many ways to be Catholic, as Catholic comedians demonstrate. When he was asked how he dealt with the incongruities and "contradictions" between the Church's teachings and his own interpretations of those issues, Colbert explained that the "American Catholic Church is not homogeneous and does not aim to make zombies or unquestioning people."[99] Instead, the institutional Church, according to Colbert, values critical loyalty.[100] Critical loyalty—an apt descriptor for Colbert's type of Catholic comedy.

As illustrated through these Catholic comedians, Catholic comedy is most definitely a form of humor worthy of further study. Catholic comedians from Novello and Carlin to C.K., Gaffigan, and Colbert use their Catholic upbringing and identity to confront and bolster the Catholic Church's religious authority. These comedians may have varying levels of discontent with the Catholic Church, but in the examples discussed here, their dissatisfaction is belied by their own occupation of white, heterosexual, middle-class, male authority. There is no uniform way in which to be a Catholic comedian, and each comedian charts his (or less likely, her) own path on the nuanced map of Catholic humor. The institutional Catholic Church may prescribe certain doctrines and dogmas, but lived religion tells us that Catholicism looks very different depending on individual comedians' authentic religious identities. The next chapter explores the multiple ways to be Catholic in contemporary America and how Colbert grapples with somber and sobering issues in the Catholic Church through comedy.

5   Colbert Catholicism

What does the religious humor expressed by Colbert, as the *real* person and the character persona, reveal about the conflicts and tensions in contemporary American Catholic life? Colbert and Colbert both trade in stereotypes. The comedy about Catholicism comes from audiences' stereotypes, presumptions, and perceptions of Catholicism and the emphasis or reversal of expectations. Of course, many of these perceptions are incorrect, ahistorical, and ignorant of Catholic heterogeneity. One such stereotype considers Catholics to have routinized faith by rote memorization of the catechism. The stereotype assumes that Catholics do not really believe what they say they believe but have a "doctrinal orthodoxy" shaped by a catechism taught to all American Catholic children in parochial schools.[1] But, as noted in earlier chapters, Catholics like Colbert often play with the catechism, such as in his "Catholic Throwdown" with Jack White. Jokes, comedy, and humor about religion often rest upon stereotypes and assumptions that, although false, hold a specific place in the public imaginary, enough of a space to make inversions of those presumptions legible as comedy.

American Catholicism is not a unified entity, and the multiple personae of Colbert(s) align with the heterogeneity and diversity in American Catholic identities. Colbert represents more of the white middle-class Catholic identities (Irish, Italian, German, or Polish Catholics whose families emigrated to America more than a century ago) and, as such, does not represent Catholic demographic and socioeconomic diversity. However, Colbert does still illustrate a particular type of Catholic multiplicity: thinking Catholics, cultural Catholics, cafeteria Catholics, and lukewarm Catholics (a phrase used by the chaplain of the Colbert Nation, Father James Martin). I put Colbert's theological musings in context with his humor to define "Colbert Catholicism" as part of the multiplicity of the Catholic Church, a type of Catholicism that sees humor as beneficial to one's faith.

I also argue that Colbert and his television programs elucidate American Catholic choices by presenting a proud, vocal, and knowledgeable Catholic through mass media, who also uses humor to both affirm and question presumptions about what it means to be Catholic in America. This chapter historically contextualizes Colbert's place in American Catholic history and sociology, defines Colbert Catholicism, and analyzes how Colbert grapples with twenty-first-century conflicts in the Catholic Church.

American Catholic History and Sociology (Abridged)

Colbert's multiple identities and presentations of Catholicism illustrate some of the ways American Catholics grapple with the multiplicity inherent in their history and current moment. This diversity of Catholic opinion, thought, and theology is not new, but Colbert's use of humor to confront, examine, and present his lay Catholicism to digital and televisual audiences is a distinctively late-twentieth- and twenty-first-century expression. Colbert comes at a point in American Catholic history where Catholics are an accepted part of the American religious landscape. However, this has not always been the case, which is what makes Colbert's presentation of religious identity so intriguing. Colbert's understanding of Catholic exceptionalism, tied to his personal family history, springs from an earlier historical moment, when American and Catholic identities were not woven together easily. While COLBERT as a conservative persona braids together ultra-American and ultra-Catholic identities, he does so in a way that implicitly combats hidden forces of anti-Catholicism, an issue that could arguably be considered moot in the later twentieth and twenty-first centuries. But COLBERT revives it as a pundit combating anyone he sees as a threat to his Americanism or his Catholicism.

Arguably, the history of Catholics in the Americas begins with French and Spanish missionaries in the fifteenth, sixteenth, and seventeenth centuries. As this book geographically and politically delineates "America" as the United States of America, the narratives of the eighteenth and early nineteenth centuries relegated Catholics in British-colonized America to enclaves such as the predominantly Catholic colony of Maryland. A prevalent narrative regarding the foundation of the United States describes the early Massachusetts Bay colonists as religiously persecuted under European Christian rule. Religious voluntarism and denominationalism became the cornerstones of America's religious freedom laws and language, but of course this language is fraught with hypocrisies, inaccuracies, and problematic otherings. Catholics, however, have been trying to be "American" since the time of John Carroll, the first Catholic bishop born in what would become in his lifetime the United States of America.[2]

From the 1820s through the 1920s, an influx of Catholic immigrants from Germany, Ireland, Italy, and eastern Europe led Protestant groups to begin nativist initiatives and smear campaigns against Catholics. Anti-Catholicism took a variety of forms: "Irish need not apply" signage, the 1836 sordid tales of *The Awful Disclosures of Maria Monk*, and Thomas Nast's 1871 cartoon "The American River Ganges," depicting the pope as a vicious alligator devouring the helpless Protestant Americans.[3] *Real* Americans were not Catholic. Popish piety and devotion were antithetical to the American way of life.

In many ways, that language continued into the late nineteenth and early twentieth century. With the incoming Italian, Polish, and other European Catholic immigrants, the Know-Nothing Party advocated bans on immigration and naturalization.[4] In response, many Catholics stuck to their self-created enclaves. In the Catholic ghetto, Catholics self-segregated and had their own clubs, groups, rituals, and schools. By the 1920s and 1930s, a few Catholics began to emerge from their seclusion. Dorothy Day and the Catholic Worker movement were on the front lines of social justice initiatives. Alfred E. Smith became the first Catholic to run for president in 1928, though his unsuccessful campaign created an uproar against Catholic involvement in politics.

World War II efforts united many American minorities and opened the mainstream to include Jewish and Catholic groups into the Judeo-Christian worldview. As sociologist Will Herberg argued in the 1955 book *Protestant, Catholic, Jew*, the three dominant religions could and should be combined into the "American Way of Life."[5] In Herberg's imagination, the ethnic and religious tensions of the prewar period had softened into a unity that made America stronger. As scholars would later point out, this supposed "unity" never really existed, and any perception of it was predicated on liberal Protestant hegemony and American exceptionalism.[6] Herberg's thesis was widely received, though it overlooked religious discord in the postwar eras.

Nonetheless, as historian Kevin Schultz points out, Catholicism was part of the popular triad of private, individual religions.[7] Much of the unification of what was considered *good* religion came on the heels of the threat of communism in the 1950s and 1960s, which encouraged religious groups to join together to fight the godless "others." Catholics became part of the religious norm, especially after presidential candidate John F. Kennedy's 1960 presentation in Houston in which he clarified that even though he was Catholic, neither the Vatican nor the pope would control him when it came to matters of state. Being Catholic was no longer seen as an overwhelming detriment for presidential nominees, as Kennedy won the election in 1960. Catholics had become key players in the public sphere.

To this day, Catholicism is sometimes perceived as "other" within the pluralism and diversity of American society. In contemporary life, some Catholics see the need for organizations to combat anti-Catholicism in the United States. COLBERT, as an extremely zealous conservative Catholic, sees terror and suffering everywhere for Catholics. On *The Colbert Report*, COLBERT exclaims, "There's a lot of discrimination out there against Catholics, I grew up in the American South," a phrase that alludes to the nativism of the KKK as well as other stereotypes about the evangelical and Protestant Christian stronghold in that region.[8] COLBERT's was an interesting mix of ultra-patriotism and ultra-Catholicism. Of course, ultra-patriotic Catholicism is not the only way to be Catholic in the United States.

Stereotypes and Sociological Categories

COLBERT often presents as a conservative Catholic who disapproves of non-traditional Catholics. At times calling them "lapsed" or "ex-Catholics," he seems to lump all these sociological and intellectual Catholic categories into one group.[9] That group is inherently other to *good*, conservative Catholics like him. Out of character, Colbert actually becomes a model of these shifting, overlapping categories: a person who identifies as Catholic but still questions and criticizes aspects of the Catholic Church and hierarchy.

While often perceived as such, Catholics have never been a fully cohesive and united group, receiving orders from Rome and abiding them wholeheartedly and fully without discord. Historian James P. McCartin concisely asserts, "[D]iversity has been an enduring hallmark of Catholics in the United States."[10] Not that Colbert is necessarily the most diverse Catholic; he is not. He is often race- and diversity-blind in problematic ways. While much of Catholic diversity can be linked to different ethnic, racial, and socioeconomic groups, Colbert's diversity focuses on the lived theologies, the intellectual identities individual Catholics associate with themselves, and the labels used to construct borders around *good* and *bad* Catholics—what American religious historian Jon Butler calls "spiritual heterogeneity," in which the emphasis is on the individual.[11]

Such emphasis on individual religious praxis can be traced to several key strands of American religious history. First, the post–World War II American landscape changed as people moved out of the cities (the Catholic ghettos) and into suburbia. As McCartin describes, for some Catholics the changes in suburban migration "undermined patterns of communal life and spiritual practice."[12] Of course, this emphasis on personal and individual Catholicism is not the only way in which Catholics experienced their religion, but individual religious understandings were becoming prevalent in many faith traditions during postwar eras. These new ways of being Catholic focused on the individual, as evidenced by retreat centers in Boston and San Francisco areas that underscored "personal responsibility" and "appeals for individuals to deepen their unique connection to God."[13]

Another moment that inspired theological, ethical, and cultural diversity was the Second Vatican Council, which convened between 1962 and 1965. Many commentators and historians consider Vatican II to be a significant moment for Catholics, when the Church experienced *aggiornamento* and was "brought up to date" and modernized. In many ways, Vatican II allowed clergy to enter the "secular" world and encouraged laity to be more active in their spiritual lives. That empowerment, among other things, led many to question their place in the Church and make individual choices about aspects of Catholicism. *Nostrae Aetate* (the Declaration on the Relation of the Church with Non-Christian Religions), for example, urged Catholics not to discriminate against or hate any other religious group, a seeming endorsement of American Catholics' interfaith initiatives. No longer seeing other religions as demonic, satanic, barbaric, or Christ-killers changed how some Catholics interpreted their own religion. If others were not evil, what made Catholics specific, unique, and good? Other questions arose as well, especially considering the clergy. If priests and nuns should now be fully enmeshed in the "secular world," then how were they distinct from other Catholics? What was the usefulness and purpose of the institutional hierarchy if not to perform the Latin Mass? If the Church could update itself, could individual Catholics modernize as well, and what could that actually mean?[14]

Individualism and modernizing connect to another historical transition: what sociologists of religion describe as the "new voluntarism" and "seeker-centered" generational shift.[15] Of course, all individualisms are not the same. The focus on the individual, rather than on the communal, was emphasized during the 1960s and onward in American life more broadly. Catholics are one part of that evolving emphasis on individuality. This larger trend demonstrates an increase in supposed religious choice and questioning of traditional authority among those in the "seeker" generation(s). American Catholics, although often thought of in terms of Catholic exceptionalism, were not immune from seeking, searching, or selecting their own religious expressions and understandings. This is not new, as evidenced in other lived religion and popular religion histories that explore how individuals actually express and experience their religion rather than the idealized, normative view of how religion should be expressed and experienced.[16] Catholics may have always chosen how to express themselves religiously, but the *perception* is that this is a new, unfamiliar land contemporary American Catholics now dwell within: the tension of choosing whether or not to take birth control or sanction gay marriage and possibly ignoring Catholic hierarchy with their individual choices.

As sociologist Mary Ellen Konieczny deftly articulates, public polarization from the culture wars and individualized religious preferences happen on "local-level social processes" as well as major religio-political settings.[17] Debates and choices do not just happen at institutional levels, in regard to the hierarchy. Nor are these individual choices made without influences. Stephen Colbert and *The Colbert Report* are often such influences for twenty-first-century Catholics.

As previously mentioned, in the public sphere, traditional, orthodox-leaning Catholics frequently berate those they describe as "cultural," "lukewarm," or "cafeteria" Catholics. Even sociologist Andrew Greeley adopted a binary typology in the wake of Vatican II. Greeley posited that the main split among lay American Catholics was between "institutional Catholics" who obeyed all the rules of the Church and "communal Catholics" who were still invested in the Church community but not necessarily in all the regulations given by the hierarchical authorities.[18] The term "Communal Catholics" never received the same public acceptance as other terms. While these categories are complicated, a simple connection between them is that most of these terms reference a rejection of authoritative orthodoxy and institutional conservatism over an individual's religious preferences and self-identification.

In February 2013, Garry Wills, a historian whose books *Bare Ruined Choirs: Doubt, Prophecy, and Radical Religion*; *Under God: Religion and American Politics*; and *Why I Am a Catholic*, among many others, give him the status of Catholic intellectual, appeared as a guest on an episode of *The Colbert Report*. Wills was there that evening to discuss *Why Priests? A Failed Tradition*, which argues that the body of Christ is the community, not the sacrament of transubstantiated bread and wine. Wills is considered a radical liberal Catholic by some, and COLBERT's conservative understanding of Catholic doctrine immediately took umbrage at the "blasphemy" and "heresy" he heard Wills spouting.

> COLBERT: Your new book is called *Why Priests? A Failed Tradition*. What do you mean, a failed tradition? It's a tradition that has lasted for over almost two thousand years.
> Wills: Yes.
> COLBERT: . . . They are the conduits of the sacraments, the miracles of God. What's failed about that?
> Wills: Well, they can continue to pretend to turn bread and wine into the Body and Blood of Jesus, which doesn't happen.[19]

Sitting in front of a huge stained-glass background sacralizing and glorifying COLBERT and America, COLBERT immediately points his finger accusatorially:

> COLBERT: You hold it right there, buddy. Are you Catholic?
> Wills: Yes.
> COLBERT: OK, and you don't believe in transubstantiation?
> Wills: No.[20]

This interview expresses what we continue to see in COLBERT and Colbert—a playing with terms like "conservative" and "liberal," "traditional" and "progressive." While COLBERT vilifies Wills for what COLBERT considers to be un-Catholic beliefs, Colbert does allow Wills to explain his point of view. Colbert becomes an unofficial gatekeeper for defining who and what is Catholic, which includes cultural, lukewarm, and cafeteria Catholics, along with COLBERT's own presentation as a conservative, traditional Catholic.

"Cultural Catholicism" is a porous, amorphous term that pits self-identification against orthodox practice and belief. Scholar Thomas Ferraro describes cultural Catholicism as a shift in Catholic habits and ways of knowing that are constructed and adopted outside the institutional Catholic Church. For Ferraro and others, cultural Catholicism enhances the sacrality in the contemporary world because "elements of Catholic belief continue to appear in everyday living."[21] Other scholars have used the term to examine the lived experiences of Catholics, experiences in which the practices at home or outside the institutional Church have been ignored or stigmatized until the cultural turn in anthropology and religious studies in the 1980s. Those are definitely part of Catholic culture, but I argue that the term "cultural Catholic" denotes something a little different.

People sometimes refer to themselves as cultural Catholics (or interchangeably as "cradle," "non-observant," or "ethnic" Catholics) if they were raised in the Catholic traditions but have since stopped going to Mass, have not been married in the Catholic Church, or oppose certain doctrines by, for example, advocating for female priests. The culture into which these people were formed had Catholic influences, but they may not follow every aspect of institutional Catholicism as defined by the hierarchy and dogma.

Take, for example, the idea of Catholic guilt. The perception is that Catholics have a special type of guilt associated with authority, strict binaries of right and wrong, and categorizing of sins. Individuals who say they are cultural Catholics may not attend Mass weekly, use rosaries in prayer, or be members of the Knights of Columbus, but many will often agree that they have experienced Catholic guilt as part of their cultural experience.[22]

The Pew Research Center surveyed U.S. Catholics for a report published in September 2015 and discovered that approximately 9 percent of those surveyed "consider themselves Catholic or partially Catholic in other ways, even though they do *not* self-identify as Catholic on the basis of religion." How are they culturally Catholic while belonging to other faith traditions or are "nones" (those who consider themselves to have no religion)? For them, Catholicism becomes a heritage, family lineage, and culture (seen as oppositional to religion), so food, clothes, holidays, and rituals are separated from "religious" connections. Some might even be "CEOs" (Christmas and Easter Only). Cultural Catholics, as opposed to ex-Catholics, do not disagree entirely with the church. According to the Pew survey, these self-identifiers felt "warmly" about the Church and would become more of a "practicing" Catholic at a later point.[23] Of course, these binaries between practicing and cultural Catholic are arbitrary and especially difficult to decipher through surveys, but the presumptions about cultural Catholics remain. They are a sociological group of Catholics neither in opposition to, nor full support of, the institutional Catholic Church and its teachings.

"Cultural Catholicism" is one of many labels for intellectual diversity in the Catholic community. Another is "lukewarm." Theologian John W. Martens attributes the phrase "lukewarm" to Archbishop John Nienstedt, who in 2010 was archbishop of St. Paul and Minneapolis, Minnesota.[24] Nienstedt claimed that Jesus Christ directed his followers to "either be hot or cold, but if you're lukewarm," that was unacceptable.[25] The archbishop referenced this as a response to parish closures in Minnesota, further claiming that he believed

> [t]hat it's important that if you're going to be Catholic, that you have to be 100% Catholic. That you stand by the Church, you believe what the church believes and you pass that on to your sons and daughters and your grandsons and granddaughters.[26]

Martens challenges the archbishop's comments through biblical exegesis, claiming that lukewarm Catholics are not in opposition to the Church by dissenting, but rather that dissent makes them "100% Catholic."[27] Of course, this article did appear in the relatively liberal-leaning Jesuit magazine, *America*, and Martens does contend that "conservative Catholics" seem to indicate that "they are quite certain they know who belongs and who does not" to the *real, true, authentic* Catholic Church.[28] Whether dissenters are 100 percent Catholic or not, the term "lukewarm" is still used.

The "chaplain of the Colbert Nation," Father James Martin, self-described as a lukewarm Catholic before he entered the Jesuits in the 1990s. Lukewarm, as a category, does not mean against, in competition with, or opposed to Catholicism. It means less fervent, less hot, less all-or-nothing. "Lukewarm" does not solely mean someone is not a Catholic, just not a conservative, traditional, orthodox Catholic (while there is no specific reason why there would not be a lukewarm liberal Catholic, the instances in which the term has been used usually refer in some way to one's being not conservative enough). Colbert's split personae, the multiple Colbert(s), obscure the all-or-nothing attitudes of conservative or liberal Catholic, similar to the lukewarm classification.

The derivation of "lukewarm" also connects to the phrase "cafeteria Catholics." Greeley was one of the first to use the term "cafeteria Catholicism" in 1985. In "Cafeteria Catholicism: Do You Have to Eat Everything on Your Plate?," the editors of *U.S. Catholic* magazine interviewed Greeley about the "do-it-yourself Catholics" who "stick with the church" even as they disagree with certain aspects of the Church's teachings. Greeley praises what he said was "the best thing that's happened to the church in a long time."[29]

Others did not agree with that assessment. Catholicism *à la carte*, the picking and choosing of the specific aspects of one's Catholic identity, was seen by some as a negative: a consumerism model of religion that did not follow the faith properly.[30] As such, the term "cafeteria Catholic" is almost always used pejoratively. Conservative, traditional Catholics would call their liberal, progressive, and dissenting counterparts "cafeteria Catholics," meaning that they pick and choose what aspects of Catholicism they prefer. Sometimes mixed with "nominal," "lapsed," or "ex-" Catholics, cafeteria Catholics may not attend Mass every week, might not go to confession, and likely disagree with the Church's stance on reproductive technologies. Because this is not an official category from the Vatican, it becomes more of an on-the-ground label. *Huffington Post* blogger Rea Nolan Martin deftly and mockingly describes the stereotype of the cafeteria Catholic:

> Shame on me for ordering my doctrine off the à la carte menu when the prix fixe would buy me so much more salvation, right? If only my conscience weren't so lax, my lifestyle so self-serving, and my spiritual

practice so undisciplined. If only I weren't so lazy, ignorant and uneducated about my religion, I might understand the benefits I'm missing when I refuse to order the items that stick in my throat.[31]

Although most people recognize these terms as intrinsically pejorative, some lay Catholics have now reclaimed the term.

Isabella Moyer, a writer and past president of the International Organization of Marianist Lay Communities, says she is proud to be a cafeteria Catholic. According to the organization's website,

> Marianist Lay Communities are a canonically recognized private association of the faithful in the Catholic Church. We gather in mission with Mary as our model and guide to bring Jesus into a world in need of justice and peace. Our favored means is by forming communities of faith-filled women and men. Our communities are in permanent mission for the needs of the Church and the world.[32]

In the USCatholic blog in July 2015, Moyer argues that "because the church says so" does not fulfill her search for knowledge of and understanding in faith. Furthermore, she asserts that the cafeteria Catholic has become the twenty-first century's "heretic" with online blogs and discussion boards trolled by zealous traditionalists who attack people "who do not give their full assent to each and every teaching of the Catholic Church." She even puts cafeteria Catholicism into use for evangelization, as "gone are the days of blind, unquestioning obedience" and in their place there is a "real dialogue."[33]

Comedy writer and blogger Sarah del Rio also embraces the term as a point of pride. Originally derided and pejoratively called a cafeteria Catholic, she now claims to be its "head lunch lady." Del Rio dissents with the Catholic Church on issues she feels are important to reforming the Church, particularly regarding sex. She describes the "sex stuff" as connected to the shame cafeteria Catholics are made to feel for wanting to change the Church's stance on masturbation, gay marriage, and birth control. "CINOs—Catholics-in-name-only," which del Rio considers to be the same as cafeteria Catholics, are not irreligious or picking and choosing for convenience.[34] Instead, she argues that cafeteria Catholics are selecting based on changing social mores, which returns us to the larger argument. Colbert, like other comedians and mass-media personalities, helps people think through Catholic conflicts. What makes him different is the split persona, the multiple Colbert(s) who embody different aspects of American Catholic identity. The Catholic Church is not a unified institution but a site of human negotiation between authorities, communities, and individuals. There have always been folk, regional, and "unauthorized" aspects to Catholicism, but now they exist on a broad scale and in mass media. The idea of a unified party line is gone, and Catholic heterogeneity is broadcast through multiple platforms.

Scholars have also tried to categorize this nebulous group of American Catholics, those who value questioning over blind faith or who at least are perceived as such. William D'Antonio, Michele Dillon, and Mary Gautier's *American Catholics in Transition* describes the historical use of the term "cafeteria Catholicism" as descriptive of Catholics who "selectively value" certain theologies and traditions.[35] Conservapedia.com has listed Stephen Colbert as a cafeteria Catholic. This "selectivity" is part of a larger trend in American religious history, specifically the individualism and "seeking" that enraptured sociology of religion for the past few decades. Catholicism is not a fundamentalist tradition, as D'Antonio and his co-authors explain. It is a "living theological tradition that blends faith and reason."[36] Sociologist Michele Dillon, in *Catholic Identity*, presents this blending through three pro-change groups in the American Catholic Church who maintain their Catholic identities while still confronting specific Church teachings and practices, in particular Catholics who are "gay or lesbian, advocates of women's ordination, or pro-choice on abortion."[37] Sociologist Jerome Baggett has also tried to explain the inconsistencies scholars see in their interlocutors' positions. Baggett tells the story of an openly gay Catholic man, Bill, who loved the traditions of the Catholic Church, but "on the other hand, though, he [was] adamant about his freedom, even obligation, to mine those riches on his own terms and in accordance with his own needs."[38] Interlocutor Bill and Stephen Colbert identify with the Church and yet critique it in ways often popularly associated with the vernacular term "thinking Catholics."[39]

Stephen Colbert exemplifies this blending of faith and reason through his satirical character and his personal affirmation of Catholic identity. His satire challenges and criticizes aspects of Catholicism but still affirms institutional authorities in the Catholic Church. Colbert plays with the liberal/conservative boundary as a Catholic on a television faux-news show who comes to work with ashes on his forehead on Ash Wednesday but still mocks Pope Benedict's expensive Prada red shoes.[40] Colbert walks a fine line between the progressivism of the pro-change groups in Dillon's research and the traditionalism of those he reflects with his over-exaggerated persona.

Media critics, bloggers, and posters to online discussion boards often discuss Colbert's cafeteria Catholicism. For example, on the discussion forum website *Reddit* many commentators noted Colbert's dissenting Catholicism in an archived post from 2015 entitled "Stephen Colbert Gets Celebrity Faith Right (relevantmagazine.com)." *Reddit* is an online community where anonymous users vote on the popularity, importance, and validity of content. They also produce and comment on that content. Using anonymous online discussion boards as an area of defining religio-sociological categories is relatively new and particular to the contemporary moment of the twenty-first century. One *Reddit* user, with the handle Trinity, was frustrated by how people claim Colbert as their own on both sides of the traditional/progressive dichotomy:

> Frustrating how he is claimed by Catholics as a positive Catholic voice on television, something recognized by none other than Timothy Cardinal Dolan, and then simultaneously derided by the Catholic right for being an advocate for LGBTQ people and other liberal causes . . . celebrating and claiming him in public when convenient, then deriding him as a faux cafeteria Catholic in conservative Catholic spaces.[41]

Another *Reddit* user, mysanityisrelative, responded, "its [sic] almost like there are almost 70 million of us in the United States alone or something!" Mysanityisrelative directly confronts the question of Catholic unity, mocking the assumptions that Catholics are not individuals with their own religious preferences and choices.[42] A third *Reddit* user, Saint_Thomas_More, chimed in, claiming it made sense that conservatives could claim Colbert as a public Catholic while simultaneously deriding him for his actions because "They want Catholic public figures to be good examples of people who subscribe to the Church's teachings, not someone who will cause confusion not only for Catholics, but for non-Catholics who often do not know a lot about what the Church teaches."[43]

On *Reddit* and other blogs and discussion boards, Colbert's Catholicism becomes a site of discussion and debate. And Colbert's label as a cafeteria Catholic opens up space for semi-anonymous audiences to grapple with their own understandings of American Catholicism. As Trinity asserts, if there were really a "closed cafeteria" comprising only those who follow Catholic doctrine and dogma to the letter, then it would be a "very small church indeed [as] diversity and doctrinal dissent have always been normative parts of Catholic life."[44] In the twenty-first century, Internet commentators, scholars, and Catholics are all trying to define this amorphous group known as "cultural," "cafeteria," or "lukewarm" Catholics. One could categorize Colbert as such a Catholic: a nominal, fair-weather religious follower who chooses which ideologies and doctrines to abide by. This rhetoric has negative implications, the indication that Catholics are no longer a unified body. Alternatively, these labels can be viewed positively, as Catholics thoughtfully struggling with moral and ethical choices and utilizing all the options in the American and global religious landscapes. Although neither option fully captures the tensions inherent in American Catholic life, they both demonstrate that Stephen Colbert's influential commentary on and presentation of Catholic life are important sites for exploring those tensions.

Colbert Catholicism

Colbert's own brand of Catholicism highlights the multiplicity of American Catholicism and Colbert's power to present Catholicism to a larger audience. One fan of *The Colbert Report* aptly illustrated Colbert's Catholic influence with a meme image. In this meme, there is a picture of COLBERT looking stoic, his eyes piercing the viewers.[45] The bold lettering mimics COLBERT's own preference for bold, capitalized, yelling punditry. The upper text reads, "'Are you a Liberal Catholic or a Conservative Catholic?'"; the bottom text responds, "I'm a Colbert Catholic." There is not enough rhetorical, material, or digital evidence to answer how many people identify as "Colbert Catholics." The meme described here presents one example in a larger understanding of Colbert's Catholicism as different, distinct from other Catholic labels.

The first line, a question, forces a choice upon the viewer. You are either/or; there is no in-between. But the meme creator has found a different path, a way that both invalidates the line between liberal and conservative and extends outside that binary. This brand of Catholicism pushes against the boundaries of conservative Catholic orthodoxy and lib-

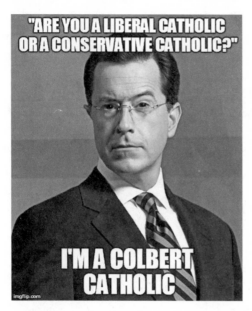

"I'm a Colbert Catholic" meme

eral or ex-Catholic identity. Colbert Catholicism is one example of push-ing against those binaries by articulating Catholic issues, identities, and experiences through humor.

It is important to draw a distinction between the two aspects of Col-bert Catholicism: Colbert's Catholicism and "Colbert Catholicism." The first pertains to the theologies and philosophies of the human being, Stephen Colbert. The second part concerns how Colbert approaches those ideas—and that is through humor, comedy, and laughter. Colbert Cathol-icism mocks aspects of Catholic culture, institutional hierarchy, and doc-trine without dismissing Catholicism or religion entirely. As Colbert explained at the Fordham event with Cardinal Dolan and Father Jim Martin, he mocks not religion but how people use religion. He mocks the insincere, the inauthentic, the unreal religious expressions, but one prob-lem arises: Who decides what's real or not? In Colbert Catholicism, the decider is Colbert himself.

Colbert's own Catholicism, which provides much of the basis for "Col-bert Catholicism," has been well documented. When he transitioned from *The Colbert Report* to *The Late Show with Stephen Colbert*, hundreds of interviews emerged, some of which were with smaller, religious news outlets and some with popular mass media. These interviews provide a glimpse into Colbert's theological underpinnings, which are constructed through his American Catholic identity, family relationships, and life experiences.

In the religious news outlets, one of the most popular interviews occurred in March 2015 at the very beginning of the Lenten season. Entitled "Colbert Catholicism," it was a video segment filmed at the *America* magazine office with its editor, Father Jim Martin. In the interview, the two men joked about Colbert's newly grown beard, questioned the intelligence of St. Peter, and sang 1960s Catholic hymns. Martin asked Colbert many questions about his faith and religious preferences; for example:

> Martin: What's your favorite scripture?
> Colbert: Favorite scripture? To quote another gospel, *Dune* by Frank Herbert . . .
> [*both men laugh*]
> Martin: Which is where Jesus got a lot of his stuff, I think.[46]

Throughout this laughter-laced interview, audiences began to see Colbert out of character. This was one of the first interviews he had done since leaving *The Colbert Report* three months prior. Martin asked relatively easy questions like "Who's your favorite saint?" Colbert replied thoughtfully that he liked "St. Peter . . . because he's super flawed . . . and yet he gets the big job."[47] These personal questions stress the individualism and authority Colbert demonstrates in choosing his own religious practice and beliefs outside the exaggerated conservative character he had portrayed for more than nine years. As of October 2018, more than 360,000 viewers have watched the 2015 Martin–Colbert interview on YouTube and were able to hear Colbert's thoughts on Catholicism in *real* life.

One tenet of Colbert Catholicism describes finding joy and humor after tragedy, as evidenced in Colbert's real life. One of the most popular articles about Colbert's religious conceptions was in *GQ* in August 2015. Writer Joel Lovell remarked that the most prevalent thought he had during and after the interview was *loss*. Lovell asked Colbert about his losses of loved ones, claiming the author had "never met anyone who's faced that reality [of loss] more meaningfully than Stephen Colbert." Colbert articulated that he abhorred playing with others' loss. While audiences and journalists often clamored for COLBERT's take on the day's news, Colbert felt that "tragedy is sacred . . . people's suffering is sacred."[48] He disliked having to make jokes when tragic events occurred, specifically referencing the 2015 shootings in Emanuel AME Church in Charleston, South Carolina. "Sacred," to Colbert, refers to the intimate and the untouchable, a classification that means that a subject, object, or topic is off limits and he does not want to poke fun, mock, or satirize what he qualifies as *real* pain, *real* sadness. The line of personal tragedy appears to be one Colbert claims he does not like to cross with his jokes.

Colbert's own family's suffering shaped him, and Lovell's article in *GQ* was one of the few instances where Colbert discussed his personal tragedy in great detail. Colbert grew up the youngest of eleven kids in Charleston, South Carolina, in the 1960s and 1970s. When he was ten years old, Stephen's father and two brothers closest in age to him were killed in a plane crash. While he was growing up after the plane crash, his older siblings were all out of the house and so it was just he and his mother alone at home. Initially, Colbert's trauma manifested by "contending with the cruel indifference of the universe" by returning the indifference and reading alone every day. When Lovell pressed him in the *GQ* interview to explain how, after such trauma, he could be so funny and "genuinely grounded and joyful," Colbert responded that he is not angry but instead is "*mystified*." Colbert also credits his mother for exemplifying how to draw on her faith and "not be swallowed by sorrow."[49] The books he read also helped Colbert think about suffering. J. R. R. Tolkien, in particular, is one of Colbert's favorite writers as evidenced by Colbert's encyclopedic knowledge of *The Lord of the Rings* and Middle Earth.[50] Colbert told Lovell about Tolkien's letter to a priest who questioned if the writer's "mythos was sufficiently doctrinaire" because death was viewed as a gift. Tolkien rebutted, "What punishments of God are not gifts?" Colbert's eyes "filled with tears" when he said he would be "ungrateful not to take *everything* with gratitude." That does not mean that he wants the suffering, but he can be grateful for everything. This does not cause Colbert cognitive dissonance; Lovell argues that Colbert "can hold both of those ideas in [his] head."[51]

Colbert's theology combines suffering and joy; in fact, he claims that "our sorrow is inseparable from our joy." "Joy," in this sense, refers to humor, mirth, and laughter. In his office, the comedian had a note taped to his computer featuring the quote "Joy is the most infallible sign of the existence of God." What is this suffering, Colbert ponders, "in the light of eternity" and the awesomeness of the world? Colbert is "grateful" for the suffering not because "the Gospel tells us" to be grateful. Rather, Colbert asserts that his gratefulness at the inseparability of joy and suffering stems from an inner human impulse. Colbert believes that what makes him grateful is an impulse potentially external to religion, spirituality, and human thought. Colbert's personal theology, influenced by the Gospel, interprets that gratefulness impulse as centered on an object he names "God." Colbert also argues that his theology is limited to his own understanding of that object as God, and he acknowledges that for others, the object which encourages inner human impulses to be grateful about their suffering, "could be many things" and take other forms.[52] Colbert's theology places God at the center of his gratefulness for the human emotions of suffering and joy. But Colbert recognizes that in the pluralistic American context, a singular understanding of suffering, joy, and God simplifies others' experiences.

Colbert Catholicism has its roots in his Catholic upbringing but does not call for Catholic exceptionalism or distinctiveness. Catholic exceptionalism or distinctiveness is evident is the historiography of American Catholicism and American religion writ large. Nineteenth- and early-twentieth-century scholars viewed Catholics as different and distinct from Protestant Christian denominations. By the 1940s and 1950s, Catholic scholars were writing Catholic histories and sociological studies. Catholic scholarship into the 1980s often self-described as "unique" and focused on specificities found only in Catholic life, for example parishes and parochial schools. That uniqueness often connoted separation and exceptionalism. The exoticization of Catholic practice and belief was often held in tension with American Catholic assimilationist tendencies. Rather than exceptionalist rhetoric, Colbert calls it his "context for [his] existence" and that he exists to "know God, love God, serve God, that we might be happy with each other in this world and with Him in the next." In other words, the Catholic catechism "makes a lot of sense" to Colbert.[53] It is an inherited and enculturated theology of the fullness of suffering and joy as complete understandings of the human condition. His theology incorporates the particularities of Catholicism as his "context" but does not diminish others' search for meaning in different systems.

As such, Colbert Catholicism is open to multiplicity and diversity in Catholic American life and global religions more broadly. The comedian, according to Lovell, is one of America's "few public moral intellectuals," which Colbert dismisses by claiming that he has "*a* morality" but does not know if it is "the best morality." Colbert says he likes "thinking," and "if people perceive that as a moral intellectualism, that's fine."[54] But his morality is not the point of his public commentary. Instead, he assures Lovell, his job is to entertain. While Colbert Catholicism entertains, at the same time Colbert also intellectually dissects and presents certain religious activities, beliefs, and identities as a Catholic and through his own moral, theological, and religious lens.

Because he is a public moral thinker who entertains others, Colbert's theological and anthropological stances are popular because he does not take himself too seriously. His morality differs from a perception of traditional religious authorities as those who claim to know all the answers or who present their path as the only path. In a pluralist, seeker-centered, American landscape, why not make a few choices that are influenced by a witty, intellectual, satirical entertainer? Colbert's responses to current events and his way of conceptualizing faith speak to individuals, so those individuals choose to listen to him. Colbert influences without the hubris and pomp that his character COLBERT so deftly portrays. By his satirizing religious authority through hyperbole as COLBERT, audiences were primed to appreciate the subtle thoughtfulness of Colbert Catholicism.

Stephen Colbert and STEPHEN COLBERT are two sides of the same embodied being. COLBERT performs the hyperconservative side of the American cultural divide. Stephen Colbert stays in a more middle space. He is not as conservative as his character counterpart, but he is also not as liberal as he appears. Colbert, in an interview with fellow comedian Paul Provenza, describes how he uses *The Colbert Report* platform to entice audiences to think outside the binaries of conservative and liberal:

I enjoy that occasionally the audience gets a whiff of my *personal* honesty out of the character's mouth, and they may not even be aware of it. . . . If my game is continuous, if I'm continually merely saying the opposite of what I mean, that becomes a well-worn rut . . . . [55]

Colbert, the real person, plays with the boundaries of Catholic identity and experience in ways similar to how he plays with American political life. Colbert's theology colors within the Catholic lines but creates a space for questioning Catholics. Some viewers describe this type of Catholicism, one that undermines the line between conservative and liberal, as "Colbert Catholicism."

Colbert's theology does not just blur the lines within Catholicism but also adds in other elements of American life, including non-Christian religions and popular culture. When discussing the process of making a TV show, Lovell correlated Colbert's focus on intention and process to "Buddha's *sutras*."[56] At the Fordham conversation with Cardinal Dolan, Colbert responded to a question from the audience, "So many Christian leaders spread hatred, especially of homosexuals. How can you maintain your joy?" After Cardinal Dolan responded with anecdotes about meeting with Muslim leaders, and another about encountering demonstrators outside St. Patrick's Cathedral, Colbert retorted unequivocally, "If someone spreads hate," he said, "then they're not your religious leader."[57] Colbert epitomizes the do-it-yourself, mixing, and self-construction aspect of contemporary religion in the United States, a perspective which purports that individuals are entitled and expected to make their own religious choices based on anything that calls to them. If religion is a cafeteria, Colbert Catholicism makes choices on the American menu, not just on the Catholic menu.

Besides the philosophies and theologies of the actor Stephen Colbert, a second aspect of Colbert Catholicism is how those thoughts are presented, which is wrapped up in humor. Mocking, satirizing, and joking become the primary modes of understanding the incongruities in the religion. Some comedians dismiss religion. Bill Maher, in particular, personifies an atheistic fanboy of Richard Dawkins and Christopher Hitchens. Colbert, on the other hand, sees his Catholicism as integral to his identity and his comedy. At the Fordham event in 2012, Colbert said he did not make jokes about the sacraments "or put a picture of the crucifixion on-screen." But, as Laurie Goodstein of the *New York Times* reported, Colbert "liked to poke fun at the use and misuse of religion, especially in politics," because then he's not "talking about Christ," but rather, he's "talking about Christ [used] as cudgel."[58]

What an amusing image, the idea of using Christ to bludgeon those who disagree with one's politics. In fact, one would expect to see that image used in a segment on *The Colbert Report*. Colbert sees what he does as extracting the religion from the politics, but that is perplexing because COLBERT intermingles the political and the religious. For Colbert, his version of Catholicism, and of religion in general, can be read as more pure and more *real* because he believes he separates his individual religion from his political beliefs. For example, he claims not to use Christ to berate others for not following his own interpretation of the Gospels. He implicitly contrasts himself with conservative evangelical Christians, such as Moral Majority leader Jerry Falwell or Christian Broadcast Network's Pat Robertson, who use their individual religion to fight their political battles. But mixing religion and politics is just what Colbert does when he testifies before Congress on social justice issues, such as the plight of migrant workers. The personal, the political, and the religious are all tied together, whether or not Colbert is aware of his integration of those three elements. Just because he can stand behind humor and comedy does not negate the fact that he also "uses" religion for his own political messages.

No hierarchy, Catholic life, or religion has been harmed in the making of his comedy, according to Colbert, because it is all in good fun, and because jokes are meant to encourage thinking and not meant to be hurtful. But that may not be true. The investment in religion and identity, while still satirizing aspects one individually disagrees with, is a popular mode of American Catholicism today and is one definition of Colbert Catholicism. Colbert Catholicism is not a new religious movement, nor a sociological category of American Catholicism, but the label is useful when one is discussing individuals, like Colbert, who use satire, comedy, and humor to understand their own religious identity and investment in religious institutions.

Colbert articulates, embodies, and performs his lay religiosity by choosing what parts of Catholicism to take and what parts to question. The difference between Colbert and other lay Catholics is that he has a larger, more public stage on which to portray his Catholic identity. Colbert does not dismiss religion by discussing it with humor; rather, Colbert Catholicism embraces humor as a means to engage with, question, and reinforce issues of contemporary Catholic life. Colbert Catholicism is one form of the larger heterogeneity of Catholic thought and identity and can be situated alongside other labels such as "lukewarm," "cafeteria," and "cultural" Catholicism. This Catholic subjectivity is somewhat revolutionary compared with the fervor of COLBERT's response to anti-Catholicism.

Colbert's Response to Anti-Catholicism

Colbert Catholicism, then, is a type of Catholicism that weaves Catholic issues into larger American narratives and contends with distinctions between liberal and conservative ideologies. Engaging the history of Catholicism directly, some of the *Colbert Report* guests explain why they see a continuation of Catholic persecution. Colbert addresses their extreme statements with comedy while COLBERT encourages them to express their thoughts on perceived anti-Catholic sentiments. One such guest was William Donohue in an interview conducted in the first year of *The Colbert Report*. Donohue is the president of the Catholic League for Religious and Civil Rights (Catholic League). He is a conservative politically and religiously. Journalist John L. Allen Jr. describes Donohue as a sociologist with "sterling conservative credentials." Prior to his work at the Catholic League, Donohue worked at the Heritage Foundation, "where he focused in part on the activities of civil rights groups, most notably the American Civil Liberties Union."[59] COLBERT described Donohue succinctly: "[H]e's been putting the fear of God into God-fearing Americans for over ten years now."[60]

In the interview, COLBERT and Donohue are seated at a conference table in front of a stained-glass window representing symbols sacred to *The Colbert Report*, including bald eagles flanking the "C" and "R" of *The Colbert Report* and the Washington Monument and the Capitol above a flag pointing downward with five white stars on a bright blue background and red and white stripes, imitating the American flag. "You're the first guest to have our new back window here," COLBERT informed Donohue as the two men sat down for the interview.[61] This stained-glass window was used often throughout the program's nine-year run, especially when interviewees came on the show specifically to discuss religious issues.

As the interview begins, COLBERT says that he has wanted Donohue to be a guest since the first show, to which Donohue responds that *The Colbert Report* is the "hottest thing on TV." COLBERT appears flattered: "Not only are you a holy man, but you're a wise man."[62] Donohue is a lay person and speaks with the authority of a lay foundation, but he is also a media creation. Donohue's persona rivals COLBERT's, but without the overt comical nature. Donohue does not have a comedy program and is not performing an ironic character.

Donohue often finds what he perceives to be anti-Catholic sentiments in the entertainment industry, making him an excellent interviewee for COLBERT, a character who epitomizes infotainment. The fact that Donohue concedes to come on *The Colbert Report*, a comedy program, but actively tries to censor *South Park*, another comedy show on Comedy Central, illustrates how Colbert and COLBERT are not seen as solely comical. Colbert is perceived, at least by Donohue, as a *good* and *real* Catholic public figure.[63] Donohue is the spokesperson for the Catholic League for Religious and Civil Rights, an anti-defamation and civil rights organization specifically defending "the right of Catholics . . . lay and clergy alike . . . to participate in American public life without defamation or discrimination." The Catholic League uses the language of legal and constitutional freedoms to describe its motivations. The organization is "motivated by the letter and the spirit of the First Amendment" to defend the rights of Catholics "whenever and wherever they are threatened."[64] In the public sphere, the rights of Catholics are often conflated with an opposition to perceived blasphemy, attacks on Catholic dogma, and irreverence toward Jesus, Mary, the saints, or institutional hierarchy and clergy. Whether or not Donohue and the Catholic League have created a strawman argument defending Catholic rights is another issue entirely.

Since 1993, under Donohue's leadership, the Catholic League has been perceived as more aggressive and prominent. Religion scholar Mark Silk called Donohue a "thug" who "reverts to bullying because he thinks that's what the job entails." In 2000, *America* magazine editors chastised Donohue for judging films without viewing them, explaining that the Catholic League "reinforces stereotypes" of the Catholic Church as judgmental and paranoid. As Catholic studies scholar Mark Massa, S.J., underscores, Donohue does not seem to understand that "not everyone who criticizes the church is anti-Catholic."[65] Of course, the Catholic League and Donohue do not represent all Catholics, and liberal and progressive Catholics "view the league with suspicion."[66] The Catholic League considers initiatives to be anti-Catholic if they promote school programs for sex education, government-funded contraception or abortion, media bias, restrictions against pro-life activism, and restrictions on religious schools.[67] That puts the Catholic League firmly on the side of traditional Catholicism, and of American social and political conservatives in general. And although they claim not to speak for all members and sectors of the Catholic Church, by their being one of the most prominent organizations, they encourage the perception that their brand of Catholicism (that which opposes perceived anti-Catholic rhetoric or sentiments) is fighting for all American Catholics—a unified religious group.

Donohue claims that the Catholic Church is a unified religion when it comes to anti-Catholicism:

> Most of the problems that I see in our society today is [sic] not a matter of anti-Catholicism visited against individual Catholics at work or at school, it's a matter of defamation, cheap shots, gratuitous shots. I'm not talking about disagreements with the Catholic Church and its teaching. You can disagree all you want. I'm talking about derision. I'm talking about insult. The kinds of untoward comments that are not made about other segments of our society and I'm a little bit fed up with . . . the Bill Mahers for the lousy little jokes about Catholics, which they wouldn't tell about Jews or blacks or gays. That's why I tell you about the secular left. They've got an agenda and I'm out there to stop 'em.[68]

COLBERT applauds Donohue's description of contemporary American society as a place where the diversity and pluralism arguments have made Catholicism a punching bag. During COLBERT's 2006 interview of Donohue, he asked why Donohue and "evangelical Protestants and Orthodox Jews" were "strange bedfellows," to which Donohue replied, because they were "putting aside theological differences so that we can come together against the people on the left." COLBERT then retorts, "You know what I think the most heinous example is? Lapsed Catholics, those are the ones who hate Catholics more than anybody else."[69]

COLBERT is seen as being on Donohue's side, arguing the same line of a unified Catholic Church that still is an underdog on the American religious stage and whose greatest threats come from those who oppose Catholic orthodoxy and orthopraxy. The persona versus the *real* person comes to bear on the issue of anti-Catholicism. Colbert rebuts the idea of overt

Catholic persecution through humor by his over-exaggerated persona's agreeing so fervently with Donohue. Colbert models a way to present Catholic identity beyond the outsider status. One way to understand the contemporary moment is through a bifurcated, fearful lens. With this lens, Donohue's and COLBERT's perceptions of anti-Catholicism are still a relevant fear in American public life. Another way to approach the contemporary moment is evident in the ambiguity of Colbert's humor. Rather than their taking oppositional sides, Colbert's polysemous interview with Donohue rebuts the latter's goal of Catholic orthodox uniformity and instead considers the multiplicity and heterogeneity of the twenty-first century. The rhetoric of "lapsed Catholic" opens the discussion of a contemporary era filled with labels and stereotypes used to define and categorize the multiplicity of Catholic identities. Those multiple identities become more porous with the conflicts brought to light in the early decades of the twenty-first century.

A Twenty-First-Century Conflict within the Catholic Church

Because Colbert knows so much about Catholicism (by being a Catholic), he feels qualified and justified in making jokes about some of the issues that lead to internal conflicts within the Catholic community. Those include issues of same-sex marriage, abortion, birth control, and sexual abuse scandals. For some issues, like same-sex marriage, the conservative, traditionalist, Catholic character COLBERT argues against popular gay rights activists, like Dan Savage. Birth control and abortion become one-line jokes, a way for COLBERT to demonstrate his conservative religio-political leanings. In a segment about the possibility of Spider-Man's being the pope, COLBERT joked that Spidey-Pope's senses would tingle whenever anyone used birth control.[70] All of these jokes and interviews are part of Colbert's schtick on *The Colbert Report*. COLBERT toes the line on issues in the Catholic Church, siding most often with traditionalist doctrine and the hierarchical authority of the institution.

However, the clergy sexual abuse scandals are another matter. The jokes made in regard to these scandals are treated very differently. Colbert rarely covers this material, which was abundant between 2005 and 2014, when *The Colbert Report* was on the air. Perhaps, as mentioned earlier in this chapter, Colbert believes "suffering is sacred," but does COLBERT share that belief? And does either Colbert(s) believe that the suffering caused by sexual abuse committed by Catholic clergy is sacred?

Arguably, the biggest issue of twenty-first-century Catholicism thus far has been the sexual abuse scandals' coming to light. Only one major *Colbert Report* segment is devoted to the sexual abuse scandal, whereas gay marriage, for example, has had more than fifty separate segments. Perhaps this is because the other issues, like birth control, abortion, and gay marriage, also involve non-Catholic conservative Christian groups. The issues regarding California's gay-marriage laws and Proposition 8, which aimed to ban gay marriage, were more connected to Mormons, evangelicals, and African-American Christian groups. Catholics were somewhat on the periphery, and even then, it seemed as though only conservative Catholics were opposed. Cafeteria, liberal, progressive, lukewarm, and other politically left–leaning–labeled Catholics were not as central to the story. However, the priest sexual abuse scandals are entirely a Catholic story. No other religions have come close to the same number of allegations and horrors. Here was a moment when Colbert could identify as a Catholic, one hurt and saddened by the events that occurred, and still be frustrated and irate at the Catholic Church's cover-ups. For his age, demographic, and public personality, Colbert might be expected to comment on one of the biggest stories in American Catholic life, but he did so only sparingly and without the satirical bite expected of someone who took down (through satire) the president of the United States while sharing a lectern at the White House Correspondents' dinner in 2006.

Awareness of the Catholic sexual abuse scandals has dominated the conversations about Catholicism in the twenty-first century. As Bishop Accountability.org reports, since 1950, "thousands of Catholic clergy and religious have raped and sodomized tens of thousands of children—perhaps more than 100,000 children."[71] Priests and their superiors kept these crimes secret for decades. More than 17,000 survivors have broken that silence, and popular films like 2015's *Spotlight* capture that silence and the cover-up of the abuse. By the mid-2000s, when *The Colbert Report* began, hundreds of articles and personal stories had come to light. The Catholic Church has been embroiled in legal cases regarding this issue since the late 1990s.

As revelations about the extent and nature of the clerical sexual abuse scandal emerged, many comedians, Catholic and non-Catholic, made jokes, puns, and off-color remarks about the crisis. Some focused entire segments of their stand-up routines on the issue, such as comedian Christopher Titus, who performs a segment on his Comedy Central program that describes violent ways of dealing with hypocritical, sexually abusive priests.

> One priest in Boston, one dude, messed with over one hundred kids, a hundred kids. Yo, Father Grope-y, it's not an Olympic event. How sick is that dude? . . . Don't you think if you're jonesing for a Boy Scout or you have an altar boy monkey on your back, you should find a way to stop, man. . . . Go to the Home Depot get a sledgehammer. [*mimes hammering his penis*] Kill the urge. I feel bad for these priests, you know, . . . I wish they had, had like, like a God to pray to for guidance. Or maybe like a book with some rules in it they could read.[72]

Other comedians, such as Robin Williams, use the sexual abuse scandals as a small part of their larger act. Williams, in his 2002 HBO stand-up special, *Live on Broadway*, incorporated jokes about "problem priests" being part of the "divine witness protection program" and that one way to fix the problem would be "shock collars" for priests.[73] George Carlin, in his 2004 book, *When Will Jesus Bring the Porkchops*, wrote about ways Catholic children could be more aware of the dangers around the pedophile priests:

> Catholic kids are stupid; they don't know how to handle a pedophile priest. Here's what you do: First of all, you don't get all scared and do whatever he tells you. Who wants to get sucked off by a forty-three-year-old clergyman with beard stubble? Not me. Instead, what you do is kick him in the nuts. You kick him squarely in the nuts, and you get the fuck out of there as fast as you can, and you go tell somebody right away; you tell as many grown-up people as you can—one of them is bound to believe you. That's what you do. You don't wait thirty years. You kick the priest in the nuts and say, "Fuck you, Father, I don't do that shit" . . . . And you're out the door.[74]

Louis C.K. writes, directs, and stars in a 2007 intense satirical short video mockumentary about the purpose of the Catholic Church. In this piece, C.K. interviewed Father Ike McCready, a faux-spokesperson for the archdiocese of New York who claimed that the Church is "an ancient, worldwide organization dedicated to the constant goal of fucking young boys."[75]

In this mockumentary, C.K. plays the straight man, never breaking character at some of the more ridiculous comments, such as the priests' excrement becoming pulp for the Bible to be printed on. These mostly male comedians describe the sexual assaults in horrific, visceral depiction. They explain how they would have reacted, give advice, and generally berate the abhorrent abuses ignored and hidden by the Catholic Church authorities. On the other hand, the "ultimate Catholic," the "truth-teller" who resists authority and speaks truth to power, Colbert, did not have a separate segment on *The Colbert Report* about this Catholic issue until 2011.

COLBERT begins the segment with a joke about popular fiction author Dan Brown and his highly popular but substantially incorrect novels:

> Folks, the Catholic Church has been rocked by scandal over the past decade and I'm not just talking about those sickening Dan Brown novels. I've known many clergymen, Mr. Brown, and very few of them had access to anti-matter technology.[76]

Next, COLBERT segues into the real issue, the "horrible, horrible, shameful chapter" in the Catholic Church's long history: the sexual abuse scandals. Unlike other issues, COLBERT does not give any background about the history of the scandals. He does not use any video clips from other news organizations the way he does with most news stories, including different issues in Catholicism and other religions. Instead, he moves into how the Church authorities dealt with the scandal:

> The United States conference of Catholic bishops has released the results of an exhaustive, $1.8 million study examining the root causes of this tragic abuse of trust. And I'm relieved to report that they have found the courage to place the blame where it belongs—on "free-love in the 1960s." It's the damn hippies.[77]

COLBERT then jokes about the "summer of love" turning into the "debauchery of Prieststock," a fake event depicted with stock photo images of priests and bishops praying and posing near the stage at a music festival under a banner bearing the name "Prieststock."

COLBERT then makes a peace sign (or V sign) with each hand and says in a hippie-style voice, "Don't eat the brown Eucharist, man." As he waves his fingers around, evoking images similar to the iconic ones of Presidents

Dwight Eisenhower and Richard Nixon (who each used it for victory and peace at very different historical moments), a dejected, sighing COLBERT continues to lament the 1960s' impact on priests.

> And folks, it could all have been avoided. As the study said, "Poor training of priests—likely contributed to the abuse problem." You see, this is not a moral failing by the leadership of the Church; it's simply a training issue. Like the new guy putting the wrong type of paper in the photocopier. Except it's not paper, and it wasn't a photocopier.[78]

Here is where the joke becomes tricky. On the one hand, Colbert mocks the Church report's feeble attempts to lay blame at priests' training rather than at the "moral failing" of Church leadership. But in the second half of the segment, when Colbert and his writers move closer to mocking the actual abuse by alluding to sexual assault with allusions to mundane office supplies, viewers could become uncomfortable.

COLBERT then comes back into his egomaniacal self, claiming that "once again it falls to me to fix this thing." He then introduces his "new comprehensive, preventative training program," jumps up from his desk, and sprints to a touchable screen by the bookcases. "Welcome to the Ecclesi-Action Center with its patented do-not-touch screen. Now if you're a man of the cloth, I want you to pay close attention."

Clergy-Matic Ecclesi-Action Center 3:16

COLBERT speaks slowly and articulates every syllable, as if talking to a child. He creates two lists regarding priest behavior. In the "Do" column, COLBERT shows a picture of a priest in white robes, speaking at a pulpit. COLBERT lists the behaviors Americans want from priests: "give sermons, counsel your flock, preach the good word." The screen then changes to "Don't," under which COLBERT writes and says emphatically, "molest anyone."

The crowd applauds, just as they did when he introduced them to the Clergy-Matic Ecclesi-Action Center 3:16, but now the camera scans the audience and an actor, wearing a priest's collar, raises his hand. "Excuse me," the fake priest interjects.

COLBERT: Yes,
Fake priest: Stephen, I have a question.
COLBERT: No, there are no questions.[79]

The fake priest then sheepishly raises his hand again, to which COLBERT immediately thwarts his request with an emphatic, "Ever!" Colbert has decreed it; priests should obey it.

Colbert's response is troubling for a number of reasons. First, he did not address this issue in any overt way until 2011, almost a decade after the scandal broke in Boston and twenty years after earlier cases were reported in New Orleans. For someone so explicitly Catholic, it seems strange that the subject was not the focus of specific segments sooner. Additionally, using the language of "molest" instead of "rape" again demonstrates a softer stance on the Catholic Church's moral role in this, not necessarily as though he is trivializing the trauma but looking at it from the institutional and legal perspectives, rather than the vantage points of survivors. He waited until the Council of Bishops discussed the issue, not when comedians or pundits had discussed the story. Few news outlets or comedy shows ignored the scandal as long as *The Colbert Report*. The rage and ferocity normally associated with COLBERT sobers to a solemn and quieter anger.

Interestingly, very few bloggers, commenters, or redditors wrote about this segment, and those who did said things like, "It's that simple" or "This is great!"[80] In fact, this was surprisingly uncommented on, which could mean a few things: first, that viewers did not watch it. That is highly unlikely considering that in 2011, Colbert's ratings were quite high.[81] Another reason could be that people did not understand the jokes, which is also unlikely because the sexual abuse scandals made international headlines. Instead, I think few people commented because Colbert hit upon a nerve more raw than other nerves. Some, especially non-Catholics, wanted to mock the rigidity and traditional doctrine of the Catholic Church; wanted a moment of *schadenfreude* against an organization that seemed holier-than-thou. Other viewers, including many Catholics, agreed with Colbert about the tragedy of the situation while still feeling raw themselves. Commenting would not have helped ease the discomfort, even the pain, of the issue. And no one wanted to sound in favor of the sexual abuse, so this issue was effectively one-sided.

The sexual abuse scandal segment exemplifies how reluctant Colbert can be when confronting the Church's authority. Colbert's subsequent conversations with Cardinal Dolan further demonstrate the extent to which Colbert celebrates and affirms Catholicism's institutional hierarchy. Even before he was appointed archbishop of New York, Cardinal Timothy Dolan was among the most controversial prelates within the sexual abuse scandal, widely criticized by journalists and survivors alike for his active role in the Church's cover-ups. In May 2012, the *New York Times* reported that as archbishop of Milwaukee, Cardinal Dolan had authorized payments to "sexually abusive priests as an incentive for them to agree to dismissal from the priesthood" quietly, and without public notice. The incentivizing can be read both as a cover-up of the sexual abuse and as dismissal of victims' trauma. In a letter of protest, Survivors Network of those Abused by Priests (SNAP) asked, "In what other occupation, especially one working with families and operating schools and youth programs, is an employee given a cash bonus for raping and sexually assaulting children?"[82] A mere sixteen months later, *The Colbert Report* invited Cardinal Dolan for an interview, one that ignored the sexual abuse scandal and instead, affirmed the Catholic Church hierarchy.

Cardinal Dolan appeared on *The Colbert Report* to promote his memoir about the recent election of Pope Francis. COLBERT introduced the book as a tell-all that "blows the lid off the papal conclave." Then COLBERT asked Cardinal Dolan about all the secret behind-the-scenes knowledge about choosing the next pope.

What's it like for the people who haven't been in there and that's every-body except you cardinals. . . . When the doors shut and they put that seal on there, what's the first thing that happens in that room? Is it smoke 'em if you got 'em? What's going on in there?[83]

Dolan explains that they pray and "ask for the inspiration of the Holy Spirit" because the Holy Spirit has "already chosen a new pope" and the cardinals just need to "figure out who he's chosen." Both COLBERT and Dolan come across as jovial, charismatic, and friendly. They interrupt each other's sentences, as one would expect of what COLBERT refers to as the first and "the second most famous Catholic[s] in America"—COLBERT be-ing the first and Dolan being the second.[84] COLBERT does not berate Dolan for his lack of support for sexual abuse victims. He does not satirize Dolan for the institutional hypocrisies around gender roles, birth control, or abor-tion issues. COLBERT appears as a fanboy, one who eagerly accepts an au-thority figure without reticence, a white male Catholic idolizing a charismatic religious figure.

The only moment in the interview when COLBERT demonstrated any dislike for certain aspects of the Church hierarchy came when he asked Cardinal Dolan if the latter had voted for Pope Francis. COLBERT wanted Cardinal Dolan to be pope, even going so far as to give him the "Colbert bump," a reference to an increase in popularity and show of support for a person or thing by mentioning it on the show. The Colbert bump has been given to political candidates, astrophysicists, and independent bookstores. Because COLBERT wanted Dolan to be pope, he was inevitably upset when the latter did not ascend to the papal throne.

> COLBERT: Let me be clear about something. [Pope Francis] is the Vicar of Christ. He is our direct connection to St. Peter, who was appointed the head of the Church by our Lord whilst he walked the earth in his flesh.
> Dolan: Okay, you got it right.
> COLBERT: I don't care for the guy [Pope Francis]. . . . [85]

At this line, Cardinal Dolan lets out a hearty laugh, along with the audi-ence. Dolan then discusses Pope Francis's sincerity, humility, and evan-gelizing style. COLBERT and Dolan spend the next few minutes of the interview judging atheists and the "spare" pope—Pope Emeritus Benedict XVI. By the end of the interview, COLBERT and Dolan appear to be chums, buddies who appreciate and enjoy one another's company. Dolan seems to like COLBERT so much that when COLBERT asks him what his papal name would be if he were elected pope, Dolan laughs loudly, thinks for a minute as the audience quiets down from laughter, and says, "Stephen."[86]

The collegial and jovial attitude of their encounter on *The Colbert Report* only continued off-stage as Colbert has been asked to introduce the cardinal at events, roast him at black-tie dinners, and discuss religious teachings with him for college-student audiences. All of those events and engagements take place away from *The Colbert Report*, when Colbert is out of character, where the *real* person with his individual ideas and religious leanings can emerge. It is in these moments where Colbert and COLBERT merge into one entity but still celebrate and challenge aspects of Catholic life through the humor of Colbert Catholicism.

For Colbert, the affirmation and critique of American Catholicism, the Catholic Church, and Catholic culture are inextricably tied to humor. The multiplicity of Colbert(s) embodies the middle ground between atheist/anti-Catholic/irreligious and conservative/orthodox/doctrine-abiding. That middle space can be categorized as cafeteria, lukewarm, thinking, progressive, or any other myriad labels.

The humor makes it palatable to deal with these sociological categories and differences, as well as question certain conflicts. Although Colbert and COLBERT criticize the Catholic Church, Colbert Catholicism un-satirically reinforces the power and authority of the Church hierarchy. The humor and comedy of Colbert do not simply reject or embrace. The tension between Colbert and COLBERT thus rejects the popular depiction of Catholics as either liberal/conservative, progressive/traditional, and in doing so has significantly shifted public dialogue toward a more diverse understanding of American Catholic culture. On *The Colbert Report*, he portrays a hyperconservative exaggerated traditional Catholic figure who advocates for Catholic institution-based religion, whereas outside the comedy show the actor Colbert publicly portrays himself as a devout Catholic. The reversal and embodiment of expectations change the perception of American Catholicism for both Catholics and non-Catholics. This diversity that Colbert embodies is an intellectual diversity, demonstrating to the American public that Catholics in the United States are not unified intellectually, morally, aesthetically, or pragmatically.

6   Colbert as Cultural Warrior

America's Religious Culture Wars

COLBERT resides in a world infused with the language of the culture wars. While some see this language as an antiquated framing device activated at moments of tension, COLBERT sees those moments as part of everyday life in the United States. Mass media portray the American political and religious climates as wars between cultures: Republican/Democrat, urban/rural, religious/secular. Of course, these are exaggerations. Nevertheless, mass media, with which entertainer Colbert is intimately intertwined, portray religion and politics through a bifurcated culture wars lens.[1] Colbert's humor expands the definition of religion beyond the culture wars binaries.

The term "culture war" originated in 1870s Germany. *Kulturkampf*, literally meaning "culture struggle," described the political, ideological, and religious confrontation between the Roman Catholic Church and German Chancellor Otto von Bismarck. U.S. political culture co-opted the term, and popular media use it retroactively to describe historical moments of cultural, political, and religious polarization. For example, E. J. Dionne of the *Washington Post* wrote an op-ed describing the 2008 election as one in a long line of political culture war moments. Popular journalists and writers place the start of the U.S. culture wars in the 1960s, as one such instance of confrontation between seemingly opposing viewpoints: liberal, peace-loving "hippies" and conservative, "prudish" traditionalists.[2] Starting in the 1970s, conservative groups such as evangelical Christian pastor Jerry Falwell's Moral Majority and Republican President Richard Nixon's Silent Majority cultivated a conservative rhetoric that emphasized a bifurcation of American ideologies.[3]

Sociologist James Davison Hunter's 1991 book, *Culture Wars: The Struggle to Define America*, popularized the term "culture wars." As Hunter argued, the term describes the polarization in American politics between the right and the left.[4] The "hot-button" issues Hunter associated with the culture wars often connected religion and politics; topics such as abortion, gay rights, and censorship all took on religious importance. Political scientist Ryan L. Claassen describes the culture wars division as a "God Gap," with "secular Democrats" pitted against "religious Republicans."[5] The division polarized Americans, identifying the opposing groups as liberal and conservative, but also moral and immoral, secular and sacred, good and bad.

The culture wars rhetoric characterized by Hunter claimed that such divisiveness came from opposing worldviews, not socioeconomic, political, religious, or ethnic differences.[6] While contemporary scholars consider those differences to be constitutive of one's ideologies and worldviews, the culture wars' progressivism-versus-orthodoxy language continues to flourish in the twenty-first century. As historian Roger Chapman defines it, the leading characteristic is a "labeling and classification of issues that suggests a moralistic either/or sensibility."[7] While sociologist Irene Taviss Thomson asserts that there may not be one singular ideological schism but rather numerous factions too often lumped together, the *perception* of a culture war and a stark divide between two distinct, polarized sides remains very much alive in mass media.[8] Colbert and COLBERT dwell in this culture wars mentality.

Scholars of American religion often challenge the ontological validity of the culture wars. Many of these scholars use similar reasons to critique the culture wars and the progressive narrative of "modernity." Religion scholar Sylvester Johnson's work on modernity and colonialism frames much of my definition of the term. Johnson places studies of modernity at the center of concerns about natural rights, consumer capitalism, religious pluralism, and revolutionary technologies and scientific innovations, as well as more "benign" aspects including religious toleration, popular sovereignty, and the democratization of spiritual power as well as racialization, ethnic cleansing, and religious hatred.[9] This notion is akin to the central argument in philosopher Bruno Latour's 1991 *We Have Never Been Modern*, which argued that the construction of "modernity" set up evaluative hierarchies that privileged the European scientific, intellectual, and institutional power systems.[10] Johnson's and Latour's works counter scholars like philosopher Charles Taylor, who considered modern people as a total category to be less connected to, or "buffered" from the religious or mystical world.[11]

Nonetheless, the assumptions and presumptions of a culture wars approach still operate within the American religious landscape. The ongoing division of Americans into two sides dismisses entire groups, including politically liberal evangelical Christians. While scholarship has sought to erase these binaries of left/right and liberal/conservative, the mythic quality of difference remains, and some have argued that the 2016 presidential election illustrated that these sentiments are more than myth. The culture wars still exist and circulate in the public ethos. Culture wars stereotypes and presumptions become shorthand for media narratives. The lived religious experiences of many Americans include the mass-mediated promulgation of stereotypes about good and bad religion, conservative and liberal sociocultural interchange, and right and left religio-political sides. Granted, not every American's religious experiences are reflected in these concepts, but they still leave an impression on the American psyche writ large. Colbert's humor emerges from, challenges, and perpetuates aspects of the culture wars context.

Pundits from MSNBC and Fox News constantly battle from seemingly diverging ends of the political spectrum and use the rhetoric of the culture wars to justify their ardor. In the contemporary United States, mass media have a firm grasp on communication regarding public topics. Unlike the in-person quality of the *agoras* in ancient Greece or the lyceums of the nineteenth century, the media experience of television, radio, films, and the Internet now controls, in many ways, how people receive information and commentary about current events, politics, and religion.

Akin to the ways politics is described, mass media describe religion in contemporary American society as holding a set of binary positions. The media often portray religion only as extremism. On one end of the spectrum lies conservative orthodoxy that embraces rigidity; on the other end lies atheism in a modern, secular world. Those assumptions come from certain twentieth-century understandings of religion, such as the myth of a Protestant American nation; the seeker-centered individualism of "good" religious identity, and the liberal/conservative culture wars of the 1980s to the present. Colbert's use of humor and satire questions American definitions of religion as presented in mass media and the digital media age.

Religion is at one time great, good, and true; America is the nation chosen by God to be a beacon of light to shine upon all the other nations; real Americans are religious, unlike those ungodly atheists in Europe. In another moment, religion is awful, horrible, and ridiculous; religion is the cause of all strife and should be replaced by only rational, scientific understandings of the universe; and primitive, pre-modern peoples had religion, but we, the intellectual and thinking Americans, are beyond that now. If this bifurcation seems hyperbolic, it is. It is also patently untrue. There are more than two extremes, but some of the stereotypes still remain. The culture wars provide a context for Colbert, both as the place where his audience dwells and through his own rhetoric. Colbert perpetuates aspects of the culture wars by portraying an over-exaggerated conservative Catholic/Christian news pundit. But through the humor of that parody, his comedy also satirizes the bifurcation and realigns the sides of the culture wars. He does so on *The Colbert Report* and through affiliated celebrity antics to an audience heavily steeped in culture wars rhetoric. His comedy easily becomes a lightning rod for culture wars issues as they play out in the digital world, both televised and on the Internet. This is the American culture into which Colbert's religious commentaries emerge.

In the culture wars landscape, the *Colbert Report* audience lands firmly on the liberal side, in part because the show is on Comedy Central, a network not generally known for conservative values, as evidenced by the liberal-leaning hosts of *The Daily Show*. Additionally, while Colbert creates a complex character, the underlying mocking of certain conservative politicians and ideologies becomes clear the more one watches the show. Initially, conservatives watched *The Colbert Report* and "were more likely to report that Colbert only pretends to be joking and genuinely meant what he said," but as time went on, fewer conservatives tuned in, believing Colbert to be mocking conservatives rather than aligning with them.[12]

As I discovered while standing in line on a freezing cold November afternoon, the *Colbert Report* audience members come from all over the geographic and demographic map. There were international tourists who were sent there when they could not get tickets for *The Daily Show with Jon Stewart*. There were die-hard Colbert fans who wear American flag sweaters because they think "Stephen will like it."[13] When it comes to religion, many audience members forge their own path, seeking something different from what they grew up with. Sam, for example, road-tripped from Wisconsin for the *Colbert Report* taping. In his mid-thirties, he wanted to see it before the show ended the next month. Sam's parents are Jewish, and his mother is currently part of an ultra-orthodox sect, Lubavitch. He, however, currently identifies as an "atheist/none/whatever-he-feels-on-any-particular-day." Sam is impressed that Colbert can come across as objective but still does not hide his faith. The double-speak of Colbert intrigues him; he thinks there is not a direct point, but rather a multiplicity of points of view that adds to the show. When I asked him how he would summarize the Colbert Nation audience, Sam replied that Colbert finds his audience by "preaching to the choir."[14]

That "choir" consists of people who idealize Americans' individual choice and who engage in the larger public understanding of embedded Protestant Christianity in Western civilization. That individual choice imperative has flourished since the 1960s. Sociologist Wade Clark Roof categorized the Baby Boomer generation (hippies, flower children and the Me Generation, according to the *New York Times'* Peter Steinfels) as "seekers" who move in and out of institutions, making individual choices about religious beliefs, worship practices, and identification groups.[15] These seeker-centered individuals experienced the shifting cultural mores of the 1960s and 1970s but often looked outside their own religious heritages to find spiritual and religious practices and experiences. Seekers searched for open and welcoming religions that often permitted diversity and disliked rigidity. They embraced Zen Buddhism, Native American religions, and New Age practices. Alternative religious expressions, like the Burning Man event, correlate to seeker-practices: searching for meaning as individuals, sometimes collectively and sometimes alone.

There is almost a direct generational line drawn from Baby Boomer seekers to millennial "spiritual but not religious" (SBNRs). SBNRs are, arguably, an evolution of seeker-centered religious identity. The primary connection is that they are in opposition to staunch religious doctrines, dogmas, and dictators. Even the subtitle of religion scholar Robert C. Fuller's book highlights the opposition to religion—*Spiritual, but Not Religious: Understanding Unchurched America.*[16] Unchurched opposes church when church is understood as Christianity, particularly Protestant Christianity. SBNRs often fill the box on surveys with "religiously unaffiliated."

One member of the *Colbert Report* audience from November 2014, Alex, says he was Methodist but has no religion now. In more recent surveys, that position has been conflated with that of the "nones," those who do not identify religiously. Nones are people who may not identify as any specific religion but have a very complicated relationship with religion either because of individual seeking, family ties, or identity and subjectivity creation. When asked in interviews, "What is your religion?" they respond, "None." Seekers, SBNRs, and nones might not fit historical religious categorizations, but these groups cannot be firmly planted in the atheist camp.

Colbert's audiences blur presumed lines of religious demarcation. Hadi, a television producer on vacation between jobs, was born to Muslim parents in Algeria and was raised in the northeastern United States. His wife is Catholic, but neither spouse is "very religious." However, sometimes they join in religious events for their families. Hadi finds *The Colbert Report* extremely funny, in part because Colbert mocks and comments in an open and amusing way. He believes Colbert's super-patriotic, right-wing character's perspective is a commentary on contemporary life, and that in real life, Colbert is "as religious as he is Republican."[17] For Hadi, this comment means that Colbert is irreligious and portrays a conservative Christian as solely an act. Hadi could never imagine a way for one who mocks religions to hold sincere religious beliefs. Hadi exemplifies a group in the Colbert Nation whose members fit into the "nones" category. They may have grown up in a variety of religious backgrounds and would not claim to be atheist or agnostic, rather religiously "none," having made a choice to ignore religious institutions or labels.

Colbert occasionally references surveys about the "unchurched" individuals who probably constitute much of his television audience. In a segment entitled "Extreme Measures for Boosting Church Attendance," COLBERT bemoans contemporary sociological data about religion in America. He finds it ironic that "Pew" research finds that people are not in the pews.

Sadly, recent pew research from the Pew Research Center found that the percentage of Americans who say they seldom or never attend religious services has risen. People aren't going to church. Evidently, somebody blabbed about the "God is everywhere" loophole.[18]

Colbert infotains audiences by correlating their movement away from institutional church settings with gestures toward pantheism and natural
religion stereotypes. "God is everywhere" operates as a linguistic locus for
all that stands in opposition to traditional, institutional Christianity embedded in America's religious self-understanding. The unchurched are stereotyped as oppositional to conservative religion; the unchurched are
considered part of the liberal left side of the culture wars. Regardless of
the actual identifications of the Colbert Nation, the perception flourishes—
those who watch *The Colbert Report* are primarily the unchurched, the
seekers, SBNRs, and nones. Whatever they are called, their influence on
American religious culture is palpable. And they watch *The Colbert
Report*.

Interestingly, Colbert's discussions with ardent atheists become a way
for him to connect with the unchurched and nones. For example, COLBERT
interviewed Richard Dawkins, prominent atheist speaker, about Dawkins'
new book on evolution. Many of the nones agree with Dawkins on the
theory of evolution. As a conservative Christian pundit, COLBERT fero-
ciously argued with Dawkins, requesting evidence for evolution. Dawkins
countered, "Where's the evidence for God?" At which point, COLBERT
paused before retorting, "Reese's Peanut Butter Cups."[19] The juxtaposition
of a silly, though delicious, reference at such a heated moment encapsulates a sentiment some Americans feel: that this discussion is silly. But,
simultaneously, audiences wonder if religion is solely oppositional to modernity, science, and thinking. Or can there be a way to engage topics of
religion without atheism's antagonism? The latter path is the one promulgated by Colbert and COLBERT on *The Colbert Report*.

The Colbert Nation shares a fluid understanding of religion and religious identity. Another shared characteristic of Colbert Nation members
is that they engage with larger conceptions of religion and other hefty
terms through digital media. Regardless of an audience member's age at
a show taping (which spanned eighteen to seventy years old at one taping), everyone in line had a smartphone. People standing in line on a frigid
November afternoon found their tickets through Twitter and Facebook.
They watch *The Colbert Report* on cable television, but rarely live. Usually,
they employed TiVo, Hulu, or YouTube streaming and recording services
to get Colbert "on demand." They may not be in the pews on Sunday morn-
ings, but they are in the audience at what one audience member called

the "Church of Colbert."[20] The Church of Colbert dwells in the digital world of the culture wars marked by dueling threads in American religious history: the embeddedness of Protestant Christianity in the nation and the individualized choices of twentieth-century religious subjectivities.

Mimicking Mouthpiece

The authoritative and pontificating COLBERT is modeled after Bill O'Reilly, whom COLBERT calls Papa Bear. William James O'Reilly Jr., born in 1949, grew up in a Catholic family on Long Island, New York. He attended Catholic parochial schools and Marist College, where he majored in history. After teaching high school at a Catholic school in south Florida, O'Reilly earned a master of arts in journalism at Boston University. In the late 1970s through the 1980s, O'Reilly was a television broadcaster, correspondent, and news anchor. From 1989 through 1995, he was the host of the nationally syndicated tabloid television program *Inside Edition*. In 1996, O'Reilly received a master of public administration from the John F. Kennedy School of Government at Harvard University. Soon after his time at Harvard, he was hired by Roger Ailes at Fox News as a pundit on a daily show called *The O'Reilly Factor*. He gained national prominence by the early 2000s as a "culture warrior" fighting against those he called secular, liberal, godless progressives.[21]

According to communications scholar Geoffrey Baym, in order to understand the Colbert character, "one must begin with the O'Reilly character, a made-for-television construct that proclaims itself to be a 'culture warrior' in the fight against liberalism."[22] COLBERT makes proclamations *à la* O'Reilly that are insistently "objective," yet in the vein of a conservative demagogue. For example, COLBERT imitates O'Reilly's rhetoric when he says, "We have a very simple system in America. Republicans believe in God, and Democrats believe in a welfare state where we tax the rich."[23]

In January 2007, Stephen Colbert was a guest on *The O'Reilly Factor*. During the interview, O'Reilly called Stephen Colbert out for imitating him. Colbert retorted, "But there's a difference between imitation and emulation. Let me tell you the difference, okay? If you imitate someone, you owe them a royalty check. If you emulate them, you don't. There's a big difference."[24] When O'Reilly appeared on *The Colbert Report*, he claimed that, contrary to popular belief, he was not a tough guy and that "this is all an act." To which COLBERT/Colbert cleverly responded, "If you're an act, then what am I?"[25] In an interview printed in *Glenview Announcements* in 2005, Colbert described mocking pundits like Bill O'Reilly, saying,

> They don't need to back up anything they say. Bill O'Reilly has this quote, "How come you don't believe it when I just said it?" and that's the way it is, once he says it, it is gospel. It's admirable. I watch him with my mouth open. How does he do it? I wish I could completely take the filter off my mouth like that.[26]

When COLBERT says something, it is known to be humor, to be funny. When O'Reilly says it, there is a seriousness, a sincerity attached.

Audiences perceive Colbert's truth-teller persona through the double-speak of COLBERT's truthiness. O'Reilly's persona also becomes an ambiguous act, a sincerely insincere fear-monger. O'Reilly's persona exists to sell the news; *The O'Reilly Factor* commodified the pundit to sell the news to a specific group of people for whom the culture wars are real, and they are on the conservative side. COLBERT, the fictional pundit, is also on the conservative side of the supposed binary.

Beyond double-speak, another difference between COLBERT and O'Reilly is that neither COLBERT nor Colbert has been accused of sexual harassment. In April 2017, the *New York Times* reported on five sexual harassment settlements made by O'Reilly. In the wake of that report and further cases of sexual misconduct and harassment, advertisers boycotted and protested O'Reilly's Fox News program, and the cable network fired O'Reilly. The hypocrisy COLBERT mocks struck again, still in the culture wars arena.

COLBERT perpetuates the ideologies of dueling, warring cultural sides in America on *The Colbert Report*. On January 18, 2007, COLBERT interviewed Bill O'Reilly, and both men educated audience members about the culture wars and how they are destroying America.

> COLBERT: There is a culture war going on.
> O'Reilly: Absolutely.
> COLBERT: Let's educate the people, what is the culture war and why is it so important?
> O'Reilly: Well, the culture wars between secular progressive like yourself—
> COLBERT: I'm not a secular progressive, sir . . . . I'm a deeply religious man who will do anything you say. Go ahead.

O'Reilly: And traditionalists like me . . . who, you know, believe that this is a noble nation, well founded. We make mistakes but we have to respect the country.

COLBERT: . . . What is destroying our country more: activist judges, illegal immigrants, gay marriage, or NBC News?

O'Reilly: NBC News . . . because here's the deal. NBC News incorporates all of the others into their presentation.[27]

Here, COLBERT sides with O'Reilly, who believes that conservative Christian views are under attack in, for example, the supposed "war on Christmas." When O'Reilly calls himself a traditionalist in opposition to secular progressives like Colbert, he implies that COLBERT is a persona played by a more liberal actor, Colbert. But COLBERT quickly retorts that he is, in fact, very religious and very conservative. COLBERT relays the culture wars perception that there is only one way in which to be religious, and that is by being a conservative Christian. Conservative Protestant Christianity and conservative Catholicism also become synonymous because ideology matters more than faith. As this segment demonstrates, religion embedded in the culture wars is assumed to be conservative Christianity, Protestant and Catholic. What is so fascinating is that the Colbert(s) and O'Reilly are Catholic. Colbert, in his humor and through his character, widens the spectrum of Catholicism and the culture wars, whereas O'Reilly's earnestness narrows Catholic subjectivity, correlating it with the conservative Christian side of the culture wars.[28]

O'Reilly and COLBERT conflate Catholicism and conservative evangelical Christianity. O'Reilly even co-wrote a book entitled *Killing Jesus* about the life and crucifixion of Jesus, to go along with his other books, *Killing Kennedy* and *Killing Lincoln*. For O'Reilly's Catholicism, traditionalism within Christianity and American political conservatism are interwoven in similar ways to the myth of the Protestant Nation. COLBERT, as a parody of O'Reilly, emulates the same narratives, but with the acknowledgment from audiences that the former is a character, a comedy act, and *not real* because he is on a humorous program. O'Reilly can be classified similarly as an "act," but because he is not included in the genre of humor, the sincerity he puts forth is believable and *real*. In mass media, the culture wars are *real*, and O'Reilly portrays one side of the culture wars while Colbert, through the character COLBERT, blurs the lines through truthiness and humor. COLBERT's character is not as straightforward as a dismissal of the culture wars because Colbert trades in that language. He does not dismiss the labels or stereotypes; he dives deeper into parody and mocks them from the inside, where Catholics and conservative Christianity are synonymous. Non-Catholic audience members often do not realize that Colbert is Catholic *in real life* and are often surprised that he would even associate himself with any religious identity as he is a "liberal" in their eyes. "As religious as he is Republican," according to Hadi.[29]

Colbert traffics in these religious stereotypes because they are familiar to an American public imagination. He plays into the conservative Christian identity as a way to mock and comment on the incongruities he sees in certain religious identities. Also, presuming two distinct and stereotypical sides (as the culture wars language often does) elicits incongruity when language and action contradict each other, thus leading to some of the most humorous material, which is ripe for satirical comment. To use Freud's incongruity theory of jokes as a basis for analysis, it is just funnier if there can be a stereotyped strawman whose beliefs and actions seem to oppose each other.[30]

"Rally to Restore Sanity and/or Fear"

COLBERT's perpetuation of culture wars stereotypes goes beyond *The Colbert Report*. It exited the small screen and entered the Washington Mall on October 30, 2010, before the 2010 midterm elections at the "Rally to Restore Sanity and/or Fear." Initially, *Daily Show* star Jon Stewart crafted his Rally to Restore Sanity as a response to Glenn Beck's "Restoring Honor" rally at the Lincoln Memorial on August 28, 2010. The Fox News pundit chose that date for his march to mark the 47th anniversary of Dr. Martin Luther King Jr.'s "I Have a Dream" speech at the March on Washington.[31] Political and culturally conservative and Mormon, Glenn Beck gathered individuals to "restore honor to America" and to encourage Americans to turn to God for help in the political arena. Republican and Tea Party politician Sarah Palin and pro-life minister Alveda King (and niece of Dr. King) also spoke at the rally. Media reports speculated wildly about the number of attendees, ranging anywhere from 87,000 to hundreds of thousands.[32]

Before and during the rally, Beck also promoted a grassroots "Black Robe Regiment," a phrase borrowed from the American Revolution that would rally conservative clergy for a political and moral revival.[33] Some of its members included conservative evangelical Christian leaders like David Barton, James Dobson, and John Hagee. According to Beck, at the rally "240 pastors, priests, rabbis and imams on stage all locked arms saying the principles of America need to be taught from the pulpit."[34] He also claimed that thousands of other ecumenical religious leaders supported his cause. Beck was an interesting leader for this rally, as a conservative Mormon, another Christian group considered by many evangelicals to be "outside" mainstream Christianity. While Beck presented himself as a conservative Christian Mormon, not all evangelicals considered him to be the type of Christian they wanted expressing their political and religious views in the media. However, as O'Reilly did with his Catholicism, this Fox News pundit constructed himself as a Christian, an American set on perpetuating the idea of a Christian nation, and a member of the conservative side of the culture wars.[35]

Less than a month after Beck's rally, Jon Stewart and Stephen Colbert both announced their own live events as a response: Stewart's "Rally to Restore Sanity" and COLBERT's "March to Keep Fear Alive." The purpose of Stewart's rally was to give a voice in mass media to the Americans who do not hold extremist political views, his motto being "Take it down a notch for America."[36] COLBERT's initial goal, as expected of his over-exaggerated manner, was to promote irrationality and extremism. As evidenced in earlier sections, COLBERT perpetuated the dueling sides of the culture wars, claiming that the right, and righteous, side was one of extreme conservatism and not moderation. As the rally approached, COLBERT went on *The Daily Show* to tell Stewart that he did not have permits to have his separate rally, so Stewart offered to combine the rallies into one event.

The "Rally to Restore Sanity and/or Fear" brought more than 200,000 individuals to the Washington Mall.[37] The rally included performances by musicians John Legend, Sheryl Crow, Yusuf Islam (formerly known as Cat Stevens), The Roots, and Mavis Staples. Comedians and correspondents from *The Daily Show* helped open the rally. Jon Stewart, modestly dressed in khaki pants, a t-shirt, and a black blazer, began the main event about an hour into the live Comedy Central and C-SPAN coverage. COLBERT, on

"Rally to Restore Sanity and/or Fear"
poster

the other hand, arrived shortly after Stewart, arising from his "fear bunker" under the stage in an all-American Evel Knievel–type suit.[38] COLBERT's presence exacerbated the extremist-versus-moderate binary the rally crafted.

The ultra-American symbolism compounded with his overtly nationalist tone only perpetuated the idea that COLBERT was on the American side, the conservative side, and that Jon Stewart, in a dark blazer, was un-American by comparison. Stephen Colbert, the actor and comedian, was present at that rally only as COLBERT; he fought the reasonableness of Stewart's cause with fear-mongering. Stewart gave out medals of reasonableness to celebrated political figures, such as Jacob Isom, who thwarted Reverend Terry Jones's burning of a Qur'an. Alternatively, COLBERT awarded "Medals of Fear" to news outlets that barred employees from attending the rally.[39] The dueling sides of the rally (extremists versus moderates) mimicked aspects of the culture wars (boisterous versus sedate).

Like many rallies and protests in Washington, D.C., this one included a benediction. Interestingly, a comedian in character as a Catholic priest gave the benediction. Father Guido Sarducci (comedian Don Novello), was a *Saturday Night Live* character popular in the 1970s and 1980s. This "chain-smoking, tinted glasses–wearing priest" had also appeared on *The Colbert Report* only months prior to the rally.[40] In his benediction, Father Sarducci (wearing extravagant zebra-print vestments) joked about parking spaces and getting people safely to the Mall. Further, he asked God which was the "right religion" and asked God to show him a sign as he read off a list of world religions. Rally audiences cheered with each religious denomination named, but Father Sarducci concluded that a sign was not valid solely based on audience fervor. When he reached Roman Catholicism, he stopped, repeated the name a few times, then asked if the microphone was working. When God did not send a sign, Father Sarducci expanded it to every Christian religion, with still no sign from God. Roman Catholicism and Judaism both had large audience response, whereas Methodists and Baptists were not as popular, at least audibly. When Islam was announced, Father Sarducci called for peace between the Jews and Muslims, explaining, "They don't eat pork, you don't eat pork, let's build on that."[41] Father Sarducci concluded the benediction by thanking God for all the good things in the world, "especially dogs," and for all the good things humans do in God's name, "charity, and forgiveness . . . thank you so much and we really mean it, Amen."[42]

After the guest performances, Stewart and COLBERT wore matching American flag coats and argued about who loved America more. They battled through singing an original song describing liberal and conservative stereotypes. After a few attempts to find the correct key, COLBERT responded to Stewart's question about why he loved America and began the song,

'Cuz on my calendar each day is the fourth of July / if you cut me open
     I bleed apple pie.
Lady Liberty's the hottest girl I've ever seen / I would totally hit that if
     I were tall and green!
America is perfect and there's nothing to fix / My PIN code is 1776;
     don't tell!
Americans will eat fried anything / And that is why I sing
That it's the . . .
Greatest, strongest country in the world

It's the greatest, strongest country in the world
From the north, the south, the east, and west / And diagonally
There's no one more American than me[43]

Colbert's verse describes a nationalist, ultra-American understanding of conservatism. Personifying a civil religion fervor, Colbert sacralizes American holidays and foods.[44] He even connects his personal banking information to America's Revolutionary War. Alternatively, Stewart began his own verse after the chorus:

But I've got just as much right to wear this sweater
I'm a tolerant American; that's why I'm better
I'm not in the spirit of the founders; I know / But I watch John Adams
    on the HBO
You tax all my cash to help a stranger / But I'll sue City Hall if they
    put up a manger
I know the forty proper terms for "Eskimos" / And here's how the
    chorus goes . . . [45]

Stewart, rather than claiming to be patriotic from the start, concedes that Colbert appears more American, but that Stewart is also American. Not in competition, but additionally. He remarks on interpretations of the Constitution, America's pluralism, and political correctness. After a few more verses, Colbert and Stewart begin sparring line for line:

Colbert: I love America, from U-S-A to U-S-Z
Stewart: I'd marry Uncle Sam if I could do it legally!
Colbert: I lull myself to sleep at night by counting detainees
Stewart: I use French words like "croissant" and "bourgeoisie"
Colbert: I love NASCAR half-time shows with tons of t-n-t
Stewart: My hybrid electric scooter gets a hundred mpg
Colbert: From gay men who like football . . .
Both: To straight men who like *Glee* . . . There's no one more American
    than . . . we![46]

This litany of stereotypes ranged across social, political, religious, and cultural issues. It divided America between urban and rural, educated and folksy, populist and elitist. COLBERT and Stewart parodied the larger fight of the culture wars, not necessarily between conservative and liberal but reframed as between a moderate and a conservative extremist.

With the Capitol behind them, Stewart and COLBERT began their final segment, standing behind two lecterns and wearing suits and ties. They showed a montage of the media fear-mongering and COLBERT brought out a giant puppet "fearzilla," which was destroyed by the audience's chants. Fear was conquered by reasonableness, and Stewart was handed the victory of the rally. In a "moment of sincerity" (a play on *The Daily Show*'s "Moment of Zen" segment), Stewart explained his intentions for the rally: "We can have animus and not be enemies." He blamed the media, "the country's twenty-four-hour politico–pundit perpetual panic conflict-inator."[47] Stewart concluded that most Americans do not solely describe themselves as "Democrats, Republicans, liberals, or conservatives," and he intended to refocus the bifurcation of the culture wars to one of moderation. Neither COLBERT nor Colbert was on stage for Stewart's concluding speech. COLBERT's role had been to perpetuate the culture wars duality, not to bring it together or collapse the sides into a middle ground.

The "Rally to Restore Sanity and/or Fear" marked a moment when COL-BERT perpetuated the bifurcation of the culture wars outside of *The Colbert Report*. In other instances, Colbert's comedy realigns the sides of the culture wars battle through social media. COLBERT and Colbert both embody the racial, ethnic, sexual, socioeconomic, and religious identities that can be labeled "ultimate American" in the public's imagination. He looks and acts like the southern, Irish/French, Catholic, upper-middle-class American father that he, in fact, is. Colbert mocks the culture wars, the sociological category of the "unchurched" nones, and the embedded Christianity all at the same time, but never to the point of a revolution. Colbert's comedy does not revolt against categories but encourages audiences to laugh while thinking about the categories. His comedic style is relatively tame, and less inflammatory than the styles of many other working comedians are sometimes perceived. Colbert is certainly not a comic revolutionary who intends to upend the system through his humor. Colbert likes to push the envelope, but if he hits controversy, he pulls away, claiming that jokes are just jokes.

Colbert's Identity in the Culture Wars and beyond Catholicism

While Colbert and COLBERT articulate and influence American Catholicism through mass media, the #cancelcolbert moment in March 2014 integrated Colbert's Catholicism with other facets of his identity. Colbert's whiteness, heterosexuality, and masculinity became most evident during this incident. After a segment on the racist football mascot of the Washington Redskins that compared the racism of that team name to racist names for the Asian community, *The Colbert Report* posted a short excerpt of the script on its Twitter account. It read, "I am willing to show #Asian community I care by introducing the Ching-Chong Ding-Dong Foundation for Sensitivity to Orientals or Whatever."[48] Offensive and derogatory, especially out of context, it caused uproar among many in the Asian American community. An Asian American writer and activist whose Twitter pseudonym is Suey Park, tweeted a response to her 19,000 followers: "The Ching-Chong Ding-Dong Foundation for Sensitivity to Orientals has decided to call for #cancelcolbert. Trend it."[49] Within minutes, the twenty-three-year-old's tweets spread like wildfire, a success akin to that of one of her previous hashtags, #NotYourAsianSidekick.[50]

Fascinatingly, the #cancelcolbert movement struck a chord on both sides of the political divide, including conservative Filipino American blogger Michelle Malkin, who tweeted, "Co-sign! RT[re-tweet] @suey_park I'm sick of liberals hiding behind assumed 'progressiveness' #CancelColbert." Another tweet focused on offensive language: "I am mindful of the words i [sic] use when talking about things or making jokes, it isnt [sic] much to ask colbert [sic] to do the same #cancelcolbert."[51] Conservative and liberal labels fell away as each affiliated with their political and ideological "enemies" to conflate political correctness and progressive politics with systematic racism. Digital social media enabled individuals to respond to a television program and reform alliances all because of something that was "just a joke."

Just a joke. That was the implicit statement from Stephen Colbert, the actor, as presented through his Twitter handle @StephenAtHome. Colbert made a statement from his private, personal Twitter account the day after the initial tweet had been removed, which said:

#CancelColbert—I agree! Just saw @ColbertReport tweet. I share your rage. Who is that, though? I'm @StephenAtHome http://www.cc.com /video-clips/b6cwb3/the-colbert-report-sport-report—professional -soccer-toddler—golf-innovations—washington-redskins-charm -offensive.[52]

In Colbert's tweet, the link connected to the Comedy Central website with the entire segment, providing context for the joke itself. Colbert subtly argued that the context was part of the satire, that he was in fact mocking racism by being an overtly racist pundit.

The character, COLBERT, does not have a Twitter handle and exists solely in connection to *The Colbert Report*. Amazingly, the distinction had not been so thoroughly invoked or delineated in the previous nine years of *The Colbert Report*. But what does it mean to be separate from his show, to be Stephen at home? Both persona and actor inhabit the same body and present themselves similarly in the world as white, heterosexual, Catholic men. Because of the confusion between persona and actor, surely audience members did not see such a stark distinction. In fact, viewers interacted with both Colbert(s), often assuming they were the same entity. The persona and the actor became known as separate beings, but when Colbert defended the joke as parody without repercussions, he sanctioned the messages.

People were outraged about Colbert's hiding behind satire and comedy. Jonathan Frandzone (@NotAllBhas) tweeted, "#CancelColbert because these 'jokes' once justified exclusionary acts, internment camps, atom bombs, napalm, and the murder of Vincent Chin." He placed Colbert's satire in the same historical trajectory as colonialist, violent, and racist language that held real implications in American life. Still others tweeted messages that linked the racism they saw in the *Colbert Report* tweets to other exclusionary language and phobias. Just Jo (@grimalkinrn) tweeted, "There is a line between satire & offense that @StephenAtHome cannot dance over. He tramples it. For transphobia& racism, #cancelcolbert," while Christopher Carbone (@christocarbone) implicated the Colbert Nation as heteronormative and racist: "You think that Colbert's satire is OK? Um, no. It's disgusting & devalues the lives of Asian & trans folks. #cancelcolbert."[53] While many disagreed with Colbert's whitewashing to justify his comedy, others defended Colbert with the hashtag #IStandWith-Colbert. Those responses were often relatively benign, such as "#istand-withColbert for being a comedian, doing what comedians do," or "#IStandWithColbert Because he's brilliant, hilarious, and essential. Period." Others were more confrontational: "if you've ever tweeted #CancelColbert, you're a faggot."[54]

Park and her hashtag received enormous media attention, largely negative. As journalist Julia Carrie Wong notes,

> Writers at *The Wall Street Journal, Slate, Salon, The Washington Post, Time, The Daily Beast, Jezebel, CNN, USA Today, Huffington Post*, the *BBC, Mediaite, Entertainment Weekly*, and many, many more have all weighed in. Almost without exception . . . these articles, essays and blog posts agree that Suey Park and the hashtag she spawned are misguided, ill-informed, unable to take a joke, unaware of the meaning of satire and/or just plain stupid.[55]

Another blogger, Arthur Chu, apologized to Park for piling on to the inundation of tweets but claimed, "There was a ton of pressure on Asians in general to 'take a side' on that issue, with the sense that taking the 'wrong' side meant making an enemy of Stephen Colbert and all his fans forever."[56]

Some of the outrage went beyond siding with Colbert. It became incendiary and referenced violence and most of it directed at the first tweet from Suey Park. Suey Park is a pseudonym, but unlike (white, Catholic, male) COLBERT, a younger Asian woman, such as Park, does not get to distinguish herself publicly in the same manner. She recalled in a later interview, "I really did think that there was a chance that I could die" because of the threats she received on 4chan and *Reddit*.[57] She received death threats, had to leave her Chicago home, and stepped back from social media. As Park described the events in a later interview, her initial tweet was hyperbolic and "intentionally extremist," supposedly mocking in the same style as Colbert. However, she was not connected with television networks. Without institutional support from a television network or adoring fans, her hyperbolic tone was not authorized by the American public. Just like Colbert, she filters her identity through digital media, but her positionality did not grant her the same leniency or protection. She is not a white Catholic man but rather a young Asian American woman. The responses to her tweets could not be more different than responses to COL-

BERT's.[58] Instead of subverting the system through satire, Colbert and COLBERT perpetuated the power over women, people of color, and marginalized groups.

Park's own religious identity as a mainline Protestant Christian was not a large part of the story. "Christianity is part of who I am," Park said in an interview. "I'm culturally Presbyterian."[59] Park says she likes Presbyterians because the congregants are more open to "the idea of Christian anti-oppression politics," and she started the hashtag #NotMyChristianLeader to provoke Christian feminists who ignore the interests of women of color.[60] She infuses her activism with her Christianity. Park co-founded Killjoy Prophets, a Christian organization whose goal is to give voice to women of color in a variety of Christian settings.[61] She also uses digital media to inform her followers about her religious journey. In 2015, Park tweeted that she was "joining the welcoming and insightful students" at McCormick Theological Seminary in Chicago.[62]

Park's mainline Christianity does not protect her in the same way that Colbert's Catholicism protects him. Both Park and Colbert use their religious identities and ideologies through satire and digital media to address concerns about life in America. Park focuses on racial and gendered injustices, which Colbert, as a heterosexual, upper-middle-class, white male often ignores. Park and Colbert invoke a comical persona when they tweeted, but being part of a mass media conglomerate authorizes Colbert's character. Both use wit to get readers and viewers to think, but his humor is granted a special place as a result of his celebrity status and his presentation as a white male. Park does not have the luxury of being able to satirize without harsh retribution. Park is seen as an activist and Colbert is seen as an entertainer.

The Colbert Report's tweet became a site of racial and ethnic negotiation beyond that of most television programs. On *The Colbert Report*, Colbert himself often explains that he takes no side, that he is just a comedian playing it for laughs. This becomes an easy escape when he pushes buttons or defies something seen as sacred in American life. When the humor borders on the profane for audiences, Colbert justifies his humor, but that does not go far enough for some and goes too far for others. As the show has done but in a different way, these tweets broke the boundaries of partisanship and complicated the boundaries of religion, politics, and the culture wars, with conservative and liberal activists on each side of the Twitter debates.

7   Colbert's Continued Presence

A month after the initial #cancelcolbert tweet, in April 2014, David Letterman announced his retirement from *The Late Show.* CBS revealed the following week that Stephen Colbert would be replacing him, without his character persona.[1] On December 18, 2014, the final episode of *The Colbert Report* aired. At the end of the episode, COLBERT achieves immortality by killing the personification of death, a Grim Reaper figure COLBERT affectionately nicknamed "Grimmy." After that scene, COLBERT/Colbert, Jon Stewart, and Randy Newman sing "We'll Meet Again" with dozens of other celebrities, the *Colbert Report* staff, and Colbert's family. The camera then pans to an empty stage, with the usual portrait within a portrait within a portrait of COLBERT's visage devoid of the faux-newscaster. COLBERT enters again, holding Captain America's shield and screaming, "What do I do now?" from the roof of the studio. He encounters Santa Claus driving Abraham Lincoln and "the one with all the answers," Alex Trebek, in his sleigh. The four-some head into the moonlit night, promising to always "be there for the American people when they need us the most." COLBERT delivers a closing monologue thanking production staff, family, the network, the guests, and the Colbert Nation, concluding with a news reporter send-off: "From eternity, I'm STEPHEN COLBERT."[2] These final irreverent moments, in which character COLBERT confronts and conquers his "stage death" and achieves immortal authoritative status alongside celebrity guests and whimsical pop culture references, evoke themes from *The Colbert Report*'s nine-year run.

The conclusion of *The Colbert Report* was abrupt for audiences who did not want to see it come to an end. However, as Colbert explained in a 2016 interview with *Fresh Air*'s Terry Gross, the show's end date was set two years prior.

I began to feel like I was stumbling downhill with an armful of bottles and that I couldn't actually keep up the discipline. [Because] it took discipline to remind myself every day to, you know, be the character, don't be yourself. And I, and I began to wonder, "What would it be like to be me?"[3]

Colbert got his wish—with his new late-night program on CBS, audiences would get to meet Colbert without his character persona.

Stephen Colbert after *The Colbert Report*

Colbert's Catholic identity and interactions with Catholic institutional authority were first projected to mass media audiences through *The Colbert Report*, but his presentation of Catholicism did not end when the Comedy Central program went off the air. In 2015, as *The Late Show with Stephen Colbert* was about to premiere, nine late-night television show hosts were interviewed for a *Vanity Fair* video promoting the new and returning hosts. In it, Stephen Colbert, Conan O'Brien, Jimmy Kimmel, Seth Meyers, James Corden, Trevor Noah, John Oliver, Larry Wilmore, and Bill Maher were each asked to describe one another in one word. When Stephen Colbert was in the hot seat, his descriptions of other late-night hosts included "brilliant," "interesting," and "smart." When Bill Maher was asked to describe Colbert in one word, he chose "Catholic."[4]

More than anytime else, Catholic comedians rule late-night television programming in the twenty-first century (currently, Seth Meyers is the only Jewish comedian on a major network's late-night lineup, and James Corden at CBS's *Late Late Show* grew up in the Salvation Army in England). Previous late-night hosts, from Jack Paar and Johnny Carson to Jay Leno and David Letterman, rarely incorporated religion into their acts, and when they did, "it was always as an outside observer," remarks communications and media studies scholar Father Michael Tueth.[5] Deacon Greg Kandra, a twenty-year veteran writer and producer for CBS News, notes that this wave of Catholic comedians have a point of view "more respectful . . . toward religion, and probably toward the pope and Catholicism."[6] Catholic insiders seem to be the new normal of late-night television.

These late-night hosts present the variety of Catholic experiences in their diversity. The only female late-night host, Samantha Bee, was raised a Catholic but now considers herself more agnostic or atheistic.[7] Jimmy Kimmel was an altar boy. Conan O'Brien employs his "experience growing up Irish Catholic just outside Boston" in his comedy.[8] Jimmy Fallon was fascinated with the Church as a child and discussed the similarities and differences between show business's audiences and the Mass's congregation on a radio broadcast in 2011.[9] South African comedian Trevor Noah, who became Jon Stewart's replacement on *The Daily Show*, attended Catholic primary school. Although it was canceled, *The Nightly Show*'s Larry Wilmore was an African American Catholic late-night host. As evinced, Stephen Colbert may be one of the best-known Catholics, but he is definitely not alone.

Bill Maher's one-word descriptor for Colbert, though, should give us pause. Catholics rule late-night television, but Colbert is arguably still one of the most popular Catholic entertainers, one who incorporates his religion into his daily identity presentation. Being Colbert, finding what Terry Gross calls his "authentic voice," might have coincided with audiences' discovery of Colbert, but it also reaffirmed his interest in and representation of his Catholic identity, "un-ironically."[10]

Audiences have become more aware of Colbert's Catholic identity as he left the character COLBERT behind on *The Late Show with Stephen Colbert*. While the questioning of the authenticity of his religiosity continues, many fans and mass media outlets are becoming more familiar with Colbert's Catholicism. Alison Lesley's journalistic punctuation in her *World Religion News* article entitled "Stephen Colbert—Comedian, TV Host . . . Catholic?" may be one of the last moments of questioning his self-proclaimed faith.[11] As discussed in earlier chapters, a majority of the in-depth interviews with Colbert, published to promote his new show, mention his Catholicism. The *Late Show* studio looks like a church with a stained-glass motif as part of the set design. Even the coffee mugs sold by CBS to promote the show include the same stained-glass image.[12] While audiences in 2005 may not have known that Stephen Colbert was a Catholic, 2015 audiences could hardly miss it.

On *The Late Show*, Colbert continues his presentation of Catholicism, but it is completely his own, without a persona or mask to confuse people. Colbert references his Catholic identity multiple times a month, more often if there is a prominent Catholic news story, such as when the pope visited the United States. He often invokes his Catholicism in his interviews with guests, such as actress Patricia Heaton with whom he had another "Catholic Throwdown," with each quizzing the other on religious particularities.[13] Beyond the uncomplicated comical jokes about Catholic identity, Colbert also performs his Catholicism at more somber moments.

On September 10, 2015, Vice President Joe Biden, also a Catholic, was a guest on *The Late Show with Stephen Colbert*. This was the third day of Colbert's reign as host of *The Late Show*, with the first two days featuring actor George Clooney, former Florida governor Jeb Bush, actress Scarlett Johansson, and CEO/inventor Elon Musk. As this was 2015, and the next presidential election was only a year away, constituents and politicians from across the nation pressured the vice president, calling on him to decide whether to run for the presidency in 2016. Colbert began the interview by complimenting Biden on his authenticity: "How did you maintain your soul in a city filled with people who are trying to lie to us in subtle ways?" Biden responded that he commuted daily to his home in Delaware in an effort to stay true to himself as a politician. Colbert retorted, "I can't imagine what it would be like to spend nine years pretending to be someone that you're not," an ironic nod to his experience on *The Colbert Report*.[14] On the third day on *The Late Show*, Colbert was still trying to present his *authentic* identity, relating to audiences that he is not the character COLBERT.

Colbert then moved the conversation to a remembrance of Beau Biden, Vice President Biden's son and the Delaware attorney general, who had passed away from brain cancer three months earlier. Colbert encouraged the vice president to share a story about his son. Biden emotionally described his son as empathetic, making sure during his last weeks that his father would be able to cope after his death. At one point, Vice President Biden turned to the crowd and with arms opened and hands gesticulating, said, "I'm not making this up, I know I sound like a father," punctuating the heartwarming reminiscence and enveloping the audience with a sense of sympathy.[15]

Afterward, Biden became quiet and Colbert calmly inquired, "How is your faith? I know you are a man of deep faith, how has your faith helped you respond . . . how important is that in your life and how has that helped you?" Biden described how his wife left him a note on the bathroom mirror as he was shaving, a quote from Kierkegaard that read, "Faith sees best in the dark." Continuing, Biden explained that his religion provides him with a sense of solace. With tears welling up in his eyes, Biden described how some of his solace comes from the ritual, "the comfort of what you've done your whole life."

> I go to Mass and . . . I am able to be just alone, even in a crowd. You are alone. I say the rosary. I find it to be incredibly comforting, and so what my faith has done is sort of takes everything about my life with my parents, and my siblings and all the comforting things and all the good things that have happened, have happened around the culture of my religion and the theology of my religion . . . the faith doesn't always stick with you, sometimes it leaves me . . . [16]

At this point, Colbert interjects, concurring with Biden that he understands the feeling of not wanting to come off as pious or as "holy Joe," but that Biden has inspired Colbert because through his suffering, Biden has made beautiful things and dedicated his life to people. Biden then says that he is inspired by people who have been hurt and have suffered, like Colbert (alluding to the death of Colbert's father and brothers in 1974). Biden asks Colbert how his mother got through her pain and suffering, and Colbert replied that "she had to take care of me . . . we had to take care of each other."[17] For Biden and Colbert, their families and their faith are intertwined.

Colbert and Biden's Catholicism, as annotated briefly in their discussion of rituals and practices, becomes a backdrop for their own theologies of suffering and inspiration. These two men, whose family lives have been marked by tragedy, allow themselves to be somber and muted on a national late-night show. They discuss what others have called Colbert Catholicism, an emphasis on the joy in concert with the suffering. These are not novel ideas, but to have the vice president of the United States discuss his religious and emotional life with a comedian and late-night host shifts where and how we see religion, in particular Catholicism, discussed in America.

Colbert also illustrates his Catholic identity on *The Late Show* through recurring segments, such as "Stephen Colbert's Midnight Confessions." The basic premise is that at midnight, the camera gives a close-up of Colbert partially obscured by a latticed partition reminiscent of a Catholic confessional. Colbert then confesses his "sins" to the audience, who collectively act in the priest's role. Colbert begins by affirming his Catholic identity and discussing his ritualistic practices with the audience:

> As many of you know, I'm Roman Catholic. But I don't always have time for some of my favorite Catholic rituals, like confession. There's just something so pure about stepping into that booth and being totally anonymous after disguising my famous voice so I sound like Darth Vader.[18]

"Forgive me, audience," Colbert begins, describing his litany of things he is not certain are sins but are "things he feels guilty about."[19] He explains that he often "takes a penny, but does not leave a penny," flosses irregularly, and is focused on the truth only insofar as it is in reference to "I Can't Believe It's Not Butter."[20] The segment ends with Colbert's asking, "Forgive me, audience," and the audience yelling in unison, "We forgive you."[21] This type of humor, the silliness and pompousness, is reminiscent of COLBERT. Separating the persona and *real* person continues to mystify audiences and scholars, and segments like "Midnight Confessions" remind us of the shared characteristics of the Colbert(s).

On the January 11, 2018, segment, Colbert again self-identified as a Catholic, "a bad Catholic, the most common kind."[22] These quips recapitulate Colbert's version of Catholicism as aligned with that of those considered to be cultural or lapsed Catholics, an over-simplification of the spectrum between nonreligious and conservative/observant Catholics. Anonymous viewers interact with Colbert's joking messages by commenting on YouTube. One viewer, whose handle is New Message, exclaimed, "Sometimes [. . .] when my Mom asks if I've been going to church [. . .] I think about these segments, and say 'Pretty regularly . . .'" This does not mean that Colbert is a replacement for Catholic practice and worship, per se, but that his parody of the confessional sacrament makes a space for those who are on the spectrum between observant and atheist. This space is not necessarily for *practicing* Catholics, but it is also not antithetical to religious sentiment, values, or engagement.

In September 2017, two years since his first "Midnight Confession," Colbert and his writing staff compiled a litany of the segment's jokes into a coffee-table book. The book is dedicated "to human frailty. If you have no regrets, I don't want to know you." Besides reflecting the Catholic teaching of original sin, in the realm of Colbert Catholicism this dedication

suggests a blending of the suffering and the joyous. However, that sentiment immediately turns to one of silliness and parody. The opening text
of Colbert's Introduction reads, "Bless me, readers, for I have published.
It's been five years since my last book," a direct parody of the confessional
dialogue between a Catholic and a priest for confession. Colbert then
compares the Catholic Church to late-night television: "[O]ur shows last
about an hour, we're obsessed with reaching younger demographics,
and the hosts are almost always men." The self-reflexive comparison that
emphasizes the market-shares and systematic patriarchy of both entities
differs from the jokes contained in the book itself. The Introduction is
pithy and parodic; the book and "confessions" are trite in comparison.
Confessing "I kind of like Yankee Candle" hints at a collective truth
about a specific suburban-American public but is not sharp, nor does it
create the biting satire for which COLBERT gained prominence.[23]

This book and segment are "religion-adjacent"; they dwell near religion,
use religious themes, but are not so in-joke that the audience must have a
complete understanding of the Bible, Catholic catechism, or Christian theology. Most of the "Midnight Confessions" segments perpetuate stereotypes of Catholic guilt and sin, while also presenting those sins as
egalitarian or commonsense jokes. The mundane nature of his "sins"
points to the everyday aspects of his Catholicism. It is not particularly ex-
ceptional, but more routine. And he incorporates his audience into his
rituals in a way that familiarizes them and uses them as a vehicle for his
comedy. The penultimate section of the "Midnight Confessions" book includes reprinted tweets from ordinary viewers about their "sins" culled
from those tagged with the hashtag #lateshowconfessions. The final section implores readers to transcribe their confessions: "[A]fter filling these
pages with your darkest secrets, burn this book. Then buy another copy."
Colbert crafts a religion-adjacent community through audience interaction
and participation in Catholic rituals.

Colbert's rhetorical engagement with contemporary Catholic issues
lacks the critical ferocity some expect from a comedian. Instead, he implicitly supports the institutional Catholic Church. On *The Late Show with
Stephen Colbert*, the entertainer also grapples with issues facing the Catholic Church in the twenty-first century, including the clerical sexual abuse
scandals. This topic came up during an interview with Mark Ruffalo, one
of the stars of *Spotlight*, the critically acclaimed 2015 film about the Bos-

ton Globe writers who reported the story and won a Pulitzer Prize in 2003. Colbert acts more as a reporter in this interview, rather than as a comedian, and lets Ruffalo take the lead in explaining the story. The conversation focuses on investigative journalism rather than on the abuses of the Catholic hierarchy and clergy, even though both men were raised Catholic. The conversation turns when Ruffalo references the Catholic Church and the *Boston Globe* as "cozied up" institutions. Colbert laments the fact that the clerical sexual abuse scandal "sullied the place that would have been a solace for the kind of heartbreak or the psychic damage created by the immediate abuse [by] the priests or the people who now, when they go into a church, feel guilty for going into a Catholic church that could allow this to happen." Colbert continues by saying that the Catholic Church recognizes that "17,500 children were abused in the United States" and that the only way for the Church to heal itself is for the "truth to be known." He imagines the sexual abuse crises as something that happened to the Church (the collective body of Christ) rather than the Church and its institutional authorities perpetrating the atrocities. He compartmentalizes the clerical sexual abuse from the Church writ large. However, Colbert quickly changed from the somber tone. Instead of diving deeper into the conversation by interrogating the institutional authorities' roles and responsibilities, Colbert posed a final question for Ruffalo that abruptly shifted the subject to a sillier and less controversial topic: "Do you like playing the Hulk?," referencing Ruffalo's appearances as the Hulk in many Marvel action movies.[24]

Colbert's love for the institutional Catholic Church continues in his segments on the pope. The first month of *The Late Show with Stephen Colbert* coincided with a visit from Pope Francis to Philadelphia—this pope's first visit to the United States. In honor of that historic event, Stephen Colbert created a special "pope show" called "Tour De Francis: A New Pope: I Heart N-Y-Holy See Humblefest 2016!" and interviewed prominent American lay Catholics, such as former First Lady of California and journalist Maria Shriver, journalist Andrew Sullivan, and comedian Jim Gaffigan. When the guests sat down, Colbert thanked them for "being publicly Catholic," to which Gaffigan responded, "We'll be crucified later, right?" and Colbert retorted, "Maybe in the press." Being a public Catholic, Colbert queried, highlighted the tension he felt by "being an American and being a Catholic at the same time." Colbert even played the "Protestant

American" (an anti-Catholic devil's advocate), enticing his guests to reply to claims such as that Catholics cannot be both American and Catholic simultaneously, since "Americans have this sort of spirit of individuality and we get to do anything we want, the Catholic church has this spirit of 'ehh, not really.'" Colbert pushed forward his Socratic questioning, posing inquiries to Andrew Sullivan, a journalist and openly gay Catholic man:

> Can you do whatever you want and still be a Catholic? Andrew . . . You're gay . . . spoiler alert, that's against the rules, my friend . . . 'cuz you're an openly gay Catholic man or an openly Catholic gay man, I'm sure both of those are not easy . . . . Do you feel a tension between your sexual orientation and your faith?[25]

Sullivan removes the binary Colbert set up, instead claiming that he is openly gay because he is a Catholic: "I was brought up to tell the truth about myself and because I was taught to treat every human being with equal dignity and love and compassion."[26]

The *Late Show* audience erupted in applause at Sullivan's interpretation of Catholic faith. And although Colbert pushed further, Jim Gaffigan was quick to retort that the argument about the supposed struggle of being both American and Catholic was ancient, one that John F. Kennedy's 1960 election had dispelled. Gaffigan went on to describe American Catholics today by using himself as an example:

> I was raised Catholic but I was essentially agnostic or atheist for most of my adult life and what brought me back was the notion of mercy . . . that Francis is saying, . . . who I am I to judge? . . . And it's an invitation to imperfect Catholics.[27]

Colbert and Gaffigan embrace in their late-night and stand-up comedy the idea of being imperfect Catholics. And yet there is not a stark divide that imperfect Catholics are any less Catholic. In fact, by having a comedian, a divorced celebrity, and a gay journalist as his team of representative Catholics, Colbert proved just how different his articulation of *real,* *true,* and *good* Catholic identity was from his conservative Catholic character COLBERT's.

Pope Francis did not visit *The Late Show with Stephen Colbert* on his 2015 trip to the United States, but Colbert did interview another member of the clergy. During that week, the archbishop of Miami, Thomas Wenski, joined Colbert and presented him with a medal of St. Genesius, the patron saint of comedians. The two joked and discussed the environmental policies of the Catholic Church. While both Colbert and COLBERT are invested in the institutional Catholic Church, Colbert's love for Pope Francis is in stark contrast to COLBERT's opinion of this pope. In an interview with Terry Gross, Colbert notes that Pope Francis's vision of inclusivity, albeit with some conservative and some liberal leanings, is the Church Colbert "imagined as a child" and "was raised" in. Unlike his character, Colbert disliked the "highly politicized" papacy of John Paul II, which was "brought into the fold of the Republican coalition of the Reagan years." According to Colbert, "the Church is larger than any political moment."[28] Where COLBERT conflated the connections between church and state, even calling for an intersection of the two, Colbert visualizes the Catholic Church, its values and morals, as more important and more pressing than political tenets.

Colbert, COLBERT, and the 2016 Election

While the #cancelcolbert incident began a conversation about Colbert's limitations as a white male comedian, the boundaries of liberal political humor were tested even further with the 2016 election. More than half of the Americans who voted spent November 9, 2016 (and the years that followed) desperately trying to decipher how Donald J. Trump became the president of the United States. In many ways that query is a grope in the dark (pun intended). One question hovers over this election: Was this Stephen Colbert's fault? Had COLBERT, the beloved persona Stephen Colbert portrayed for nine years on *The Colbert Report*, desensitized Americans to factlessness and truthiness? In January 2017, journalists and bloggers began culling *Colbert Report* clips from the archives to discuss "alternative facts" in conjunction with "truthiness."[29] Did COLBERT numb us, or further endear us, to egomaniacal, xenophobic, misogynistic buffoonery? Did he train us to laugh at what should have terrified us?

When *The Colbert Report* ended, Colbert thought he was removing his character from the world. He left, in part, because it became more difficult to maintain the persona.

> I thought maybe I would make some big mistake with the character because he says, he would say terrible things, and I got away with some of the terrible things he would say or do because it was all filtered through his mask. But if I didn't maintain the mask, it would just be me being terrible. . . . I felt my discipline slipping . . . that I would simply slide into being like the thing that I was mocking.[30]

What Colbert did not realize is that there were moments when he in fact did embody the thing he was mocking. Colbert satirized a specific kind of white conservative man, portrayed as real by Fox News and other conservative news media. As such, Colbert is a white male who played a character slightly more white-privileged than the actor, and the character was much less aware of his white privilege than the actor portraying him. Colbert met every guest on the show out of character before the taping. He said, my character is "an idiot, so disabuse me of my ignorance."[31] But Colbert did not tell that to the audience. He let the persona stand in, be the fool, joke and play for the sake of satire. But as Colbert said himself on his Showtime Election Day show, "Maybe we drank the poison, maybe we drank too much."[32] Colbert was so well liked and seen as such a truth-teller that Americans did not notice when COLBERT and his truthiness became the *modus operandi* for American culture. The character and the *real* person were so intertwined that separating the satire from everyday life became almost impossible.

Perhaps this could have been foreseen. Colbert never fully articulated that he and his character share similar cultural, religious, and political privileges. Colbert is a Catholic, and while theirs has historically been a marginalized group, his whiteness overshadows any religious marginalization, especially in the twenty-first century. The jokes he makes do not come from a place of "other," as evidenced by his ascent to a throne of late-night television. White Catholic men continue to oppress other Americans, and perhaps the humorous antidote does not always work.

Beyond the representation of conservative white men on television, perhaps the expectation of a united audience is not as universal as envisioned in the American imaginary. Perhaps smiles and laughs require more critical awareness. Satire and parody encourage active thought. Satire, by nature, is predicated on the critique of the status quo. But "truthiness" betrayed Americans because it acclimated and desensitized audiences, especially when it was spoken by a white Catholic male whose persona embodied hyperconservative rhetoric. COLBERT contributed to America's comfort with buffoonery, radical right-wing extremism, and political incorrectness in the election of President Trump. Audiences trusted Colbert, legitimized his humor, and authorized COLBERT and Colbert as influential figures. By authorizing and legitimizing COLBERT, American citizens ignored the implications of Trump, calling him a joke. In the first months of his presidential candidacy, many Americans did not take Trump *seriously.*

In no way am I claiming that Colbert secretly adores President Trump. In fact, his current nightly monologues demonstrate his rebuke and admonition. Regardless of direct causality, the popularity of *The Colbert Report* and the mainstream quality of Colbert influenced American audiences for nine years. Colbert's stance post–the 2016 election has been to mock President Trump. He lampoons him, mimics his voice, and infantilizes him with cartoons and impersonations. While Colbert may be a voice of the resistance to Trump, has the damage already been done? Were American audiences and voters blinded to the rise of President Trump in part because comedians, the funny, ironic truth-tellers, were for so long invested in perpetuating truthiness?

The End and the Beginning

The truthiness of *The Colbert Report* ended in 2014, and Colbert is arguably still trying to figure out his identity on *The Late Show with Stephen Colbert.* This book begins a conversation about Colbert post-COLBERT, the actor without his persona. Part of what made writing about Stephen Colbert exciting is that he is a living, ever-changing, and complex human actor with a big stage. He is popular: Journalists, authors, and scholars write about him. Alternatively, part of what made writing about Colbert exhausting is that everyone knows him. Everyone has an opinion, a thought, or a piece written on him and his many exploits. The life and work of Stephen Colbert did not end with the conclusion of *The Colbert Report.*

This book on the intersection of religion and humor tests the limits of the field of religious studies, as well as the connection between the study of religion and the study of media and culture. Consequently, my project understands that religion happens outside the confines of our preconceived assumptions. Individuals and groups are braiding, mixing, complicating, and diversifying religious belief, practice, ritual, and identity. They are doing so in the twenty-first century with new media technologies and applications. This research pushes scholars, students, and the public to consider the intersection of humor and religion as viable for further study. Scholars cannot assume that religion must be taken *seriously*. Taking religion *humorously* refocuses where we find religion in contemporary life, allowing us to see clearly the religious elements in the work and life of comedian Stephen Colbert.

Appendix

Alphabetical List of Search Terms for the *Colbert Report* Website

Advent

Almighty

atheist/atheism

Atone Phone

Bible

Blitzkrieg of Grinchitude

Buddha

Buddhism/Buddhist

Catholic

Catholicism

Catholics

Chanukkah/Chanukah/
    Hanukkah/Hanukah

Christ

Christianity

Christian(s)

Christmas

church/churches

clergy

Devil

Easter

Easter Under Attack

evangelical

faith

God(s)

Hanukkah. *See* Chanukkah

Hindu/Hinduism

Islam

Jain

Jesus

Jewish

Jews

Judaism

Krishna

Lent

Lord

Mass

meditate/meditation

Muslim

nun(s)

papal

Passover

pastor(s)

Pentecost

Pesach

pope

pray

prayer

priest(s)

Protestants

rabbi

religion

religions

religious

Rosary

Rosh Hashana

Santeria

Sikh

sin

spirit(s)

spiritual but not religious

spirituality

supernatural

Unitarian

Voodoo

Vodun

Yom Kippur

Selected *Colbert Report* Videos

"5 X Five - Colbert Holidays: Black Friday." *The Colbert Report*, Comedy Central, 2013. http://thecolbertreport.cc.com/videos/2j97sd/5-x-five—colbert-holidays—black-friday.

"5 X Five - Colbert Holidays: Christmas." *The Colbert Report*, Comedy Central, 2013. http://thecolbertreport.cc.com/videos/2tv4s2/5-x-five—colbert-holidays—christmas.

"5 X Five - Colbert Holidays: Hanukkah." *The Colbert Report*, Comedy Central, 2013. http://thecolbertreport.cc.com/videos/bsyqlt/5-x-five—colbert-holidays—hanukkah.

"5 X Five - Colbert Holidays: Thanksgiving." *The Colbert Report*, Comedy Central, 2013. http://thecolbertreport.cc.com/videos/8qn1vx/5-x-five—colbert-holidays—thanksgiving.

"5 X Five - Colbert Holidays: Vacation." *The Colbert Report*, Comedy Central, 2013. http://thecolbertreport.cc.com/videos/groczx/5-x-five—colbert-holidays—vacation.

"5 X Five - Colbert on Religion - Buddhism." *The Colbert Report*, Comedy Central, 2012. http://thecolbertreport.cc.com/videos/hrqcio/5-x-five—colbert-on-religion—buddhism.

"5 X Five - Colbert on Religion - Catholicism." *The Colbert Report*, Comedy Central, 2012. http://thecolbertreport.cc.com/videos/3tgsfs/5-x-five—colbert-on-religion—catholicism.

"5 X Five - Colbert on Religion - Islam." *The Colbert Report*, Comedy Central, 2012. http://thecolbertreport.cc.com/videos/4ha3eh/5-x-five—colbert-on-religion—islam.

"5 X Five - Colbert on Religion - Judaism." *The Colbert Report*, Comedy Central, 2012. http://thecolbertreport.cc.com/videos/m3zujh/5-x-five—colbert-on-religion—judaism.

"5 X Five - Colbert on Religion - Scientology." *The Colbert Report*, Comedy Central, 2012. http://thecolbertreport.cc.com/videos/96le8w/5-x-five—colbert-on-religion—scientology.

"Bibles Swapped for 'Fifty Shades of Grey.'" *The Colbert Report*, Comedy Central, 2012. http://thecolbertreport.cc.com/videos/f7r4oe/bibles-swapped-for—fifty-shades-of-grey-.

"Bill O'Reilly." *The Colbert Report*, Comedy Central, January 18, 2007. http://www.cc.com/video-clips/9seimt/the-colbert-report-bill-o-reilly.

"Bill O'Reilly on America's 'Grievance Industry.'" *The Colbert Report*, Comedy Central, 2011. http://thecolbertreport.cc.com/videos/3a9611/bill-o-reilly-on-america-s—grievance-industry-.

"The Blitzkrieg on Grinchitude - Fired Santa Claus & Colbert Super PAC Christmas," *The Colbert Report*. Comedy Central, 2011. http://thecolbertreport.cc.com/videos/3krrxg/the-blitzkrieg-on-grinchitude—fired-santa-claus—colbert-super-pac-christmas.

"Blitzkrieg on Grinchitude - Mistletoe Drones," *The Colbert Report*, Comedy Central, 2014. http://thecolbertreport.cc.com/videos/lje2l4/blitzkrieg-on-grinchitude—mistletoe-drones.

"Blitzkrieg on Grinchitude - Santa Claus, IN," *The Colbert Report*, Comedy Central, 2006. http://thecolbertreport.cc.com/videos/jl58qd/blitzkrieg-on-grinchitude—santa-claus—in.

"Blitzkrieg on Grinchitude - Santa's Pipe," *The Colbert Report*, Comedy Central, 2012. http://thecolbertreport.cc.com/videos/tl4uce/blitzkrieg-on-grinchitude—santa-s-pipe.

"#BringBackOurGirls - Rosemary Nyirumbe," *The Colbert Report*. Comedy Central, May 13, 2014. http://www.cc.com/video-clips/2rgt3x/the-colbert-report—bringbackourgirls—rosemary-nyirumbe.

"Chick-Fil-A Appreciation Day," *The Colbert Report*. Comedy Central, August 6, 2012. http://www.cc.com/video-clips/w2s6co/the-colbert-report-chick-fil-a-appreciation-day.

"Clergy-Matic Ecclesi-Action Center 3:16," *The Colbert Report*. Comedy Central, May 19, 2011.

"Daniel Goleman," *The Colbert Report*. Comedy Central, December 2, 2013. http://www.cc.com/video-clips/tllp9w/the-colbert-report-daniel-goleman.

"December 18, 2014 - Grimmy," *The Colbert Report*. Comedy Central, December 18, 2014. http://www.cc.com/episodes/qofohx/the-colbert-report-december-18–2014—grimmy-season-11-ep-11040.

"Election of Pope Francis," *The Colbert Report*. Comedy Central, March 25, 2013. http://www.cc.com/video-clips/6zcxhr/the-colbert-report-election -of-pope-francis.

"Extreme Measures for Boosting Church Attendance," *The Colbert Report*. Comedy Central, April 21, 2014. http://thecolbertreport.cc.com/videos /hls49q/extreme-measures-for-boosting-church-attendance.

"Father James Martin - September 13, 2007," *The Colbert Report*. Comedy Central, September 13, 2007. http://www.cc.com/video-clips/g1gps7/the -colbert-report-father-james-martin.

"Glenn Beck Attacks Social Justice - James Martin," *The Colbert Report*. Comedy Central, March 18, 2010. http://www.cc.com/video-clips/oymi8o /the-colbert-report-glenn-beck-attacks-social-justice—james-martin.

"Green Screen Challenge - iPod + Colbert," *The Colbert Report*, Comedy Central, 2006. http://thecolbertreport.cc.com/videos/mechk8/green -screen-challenge—ipod—colbert.

"Interview with Henry Louis Gates, Jr.," *The Colbert Report*. Comedy Central, February 4, 2010. http://www.cc.com/video-clips/sm98y8/the -colbert-report-henry-louis-gates—jr-.

"Interview with Martha Stewart," *The Colbert Report*. Comedy Central, November 10, 2010. http://www.cc.com/video-clips/0cxark/the-colbert -report-martha-stewart.

"The Koran's Best Day Ever," *The Colbert Report*. Comedy Central, 2011. http://thecolbertreport.cc.com/videos/a3005c/the-koran-s-best-day -ever.

"On Topic - In the News - Gay Marriage," *The Colbert Report*. Comedy Central, 2010. http://thecolbertreport.cc.com/videos/swiftb/on-topic—in -the-news—gay-marriage.

"Paul Ryan's Christian Budget Cuts," *The Colbert Report*. Comedy Central, May 1, 2012. http://www.cc.com/video-clips/0zj7f4/the-colbert-report -paul-ryan-s-christian-budget-cuts.

"Philip Zimbardo," *The Colbert Report*. Comedy Central, February 11, 2008. http://www.cc.com/video-clips/8sjp0a/the-colbert-report-philip -zimbardo.

"Pope Francis on Baptizing Martians," *The Colbert Report*. Comedy Central, May 14, 2014. http://www.cc.com/video-clips/50b1j2/the-colbert -report-pope-francis-on-baptizing-martians.

"Pope's Baseball Cap & CatholicTV," *The Colbert Report*. Comedy Central, August 5, 2010. http://www.cc.com/video-clips/gw1rft/the-colbert-report-pope-s-baseball-cap—catholictv.

"Pope's Resignation & Papal Speculatron 7500 - James Martin," *The Colbert Report*. Comedy Central, February 11, 2013. http://www.cc.com/video-clips/v1p2wr/the-colbert-report-pope-s-resignation—papal-speculatron-7500—james-martin.

"Prophet Glenn Beck - Father Guido Sarducci - The Colbert Report," *The Colbert Report*. Comedy Central, June 23, 2010. http://www.cc.com/video-clips/3dk57p/the-colbert-report-prophet-glenn-beck—father-guido-sarducci.

"Richard Dawkins," *The Colbert Report*. Comedy Central, September 30, 2009. http://www.colbertnation.com/the-colbert-report-videos/250617/september-30-2009/richard-dawkins.

"Sign Off - Hotel Bibles," *The Colbert Report*. Comedy Central, 2013. http://thecolbertreport.cc.com/videos/9hwods/sign-off—hotel-bibles.

"Spider-Pope," *The Colbert Report*. Comedy Central, September 29, 2009.

"Sport Report - Professional Soccer Toddler, Golf Innovations & Washington Redskins Charm Offensive," *The Colbert Report*. Comedy Central, March 26, 2014. http://www.cc.com/video-clips/b6cwb3/the-colbert-report-sport-report—professional-soccer-toddler—golf-innovations—washington-redskins-charm-offensive.

"Stephen's Lenten Sacrifice," *The Colbert Report*. Comedy Central, 2012. http://thecolbertreport.cc.com/videos/krghr1/stephen-s-lenten-sacrifice.

"Syria Conflict & End Times Prophecy," *The Colbert Report*. Comedy Central, 2013. http://thecolbertreport.cc.com/videos/g7l8kk/syria-conflict—end-times-prophecy.

"Timothy Dolan Pt. 1," *The Colbert Report*. Comedy Central, September 3, 2013. http://www.cc.com/video-clips/pwzlgj/the-colbert-report-timothy-dolan-pt—1.

"Timothy Dolan Pt. 2," *The Colbert Report*. Comedy Central, September 3, 2013. http://www.cc.com/video-clips/m4po7o/the-colbert-report-timothy-dolan-pt—2.

"Tip/Wag - Catholic Diocese of Brooklyn & Stoner Dogs," *The Colbert Report*. Comedy Central, May 6, 2013. http://www.cc.com/video-clips/ltsnqq/the-colbert-report-tip-wag—catholic-diocese-of-brooklyn—stoner-dogs.

"Tip/Wag - Christmas," *The Colbert Report*. Comedy Central, 2006. http://thecolbertreport.cc.com/videos/shtpb9/tip-wag—christmas.

"Turning to Religion - Jim Martin," *The Colbert Report*. Comedy Central, February 23, 2009. http://www.cc.com/video-clips/823sva/the-colbert-report-turning-to-religion—jim-martin.

"William Donohue," *The Colbert Report*. Comedy Central, July 25, 2006. http://www.cc.com/video-clips/6xp57g/the-colbert-report-william-donohue.

"The Word—Truthiness," *The Colbert Report*. Comedy Central, 2005. http://thecolbertreport.cc.com/videos/63ite2/the-word—truthiness.

"The Word - XMas," *The Colbert Report*. Comedy Central, 2005. http://thecolbertreport.cc.com/videos/278dqm/the-word—xmas.

"Yahweh or No Way - Altered Catholic Mass, Papal Seat Belt & Offensive Vodka Ad," *The Colbert Report*. Comedy Central, November 29, 2011. http://www.colbertnation.com/the-colbert-report-videos/403247/november-29-2011/yahweh-or-no-way—altered-catholic-mass—papal-seat-belt—offensive-vodka-ad.

"Yahweh or No Way - Dinosaur Adventure Land & Black Market Kidneys," *The Colbert Report*. Comedy Central, August 6, 2009. http://www.colbertnation.com/the-colbert-report-videos/240802/august-06-2009/yahweh-or-no-way—dinosaur-adventure-land—black-market-kidneys.

"Yahweh or No Way - Father Cutie & Miss California," *The Colbert Report*. Comedy Central, May 14, 2009. http://www.colbertnation.com/the-colbert-report-videos/227664/may-14-2009/yahweh-or-no-way—father-cutie—miss-california.

"Yahweh or No Way - Legislation Prayers & Fake Shroud of Turin," *The Colbert Report*. Comedy Central, October 14, 2009. http://www.colbertnation.com/the-colbert-report-videos/252714/october-14-2009/yahweh-or-no-way—legislation-prayers—fake-shroud-of-turin.

"Yahweh or No Way - Online Christian Dating & Seven Days of Sex," *The Colbert Report*. Comedy Central, January 17, 2012. http://www.colbertnation.com/the-colbert-report-videos/406123/january-17-2012/yahweh-or-no-way—online-christian-dating—seven-days-of-sex.

"Yahweh or No Way - Roland Burris," *The Colbert Report*. Comedy Central, January 8, 2009. http://www.colbertnation.com/the-colbert-report-videos/215452/january-08-2009/yahweh-or-no-way—roland-burris.

"Yahweh Or No Way - The Blues Brothers & Glenn Beck," *The Colbert Report*. Comedy Central, June 23, 2010. http://www.colbertnation.com/the-colbert-report-videos/313496/june-23-2010/yahweh-or-no-way—the-blues-brothers—glenn-beck.

"Yahweh or No Way - Yahweh or No Way - IHOP & Antonio Federici Ad," *The Colbert Report*. Comedy Central, September 27, 2010. http://www.colbertnation.com/the-colbert-report-videos/360201/september-27-2010/yahweh-or-no-way—yahweh-or-no-way—ihop—antonio-federici-ad.

"Yahweh or No Way? - Thor and Apocalypse," *The Colbert Report*. Comedy Central, May 10, 2011. http://www.colbertnation.com/the-colbert-report-videos/385915/may-10-2011/yahweh-or-no-way—-thor-and-apocalypse-billboard.

"Yahweh or No Way? - Mormons & God's Poll Numbers," *The Colbert Report*. Comedy Central, August 10, 2011. http://www.colbertnation.com/the-colbert-report-videos/394360/august-10-2011/yaweh-or-no-way—-mormons—god-s-poll-numbers.

Acknowledgments

Religion and humor is an under-examined category of both religious studies and media/cultural studies. Because neither religion nor humor is well defined, I have had a vast array of academic and personal interlocutors, spanning disciplines, programs, and schools. In writing this book, I have received support and encouragement from countless individuals. Like an unprepared actor winning an Oscar, I am bound to forget many of those helpful souls. Please forgive me for the oversight.

First, this book would not have been possible without the support of my Northwestern University mentors, Bob Orsi and Sarah McFarland Taylor. I aspire to live up to your examples as scholars, teachers, and storytellers. Your assistance and encouragement have made me into the scholar I am today. Gene Lowe has helped me explore the possibilities of merging my academic and professional goals while always providing perceptive advice. The Rhetoric and Public Culture Cluster has given me a second academic home and thoughtful readers of this work. I am indebted to that program for introducing me to the media ethnographic methodology.

Thank you to my "primary writing group" of Misty de Berry, Meaghan Fritz, Amanda Kleintop, Brittnay Proctor, and LaCharles Ward for boosting me up and giving me the constructive criticism I needed at every stage of writing this manuscript. Thank you to Elizabeth Lenaghan for coordinating peers to edit my work and for her own editing along the way.

Northwestern University's Department of Religious Studies and the North American Religions Workshop (NARW) colleagues and faculty have been collegial, kind, and excited about my scholarship. Kristi Woodward Bain, Jen Callaghan, Brian Clites, Matt Cressler, Hayley Glaholt, Joel Harrison, Tina Howe, Ashley King, Saralyn McKinnon-Crowley, Tim Noddings, Courtney Rabada, Ariel Schwartz, Matt Smith, Stephanie Wolfe, and especially my cohort, Candace Kohli and Will Caldwell, thank you for being there for me along the way. My friend, collaborator, and personal chef, Myev Rees: Thank you for your reassurance, your confidence in this project, and the pasta.

My master's advisor, Peter W. Williams, pointed me toward academic life. I am eternally indebted to you, and I aspire to be as generous and intelligent. The mentors I met at Miami University, in particular James Bielo and Jana Riess, have provided me with guidance throughout this process. The Department of Religion and its colleagues at Florida State University sparked my interest in this topic and the academic study of religion. Thank you especially to the original readers of my work on Colbert: Martin Kavka, Amy Koehlinger, Amanda Porterfield, and Mark Zeigler.

Kathryn Lofton and Kristy Nabhan-Warren, I owe you an immeasurable thank you for your constructive engagement with my work and unending support of my endeavors. Sarah Dees, Kate Dugan, Amanda Kleintop, Moira Kyweluk, Aram Sarkisian, Hannah Scheidt, and Jeff Wheatley edited many drafts of this book. Thank you for your diligence and enthusiasm. Thank you, as well, to Fordham University Press, especially John Seitz, Fredric Nachbaur, and John Garza. I appreciate your support in turning this manuscript into a finished book.

As I revised this manuscript, I began working at The Graduate School at Northwestern, and I owe a big "thank you" to my colleagues. Your excitement for my work invigorates me. The Academic Affairs team, especially Angela Ripp and Eric Long, has helped me transition into my role as an administrator-scholar. Angela G. Ray, in particular, has become a trusted mentor and sage advisor. I aspire to your grace and integrity.

To my kindred spirits across the country, especially Shina Aladé and Hilary O'Neil, thank you for your patience and support. And last but certainly not least, my family: the Brehm, DiDio, and Jeffryes families, in particular my parents, Rosemary and Bill; my sister, Dani; and especially my husband, James (who read and thought through many drafts with me). Thank you for comforting me, cheering for me, and celebrating with me. Thank you for the encouragement and the questions. This book is dedicated to you.

P.S. I guess I should also thank Dr. Stephen T. Colbert D.F.A., because he has a minor role in this book.

Notes

1. Colbert as Character

1. *The Colbert Report*, "Tip/Wag - Catholic Diocese of Brooklyn & Stoner Dogs." Comedy Central, May 6, 2013.

2. David Gibson, "Colbert the Catechist," *Sacred and Profane*, February 13, 2013, http://davidgibson.religionnews.com/2013/02/13/colbert-the-catechist/; Patrick R. Manning, "Truth and Truthiness," *America* magazine, February 3, 2014, http://americamagazine.org/issue/truth-and-truthiness.

3. Sociologist Danièle Hervieu-Leger coined the term "lived religion" in studying what lay people believe on-the-ground and how they enact those beliefs in practice. David Hall compiled essays from Hervieu-Leger and others to explore the shape and character of the lived religion conversation. In the anthology *Lived Religion in America: Toward a History of Practice*, Robert A. Orsi encouraged scholars of religion to use multiple methodologies to look beyond religious institutions and into the everyday life of practitioners. See David D. Hall, *Lived Religion in America: Toward a History of Practice* (Princeton, N.J.: Princeton University Press, 1997).

4. Charles McGrath, "How Many Stephen Colberts Are There? - NYTimes .com," January 4, 2012, http://www.nytimes.com/2012/01/08/magazine /stephen-colbert.html?pagewanted=all.

5. Stephen Colbert, "2006 White House Correspondents' Dinner" (Washington, D.C.: C-SPAN, April 29, 2006), https://www.c-span.org/video/ ?192243-1/2006-white-house-correspondents-dinner.

6. Sharilyn Johnson, "Stephen Colbert at the New Yorker Festival," October 5, 2008, http://www.third-beat.com/2008/10/05/stephen-colbert-at -the-new-yorker-festival/.

7. When the show ended in December 2014, the official Facebook site was removed.

8. On *The Late Show*, Colbert brought back COLBERT for the 2016 Democratic and Republican National conventions but was told by Viacom lawyers that because the character originated on Comedy Central, he could not be shown on CBS. Since then, Colbert has created an "identical twin cousin" also

named STEPHEN COLBERT, and instead of his signature segment "The Wørd," *The Late Show* now has "The Werd." For more, see Tom Huddleston Jr., "'Stephen Colbert' No Longer Can Appear on 'The Late Show,'" *Fortune*, July 28, 2016, http://fortune.com/2016/07/28/stephen-colbert-late-show-lawyers/.

9. "The Annenberg Public Policy Center of the University of Pennsylvania—Stephen Colbert's Civics Lesson: Or, How a TV Humorist Taught America About Campaign Finance," *The Annenberg Public Policy Center of the University of Pennsylvania*, June 2, 2014, http://www.annenbergpublicpolicycenter.org/stephen-colberts-civics-lesson-or-how-a-tv-humorist-taught-america-about-campaign-finance/.

10. Peter Weber, "Listen to the Best Jokes from Stephen Colbert's Al Smith Dinner Roast," *The Week*, October 18, 2013, http://theweek.com/article/index/251367/listen-to-the-best-jokes-from-stephen-colberts-al-smith-dinner-roast.

11. William V. D'Antonio, Michele Dillon, and Mary L. Gautier at CARA (Center for Applied Research in the Apostolate) at Georgetown University, *American Catholics in Transition* (Lanham, Md.: Rowman & Littlefield, 2013), 47.

12. "Cafeteria Catholic - Conservapedia," Conservapedia.com, April 1, 2018, https://www.conservapedia.com/Cafeteria_Catholic.

13. Wade Clark Roof, *A Generation of Seekers: The Spiritual Journeys of the Baby Boom Generation* (San Francisco: HarperSanFrancisco, 1993); Wade Clark Roof, *Spiritual Marketplace: Baby Boomers and the Remaking of American Religion.* (Princeton, N.J.: Princeton University Press, 2001); Robert Wuthnow, *The Restructuring of American Religion* (Princeton, N.J.: Princeton University Press, 1988).

14. D'Antonio, Dillon, and Gautier, *American Catholics in Transition*, 47.

15. Michele Dillon, *Catholic Identity: Balancing Reason, Faith, and Power*, First edition (New York: Cambridge University Press, 1999).

16. Kristin Norget, Valentina Napolitano, and Maya Mayblin, *The Anthropology of Catholicism: A Reader* (Berkeley: University of California Press, 2017), 2.

17. Ibid., 11.

18. Ibid., 10.

19. Mel van Elteren, "Celebrity Culture, Performative Politics, and the Spectacle of 'Democracy' in America," *Journal of American Culture* 36, no. 4 (December 2013): 264, doi:10.1111/jacc.12049.

20. William Deresiewicz, "The End of Solitude," *The Chronicle of Higher Education*, January 30, 2009, http://www.chronicle.com/article/The-End-of-Solitude/3708/?key=KGrv9oCgTeGTek48zjwEbvdSEo5sejNeIb69WEnZItAcDFTU75GulNjZ1VdJb4SkbEJXaVo3LXBUb2lxMHMtZWQ3TFppZHkzNE9uX2t-MMmUwToZZNzdfS1Fzaw.

21. Henry Jenkins, *Convergence Culture: Where Old and New Media Collide* (New York: New York University Press, 2006), 2.

22. "Center for Media, Religion, and Culture: About the Center," http://cmrc.colorado.edu/about/.

23. Stewart M. Hoover, *The Media and Religious Authority* (University Park: Pennsylvania State University Press, 2016), 4.

24. Diane Winston, "Introduction," in *Small Screen, Big Picture: Television and Lived Religion*, ed. Diane Winston (Waco, Tex.: Baylor University Press, 2009), 2.

25. Elijah Siegler, "Is God Still in the Box? Religion in Television Cop Shows Ten Years Later," in *God in the Details: American Religion in Popular Culture*, ed. Eric Michael Mazar and Kate McCarthy (New York: Routledge, 2011), 179.

26. Joseph Boskin, ed., *The Humor Prism in 20th Century American Society* (Detroit: Wayne State University Press, 1997), 17.

27. Arthur Asa Berger, "What Makes People Laugh? Cracking the Cultural Code," in *The Humor Prism*, 29.

28. Sigmund Freud, *Jokes and Their Relation to the Unconscious*, trans. James Strachey (New York: Norton, 1889); Tony Veale, "Incongruity in Humor: Root Cause or Epiphenomenon?," *Humor: International Journal of Humor Research* 17, no. 4 (October 2004): 419–28.

29. Frederick Turner, "On Satire in the Arts," *American Arts Quarterly* (Fall 2012): 29.

30. For more, see Lawrence R. Jacobs, "The Contested Politics of Public Value," *Public Administration Review* 74, no. 4 (July 1, 2014): 487; and Kathleen Hall Jamieson and Bruce W. Hardy, "The Effect of Media on Public Knowledge," in *The Oxford Handbook of American Public Opinion and the Media*, ed. Robert Y. Shapiro and Lawrence R. Jacobs (Oxford: Oxford University Press, 2011).

31. American Dialect Society, "'Truthiness' Voted 2005 Word of the Year, American Dialect Society," January 6, 2006, http://www.americandialect.org/truthiness_voted_2005_word_of_the_year.

32. *The Word - Truthiness*, 2005, http://thecolbertreport.cc.com/videos/63ite2/the-word—truthiness.

33. Ben Zimmer, "Truthiness," *New York Times*, October 13, 2010, http://www.nytimes.com/2010/10/17/magazine/17FOB-onlanguage-t.html.

34. Jonathan Gray, Jeffrey P. Jones, and Ethan Thompson, *Satire TV: Politics and Comedy in the Post-Network Era* (New York: New York University Press, 2009), 127.

35. Jeffrey P. Jones, *Entertaining Politics: Satiric Television and Political Engagement*, Second edition (Lanham, Md.: Rowman & Littlefield, 2009), 203.

36. Heather L. LaMarre, Kristen D. Landreville, and Michael A. Beam, "The Irony of Satire: Political Ideology and the Motivation to See What You

Want to See in The Colbert Report," *The International Journal of Press/Politics* 14, no. 2 (April 1, 2009): 212–31.

37. Amber Day, *Satire and Dissent: Interventions in Contemporary Political Debate* (Bloomington: Indiana University Press, 2011), 6.

38. Robert Hariman, "Political Parody and Public Culture," *Quarterly Journal of Speech* 94, no. 3 (2008): 250.

39. Paul Provenza and Dan Dion, *Satiristas: Comedians, Contrarians, Raconteurs & Vulgarians*, First edition (New York: It Books, 2010), 28.

40. Gray, Jones, and Thompson, *Satire TV*, ix.

41. Phone interview with Adam Lowitt, senior producer at *The Daily Show*, January 9, 2015.

42. Nathan O. Hatch, *The Democratization of American Christianity* (New Haven, Conn.: Yale University Press, 1989).

43. Maureen Dowd, "Jon Stewart and Stephen Colbert: America's Anchors," *Rolling Stone*, November 16, 2006, http://www.rollingstone.com/tv/news /americas-anchors-20061116.

44. Charles McGrath, "How Many Stephen Colberts Are There?" - NY-Times.com, *New York Times*, January 4, 2012. http://www.nytimes.com/2012 /01/08/magazine/stephen-colbert.html?pagewanted=all.

45. "Stephen Colbert Commencement Address - Knox College," http:// departments.knox.edu/newsarchive/news_events/2006/x12547.html.

46. Darrell M. West and John M. Orman, *Celebrity Politics* (Upper Saddle River, N.J.: Prentice Hall, 2003), 102.

47. Kathryn Lofton, *Consuming Religion* (Chicago: University of Chicago Press, 2017).

48. Gary Laderman, *Sacred Matters: Celebrity Worship, Sexual Ecstasies, the Living Dead, and Other Signs of Religious Life in the United States* (New York: The New Press, 2010), 77.

49. I borrow this phrase from W. Clark Gilpin's work on the religious contexts surrounding the American poet Emily Dickinson. For more, see W. Clark Gilpin, *Religion Around Emily Dickinson* (University Park: Pennsylvania State University Press, 2014).

50. Jill E. Dierberg, "Searching for Truth(iness): Mapping the Religio-Political Landscape and Identity of Christian Emerging Adults through a Reception Study of 'The Colbert Report'" (Ph.D. dissertation, University of Denver, 2012), http://search.proquest.com.turing.library.northwestern.edu / pqdtft/docview/1112843336/abstract/372B17F7C1A343C9PQ/1?accoun tid=12861; Lynn Schofield Clark and Jill Dierberg, "Digital Storytelling and Collective Religious Identity in a Moderate to Progressive Youth Group," in *Digital Religion: Understanding Religious Practice in New Media Worlds*, ed. Heidi A. Campbell (New York: Routledge, 2012), 147–54.

51. Martin's most prominent work on humor and religion is James Martin, *Between Heaven and Mirth: Why Joy, Humor, and Laughter Are at the Heart of the Spiritual Life*, Reprint edition (New York: HarperOne, 2012).

52. Rebecca Pardo, Elizabeth ErkenBrack, and John L. Jackson, "Media Anthropology," January 11, 2012, http://www.oxfordbibliographies.com/display /id/obo-9780199766567-0015.

2. Colbert as Catholic Authority

1. Stewart M. Hoover, *The Media and Religious Authority* (University Park: Pennsylvania State University Press, 2016), 5.

2. Ibid., 10.

3. *The Colbert Report*, "Pope's Baseball Cap & CatholicTV," Comedy Central, August 5, 2010.

4. Jay P. Dolan, *In Search of an American Catholicism: A History of Religion and Culture in Tension* (Oxford: Oxford University Press, 2003), 4.

5. For examples of Protestant Christian usage of media innovations, see Tona J. Hangen, *Redeeming the Dial: Radio, Religion, and Popular Culture in America* (Chapel Hill: University of North Carolina Press, 2002); Susan Friend Harding, *The Book of Jerry Falwell: Fundamentalist Language and Politics* (Princeton, N.J.: Princeton University Press, 2001); Heather Hendershot, *Shaking the World for Jesus: Media and Conservative Evangelical Culture* (Chicago: University of Chicago Press, 2004); Lerone A. Martin, *Preaching on Wax: The Phonograph and the Shaping of Modern African American Religion* (New York: New York University Press, 2014).

6. Although in a 2015 episode of *The Mindy Project* he does play a fictional priest. As Sarah Butler describes, he plays "Father Michael O'Donnell," a reformed leather jacket–wearing Catholic priest who sends spaghetti emojis and wants to say Mass in Latin." See Sarah Butler Schueller, "Stephen Colbert Guest Stars as Catholic Priest on 'The Mindy Project,'" *U.S. Catholic*, March 11, 2015, http://www.uscatholic.org/blog/201503/stephen-colbert-guest-stars -catholic-priest-mindy-project-29886.

7. Stewart M. Hoover, "Religious Authority in the Media Age," in *The Media and Religious Authority*, ed. Stewart M. Hoover (University Park: Pennsylvania State University Press, 2016), 32.

8. Heidi Campbell, "Who's Got the Power? Religious Authority and the Internet," *Journal of Computer-Mediated Communication* 12, no. 3 (April 2007): 1043–62.

9. Giddens describes "high modernity" in the same way as one would describe the period the United States is currently experiencing. Anthony Giddens, *Modernity and Self-Identity: Self and Society in the Late Modern Age*, First edition (Stanford, Calif.: Stanford University Press, 1991), 194.

10. Adam B. Seligman, *Modernity's Wager* (Princeton, N.J.: Princeton University Press, 2000).

11. Wade Clark Roof, *A Generation of Seekers: The Spiritual Journeys of the Baby Boom Generation* (San Francisco: HarperSanFrancisco, 1993); Wade Clark Roof, *Spiritual Marketplace: Baby Boomers and the Remaking of American Religion* (Princeton, N.J.: Princeton University Press, 2001); Robert Wuthnow, *The Restructuring of American Religion* (Princeton, N.J.: Princeton University Press, 1988).

12. Talal Asad, *Formations of the Secular: Christianity, Islam, Modernity*, First edition (Stanford, Calif.: Stanford University Press, 2003); Courtney Bender et al., *Religion on the Edge: De-Centering and Re-Centering the Sociology of Religion* (New York: Oxford University Press, 2012); Courtney Bender and Ann Taves, *What Matters? Ethnographies of Value in a Not So Secular Age* (New York: Columbia University Press, 2012).

13. Gary Laderman, *Sacred Matters: Celebrity Worship, Sexual Ecstasies, the Living Dead, and Other Signs of Religious Life in the United States* (New York: The New Press, 2010), 64.

14. Bruce Lincoln, *Authority: Construction and Corrosion*, Second edition (Chicago: University of Chicago Press, 1994), 4.

15. Where authority was previously centered on hierarchical church structure, Schofield Clark explains that the Puritans of the sixteenth and seventeenth centuries actually created collective, communal agreements granting any leader their authority. For more, see Clark, "Religion and Authority in a Remix Culture: How a Late Night TV Host Became an Authority on Religion," in *Religion, Media and Culture: A Reader*, ed. Gordon Lynch, Jolyon P. Mitchell, and Anna Strhan (New York: Routledge, 2012).

16. Hangen, *Redeeming the Dial*, 2.

17. Ibid., 4.

18. Ibid., 6.

19. As historian Jay P. Dolan argues, Smith's presidential campaign, while momentous in further bringing Catholics into the political sphere, did leave a bitter taste of anti-Catholic hostility. Dolan, *The American Catholic Experience* (Garden City, N.Y.: Doubleday, 1985), 351.

20. Donald Warren, *Radio Priest: Charles Coughlin, the Father of Hate Radio*, First edition (New York: The Free Press, 1996), 2.

21. Ibid., 3.

22. William Vincent Shannon, *The American Irish* (New York: Macmillan, 1963).

23. Ronald H. Carpenter, *Father Charles E. Coughlin: Surrogate Spokesman for the Disaffected* (Westport, Conn.: Greenwood Press, 1998), 6.

24. Raymond Swing, *Forerunners of American Fascism* (New York: Messner, 1935), 52.

25. Warren, *Radio Priest*, 13.

26. Stegner, Wallace, "The Radio Priest and His Flock," in *The Aspirin Age: 1919–1941*, ed. Isabel Leighton (New York: Simon and Schuster, 1949), 234.

27. Warren, *Radio Priest*, 2.

28. Ibid., 1.

29. Ibid., 2.

30. Ibid., 2.

31. "The American Experience. America and the Holocaust. People & Events | Reverend Charles E. Coughlin (1891–1979) | PBS," *American Experience*, 2005, http://www.pbs.org/wgbh/amex/holocaust/peopleevents /pandeAMEX96.html.

32. Ibid.

33. David M. Kennedy, *Freedom from Fear: The American People in Depression and War, 1929–1945* (New York: Oxford University Press, 1999).

34. Louis B. Ward, *Father Charles E. Coughlin: An Authorized Biography* (Detroit: Tower Publications, 1933), 27–28.

35. "American Experience."

36. Warren, *Radio Priest*, 35.

37. Sheldon Marcus, *Father Coughlin: The Tumultuous Life of the Priest of the Little Flower* (Boston: Little, Brown, 1973), 11.

38. Warren, *Radio Priest*, 4.

39. Ibid., 2.

40. Ibid., 6.

41. Mark S. Massa, S.J., *Catholics and American Culture: Fulton Sheen, Dorothy Day, and the Notre Dame Football Team* (New York: Crossroad, 1999), 82.

42. Christopher Lynch, *Selling Catholicism: Bishop Sheen and the Power of Television* (Lexington: University Press of Kentucky, 1998), 1.

43. Noted Catholic sociologist Andrew Greeley describes the term "Catholic imagination" as seeing ". . . created reality as a 'sacrament,' that is, a revelation of the presence of God." As such, the material and physical world (including human beings) are presences and sources of God's grace. Since the inception of this term, it has come as a binary juxtaposed with the Protestant imagination. David Tracy, in his seminal work *The Analogical Imagination: Christian Theology and the Culture of Pluralism*, pits the Catholic tendency to present material through metaphor in opposition to the dialectical imagination of Protestantism. Ingrid Shafer, in her introductory article in the *Journal of Popular Film and Television*'s Catholic-Imagination-themed issue, uses Tracy's

and Greeley's models to discuss the "undeniably Roman Catholic slant" to academic works on religion and popular culture. She delineates further in applying a Protestant/Catholic paradigm, "those who reject, criticize, and reform versus those who adopt, adapt, and absorb; . . . those who see the world fractured by original sin versus those who see the world connected by original blessing . . . ." The Catholic imagination, as Greeley phrases it, is evidence of a lack of demystification and secularism in contemporary society. Catholic religiosity does not demean or belittle popular culture because it is not high art and because Catholics are not iconoclasts. Instead, the Catholic imagination senses "the sacred in such places as popular film and television" because the world can be a sacramental place; the sacred is not wholly in opposition to the profane. In fact, the profane and popular might just be where a Catholic God lurks. For more, see Andrew M. Greeley, *The Catholic Imagination* (Berkeley: University of California Press, 2001); David Tracy, *The Analogical Imagination: Christian Theology and the Culture of Pluralism* (New York: Crossroad, 1981); Ingrid Shafer, "Introduction: The Catholic Imagination in Popular Film and Television," *Journal of Popular Film and Television* 19, no. 2 (Summer 1991): 50–57.

44. David Weinstein, *The Forgotten Network: DuMont and the Birth of American Television* (Philadelphia: Temple University Press, 2006), 157.

45. James C. G. Conniff, *The Bishop Sheen Story* (Greenwich, Conn.: Fawcett, 1953), 11.

46. Lynch, *Selling Catholicism*, 7.

47. Anthony Burke Smith, *The Look of Catholics: Portrayals in Popular Culture from the Great Depression to the Cold War*, First edition (Lawrence: University Press of Kansas, 2010), 136.

48. "Microphone Missionary," *Time*, April 14, 1952: 72.

49. It is unclear why two foreign men are on this list at all, but perhaps Americans ranked all men, not just American men. For more, see George H. Gallup, *The Gallup Poll: Public Opinion, 1935–1971*, vol. 2, *1949–1958* (New York: Random House, 1972), 1113, 1296, 1387, 1462, 1536; on the 1956 ranking, see 1462.

50. Smith, *The Look of Catholics*, 2, 138.

51. Ibid., 28.

52. Lynch, *Selling Catholicism*, 27.

53. Smith, *The Look of Catholics*, 28.

54. Massa, *Catholics and American Culture*, 84.

55. Fulton J. Sheen, "How to Think," *Life Is Worth Living*. Recorded television episodes. Sheen Productions, Inc., Victor, N.Y. Kinescopes, 1955.

56. Lynch, *Selling Catholicism*, 1.

57. Ibid., 152.

58. Kathleen Riley Fields, *Bishop Fulton J. Sheen: An American Catholic Response to the Twentieth Century* (Notre Dame, Ind.: University of Notre Dame Press, 1988).

59. Lynch, *Selling Catholicism*, 2.

60. "Bishop Cloys as Critic," *Christian Century*, December 5, 1956.

61. Massa, *Catholics and American Culture*, 85.

62. Smith, *The Look of Catholics*, 26.

63. Fulton J. Sheen, "Reparation," *Life Is Worth Living*. Recorded television episode. Sheen Productions, Inc., Victor, N.Y. Kinescopes, 1952–1953 season.

64. Massa, *Catholics and American Culture*, 88.

65. Fulton J. Sheen, "Signs of Our Time," *Life is Worth Living*. Recorded television episodes. Sheen Productions, Inc., Victor, N.Y. Kinescopes, 1954.

66. Lynch, *Selling Catholicism*, 136–37.

67. Fulton J. Sheen, "Something Higher," *Life Is Worth Living*. Recorded television episodes. Sheen Productions, Inc., Victor, N.Y. Kinescopes, 1952–1953 season.

68. *Bishop Fulton J. Sheen: His Irish Wit and Wisdom* (DVD Video, 2000).

69. Ibid.

70. Fulton J. Sheen, "The Divine Sense of Humor," *Life Is Worth Living*. Recorded television episodes. Sheen Productions, Inc., Victor, N.Y. Kinescopes, 1959.

71. *The Colbert Report*, "Sport Report - NFL Fines & Colbert Super PAC's Second NBA Lockout Ad." Comedy Central, October 27, 2011.

72. *The Colbert Report*, "Yahweh or No Way - Dinosaur Adventure Land & Black Market Kidneys." Comedy Central, August 6, 2009.

73. "Stephen Colbert on Getting to Play Himself," *CBS Sunday Morning*, September 6, 2015.

74. Joel Lovell, "Stephen Colbert on Making The Late Show His Own," *GQ*, August 17, 2015, http://www.gq.com/story/stephen-colbert-gq-cover-story.

75. America Media, "Colbert Catechism: Stephen Colbert Professes His Faith to Fr. James Martin," Filmed [March 2, 2015]. YouTube video, 6:42. Posted [March 2, 2015]. https://www.youtube.com/watch?v=0-zxn-YGUI4.

76. "Yahweh or No Way - 30 Best 'Colbert Report' Bits," *Rolling Stone*, December 15, 2014, http://www.rollingstone.com/tv/lists/30-best-colbert-report-bits-20141215/yahweh-or-no-way-20141215.

77. *The Colbert Report*, "Yahweh or No Way - Father Cutie & Miss California." Comedy Central, May 14, 2009.

78. Charles McGrath, "How Many Stephen Colberts Are There? - NYTimes.com," *New York Times*, January 4, 2012. http://www.nytimes.com/2012/01/08/magazine/stephen-colbert.html?pagewanted=all.

79. Jeffrey P. Jones, *Entertaining Politics: Satiric Television and Political Engagement* (Lanham, Md.: Rowman & Littlefield, 2009), 187.

80. Ibid.

81. Nathan Rabin, "Interview with Stephen Colbert from The Onion's AV Club," January 25, 2006, http://www.jerriblank.com/colbert_onion-av-club.html.

82. *The Colbert Report*, "Yahweh or No Way - Roland Burris." Comedy Central, January 8, 2009.

83. *The Colbert Report*, "Yahweh or No Way - Mormons & God's Poll Numbers." Comedy Central, August 10, 2011.

84. *The Colbert Report*, "Yahweh Or No Way - The Blues Brothers & Glenn Beck." Comedy Central, June 23, 2010; *The Colbert Report*, "Yahweh or No Way - Mormons & God's Poll Numbers." Comedy Central, August 10, 2011.

85. *The Colbert Report*, "Yahweh or No Way - Father Cutie & Miss California." Comedy Central, May 14, 2009.

86. *The Colbert Report*, "Yahweh or No Way - Altered Catholic Mass, Papal Seat Belt & Offensive Vodka Ad." Comedy Central, November 29, 2011.

87. Ibid.

88. Ibid.

89. Ibid.

90. Bill DeMain, *In Their Own Words: Songwriters Talk about the Creative Process* (Westport, Conn.: Greenwood, 2004), 119.

91. *The Colbert Report*, "Yahweh or No Way - Altered Catholic Mass, Papal Seat Belt & Offensive Vodka Ad." Comedy Central, November 29, 2011.

92. *The Colbert Report*, "Yahweh or No Way - Thor & Apocalypse Billboard." Comedy Central, May 10, 2011.

93. *The Colbert Report*, "On Topic - The Seven Deadly Sins—Anger" compilation clips. Comedy Central, accessed October 22, 2015.

3. Colbert as Catechist

1. Fieldnotes 11.18.2014.

2. Colbert references teaching Sunday school or Confraternity of Christian Doctrine (CCD) classes in interviews both in and out of character. For an example, see *The Colbert Report*, "Philip Zimbardo," Comedy Central, February 11, 2008.

3. Fieldnotes 11.18.2014.

4. Ibid.

5. Neil Strauss, "Stephen Colbert on Deconstructing the Colbert Nation," *Rolling Stone*, September 2, 2009, http://www.rollingstone.com/culture/news/stephen-colbert-on-deconstructing-the-news-religion-and-the-colbert-nation-20090902.

6. Interview with Father James Martin, November 19, 2014.

7. Fieldnotes 11.18.2014.

8. David Fricke, "The Mysterious Case of the White Stripes," *Rolling Stone*, September 8, 2005, http://www.rollingstone.com/music/news/white-on-white-20050908.

9. CBS, 60 *Minutes*, February 8, 2005, http://www.cbsnews.com/stories/2005/02/08/60II/main672415.shtml.

10. *The Colbert Report*, "2011: A Rock Odyssey Featuring Jack White - Catholic Throwdown." Comedy Central, June 22, 2011.

11. Émile Durkheim, *The Elementary Forms of The Religious Life* (New York; London: Allen & Unwin Ltd., 1912).

12. Ann Taves, *Religious Experience Reconsidered: A Building-Block Approach to the Study of Religion and Other Special Things* (Princeton, N.J.: Princeton University Press, 2009).

13. *The Colbert Report*, "Interview with Henry Louis Gates, Jr.," Comedy Central, February 4, 2010.

14. *The Colbert Report*, "Interview with Martha Stewart," Comedy Central, November 10, 2010.

15. *The Colbert Report*, "Catholic Bender," Comedy Central, April 25, 2011.

16. Jay P. Dolan, *In Search of an American Catholicism: A History of Religion and Culture in Tension* (Oxford: Oxford University Press, 2003), 4.

17. *The Colbert Report*, "Paul Ryan's Christian Budget Cuts," Comedy Central, May 1, 2012.

18. Hillary Kaell, "'A Bible People': Post-Conciliar U.S. Catholics, Scripture, and Holy Land Pilgrimage," *U.S. Catholic Historian* 31, no. 4 (2013): 85–106.

19. *The Colbert Report*, "Pope Francis on Baptizing Martians," Comedy Central, May 14, 2014.

20. *The Colbert Report*, "Daniel Goleman," Comedy Central, December 2, 2013.

21. *The Colbert Report*, "Pope Francis on Baptizing Martians," Comedy Central, May 14, 2014.

22. *The Colbert Report*, "Election of Pope Francis," Comedy Central, March 25, 2013.

23. *The Colbert Report*, "Yahweh or No Way - Father Cutie & Miss California," Comedy Central, May 14, 2009.

24. *The Colbert Report*, "Turning to Religion - Jim Martin," Comedy Central, February 23, 2009.

25. Martin interview.

26. Ibid.

27. For more on reciprocal fandom, see Paul Booth, "The Reciprocal Relationship - How Much Is Too Much?," in *Fandom at the Crossroads: Cele-*

bration, Shame and Fan/Producer Relationships, ed. Lynn Zubernis and Katherine Larsen (Newcastle Upon Tyne, UK: Cambridge Scholars, 2012), 175–229.

28. Martin interview.

29. *The Colbert Report*, "Father James Martin," Comedy Central, September 13, 2007.

30. *The Colbert Report*, "Glenn Beck Attacks Social Justice - James Martin," Comedy Central, March 18, 2010.

31. Deirdre M. Moloney, *American Catholic Lay Groups and Transatlantic Social Reform in the Progressive Era* (Chapel Hill: University of North Carolina Press, 2003), 2.

32. *The Colbert Report*, "Glenn Beck Attacks Social Justice - James Martin," Comedy Central, March 18, 2010.

33. "Compendium of the Social Doctrine of the Church," http://www .vatican.va/roman_curia/pontifical_councils/justpeace/documents/rc_pc _justpeace_doc_20060526_compendio-dott-soc_en.html. The option for the poor also connects to the liberation theology movement first articulated by Father Gustavo Gutierrez. See Gustavo Gutierrez, *A Theology of Liberation: History, Politics, and Salvation*, trans. Caridad Inda and John Eagleson, Revised edition (Maryknoll, N.Y: Orbis Books, 1988). For more, see Rohan Michael Curnow, *The Preferential Option for the Poor: A Short History and a Reading Based on the Thought of Bernard Lonergan* (Milwaukee, Wisc.: Marquette University Press, 2014).

34. *The Colbert Report*, "Glenn Beck Attacks Social Justice - James Martin," Comedy Central, March 18, 2010.

35. Ibid.

36. *The Colbert Report*, "Pope's Resignation & Papal Speculatron 7500 - James Martin," Comedy Central, February 11, 2013.

37. James Martin, *Between Heaven and Mirth: Why Joy, Humor, and Laughter Are at the Heart of the Spiritual Life*, Reprint edition (New York: HarperOne, 2012), 3.

38. Ibid., 15.

39. Martin interview.

40. Peter Weber, "Listen to the Best Jokes from Stephen Colbert's Al Smith Dinner Roast," *The Week*, October 18, 2013, http://theweek.com/article/index /251367/listen-to-the-best-jokes-from-stephen-colberts-al-smith-dinner-roast.

41. James Martin, S.J., "The Cardinal Meets Colbert . . . and Both Meet Fordham | America Magazine," *America: The National Catholic Review*, September 15, 2012, http://americamagazine.org/content/all-things/cardinal-meets -colbertand-both-meet-fordham.

42. Laurie Goodstein, "Colbert and Dolan Open Up on Spirituality," *New York Times*, September 16, 2012, http://www.nytimes.com/2012/09/16/nyregion

/stephen-colbert-and-cardinal-cardinal-timothy-dolan-at-fordham-university
.html.

43. Ibid.

44. "'The Cardinal and Colbert' at Fordham University," *Colbert News Hub*, September 16, 2012, http://www.colbertnewshub.com/2012/09/16/the-cardinal -colbert/.

45. sam, but spooky @ NYCC. Twitter Post. September 14, 2012. https:// twitter.com/samanthaistan/status/246730383402618880; shufywithadash. Twitter Post. September 14, 2012, https://twitter.com/shufypongnon/status /246756005218770944.

46. For more, see "About Busted Halo | Busted Halo," http://bustedhalo .com/about.

47. Bernadette Davis and Rachel Roman, "#Dolbert: A Firsthand Account of 'The Cardinal and Colbert,'" *Busted Halo*, January 5, 2013, http://bustedhalo .com/features/dolbert-a-firsthand-account-of-the-cardinal-and-colbert.

48. Carl Sobrado, January 5, 2013, comment on Davis and Roman, "#Dolbert: A Firsthand Account of 'The Cardinal and Colbert.'"

49. Davis and Roman, "#Dolbert: A Firsthand Account of 'The Cardinal and Colbert.'"

50. Dennis Coday, "2014's Runner-up to Person of the Year | National Catholic Reporter," December 31, 2014, http://ncronline.org/blogs/ncr-today /2014s-runner-person-year.

51. "About S+L | Salt and Light Catholic Media Foundation," http:// saltandlighttv.org/about/, http://saltandlighttv.org/about/.

52. Salt and Light, *Stephen Colbert - Witness*, 2015.

53. Ibid.

54. Ibid.

4. Colbert as Catholic Comedian

1. John Scott, ed., *Marginalization - Oxford Reference: A Dictionary of Sociology* (Oxford: Oxford University Press, 2014).

2. Christie Davies, *Ethnic Humor Around the World: A Comparative Analysis* (Bloomington: Indiana University Press, 1990).

3. "Everyone's a Little Bit Racist Lyrics | AVENUE Q Soundtrack," http://www.stlyrics.com/lyrics/avenueq/everyonesalittlebitracist.htm.

4. "Redneck Jokes | Jeff Foxworthy," http://www.jefffoxworthy.com/jokes.

5. Sigmund Freud, *Jokes and Their Relation to the Unconscious* (New York: Norton, 1960).

6. Mikhail Bakhtin, *Rabelais and His World*, trans. Helene Iswolsky (Bloomington: Indiana University Press, 1965).

7. Mel Watkins, *On the Real Side: A History of African American Comedy*, Second edition (Chicago: Lawrence Hill Books, 1999), 26.

8. Salvatore Attardo, *Encyclopedia of Humor Studies* (Thousand Oaks, Calif.: SAGE Publications, 2014), 216.

9. Tambay Obenson, "Tyler Perry Has a White Audience Problem He'd Like to Solve," *Shadow and Act*, October 26, 2016, http://shadowandact.com /2016/10/26/tyler-perrys-talks-his-white-audience-problem/.

10. Christie Davies, *The Mirth of Nations* (New Brunswick, N.J.: Transaction Publishers, 2002), 9.

11. Watkins, *On the Real Side*, 28.

12. Joanne R. Gilbert, *Performing Marginality: Humor, Gender, and Cultural Critique*, Humor in Life and Letters Series (Detroit: Wayne State University Press, 2004), 174.

13. Ibid., xiii.

14. Ibid.

15. Ibid., 169.

16. Jarrod Tanny, "The Anti-Gospel of Lenny, Larry and Sarah: Jewish Humor and the Desecration of Christendom," *American Jewish History* 99, no. 2 (2015): 167–93.

17. Wisse argues that Yiddish humor began with Heinrich Heine and Sholem Aleichem. For more, see Ruth R. Wisse, *No Joke: Making Jewish Humor* (Princeton, N.J.: Princeton University Press, 2013); Elliott Oring, "The People of the Joke: On the Conceptualization of a Jewish Humor," *Western Folklore* 42, no. 4 (1983): 261–71.

18. Esther Romeyn, Jack Kugelmass, and Spertus Museum, *Let There Be Laughter! Jewish Humor in America* (Chicago: Spertus Museum, 1997), 2.

19. The quote is from *Psychology Today*, but the research on percentages was initially conducted by psychotherapist and author Samuel S. Janus. For more, see J. Rogers, "Pt Bookshelf," *Psychology Today* 35, no. 1 (February 1, 2002): 69; Samuel S. Janus, "The Great Comedians: Personality and Other Factors," *American Journal of Psychoanalysis* 35, no. 2 (1975): 169–74.

20. Freud, *Jokes*.

21. Davies, *The Mirth of Nations*.

22. Oring, "The People of the Joke: 266.

23. Ibid., 267.

24. Attardo, *Encyclopedia of Humor Studies*, 552.

25. Davies, *Ethnic Humor Around the World*, 2.

26. Nancy A. Walker, *A Very Serious Thing: Women's Humor and American Culture* (Minneapolis: University of Minnesota Press, 1988), 2.

27. "Catholic Humor Painfully Un-Funny," *U.S. Catholic* 69, no. 1 (January 2004): 5.

28. Ibid.

29. Ibid.

30. Eye of the Tiber, "About Us | EOTT LLC," http://www.eyeofthetiber.com /about-us/.

31. Ibid.

32. For more on SC Naoum, see Mary Rezac, "Meet the Man behind the Mysterious Eye of the Tiber," *Catholic News Agency*, January 2, 2016, http:// www.catholicnewsagency.com/news/whos-behind-the-mysterious-eye-of-the -tiber-70906/; Derek Welch, "'Eye of the Tiber' - The Catholic Answer to 'The Onion' - World Religion News," January 11, 2016, http://www .worldreligionnews.com/religion-news/christianity/eye-of-the-tiber-the-catholic -answer-to-the-onion.

33. Stephen Beale, "Stephen Colbert and America's Catholic Comic Moment," *National Catholic Register*, June 3, 2016, http://www.ncregister.com /daily-news/stephen-colbert-and-americas-catholic-comic-moment/.

34. Ibid.

35. Ibid.

36. Emily McFarlan Miller, "A Funny Thing Happened in That Joke with the Pope Contest . . . ," *Religion News Service*, October 8, 2015, http:// religionnews.com/2015/10/08/funny-thing-happened-joke-pope-contest/.

37. Paul Provenza and Dan Dion, *Satiristas: Comedians, Contrarians, Raconteurs & Vulgarians*, First edition (New York: It Books, 2010), 131.

38. "TV Priest Joins Movie Mafia," *Ellensburg Daily Record*, October 29, 1990.

39. Don Novello, *The Lazlo Letters* (New York: Workman, 1977).

40. Bob Garfield, "The Lazlo Letters," *On The Media* (WNYC, October 3, 2003), http://www.wnyc.org/story/130618-the-lazlo-letters/?utm_source =sharedUrl&utm_medium=metatag&utm_campaign=sharedUrl.

41. Provenza and Dion, *Satiristas*, 134.

42. Charles E. Cohen, "Butt Out, Guido Sarducci! Surgeon General Antonia Novello, Your Sister-in-Law, Wants Everyone to Quit Smoking," *People.com*, December 17, 1990, http://people.com/archive/butt-out-guido-sarducci-surgeon -general-antonia-novello-your-sister-in-law-wants-everyone-to-quit-smoking-vol -34-no-24/.

43. Adam Sternbergh, "Stephen Colbert Has America by the Ballots," *NYMag.com*, October 16, 2006, http://nymag.com/news/politics/22322.

44. "Don Novello," *NNDB (Notable Names Database)*, n.d., http://www.nndb .com/people/444/000024372/.

45. Provenza and Dion, *Satiristas*, 132.

46. Ibid.

47. Associated Press, "Vatican Seizes 'Father' From 'Saturday Night,'" *New York Times*, May 3, 1981, sec. World, http://www.nytimes.com/1981/05/03 /world/vatican-seizes-father-from-saturday-night.html.

48. James Sullivan, *Seven Dirty Words: The Life and Crimes of George Carlin* (New York: Da Capo, 2011), 3.

49. Ibid., 4.

50. "FCC v. Pacifica Foundation 438 U.S. 726 (1978)," *Justia Law*, 1978, https://supreme.justia.com/cases/federal/us/438/726/.

51. Sullivan, *Seven Dirty Words*, 17–18.

52. George Carlin, "George Carlin I Used to Be Irish Catholic," *Class Clown*, 1972.

53. Sullivan, *Seven Dirty Words*, 7–8.

54. Charles Taylor, "Dirty Old Man," *Salon*, April 3, 2004, http://www.salon .com/2004/04/03/carlin_4/.

55. Sullivan, *Seven Dirty Words*, 164.

56. Ibid., 165.

57. Rocco Urbisci, *George Carlin: 40 Years of Comedy*, Comedy Recording (1997).

58. Sullivan, *Seven Dirty Words*, 143.

59. Urbisci, *George Carlin*.

60. Provenza and Dion, *Satiristas*, 344.

61. Kennedy Center, "The Eleventh Annual Kennedy Center Mark Twain Prize Celebrating the Life and Humor of George Carlin | PBS," February 4, 2008, https://www.pbs.org/weta/twain2008/.

62. For more on Carlin's theology, see Kathryn Lofton, "The Theodicy of George Carlin," *Religion Dispatches*, January 14, 2010, http://religiondispatches .org/the-theodicy-of-george-carlin/.

63. Terry Gross, "Louis C.K. on His 'Louie' Hiatus: 'I Wanted the Show to Feel New Again,'" *NPR.org*, May 19, 2014, http://www.npr.org/2014/05/19 /313950799/louis-c-k-on-his-louie-hiatus-i-wanted-the-show-to-feel-new-again.

64. Louis C.K, "God," *Louie* Television Series, August 31, 2010.

65. Nathan Rabin, "Louie: 'God,'" August 31, 2010, http://www.avclub.com /tvclub/louie-god-44549.

66. Kelli Marshall, "Louie's 'God' as Cathartic Television," *In Media Res: A Media Commons Project*, March 22, 2012, http://www.criticalcommons.org /Members/kellimarshall/clips/louie_god.mp4/embed_view.

67. Melena Ryzik, Cara Buckley, and Jodi Kantor, "Louis C.K. Is Accused by 5 Women of Sexual Misconduct," *New York Times*, November 9, 2017, sec. Television. https://www.nytimes.com/2017/11/09/arts/television/louis-ck-sexual -misconduct.html.

68. Samantha Abernethy, "Interview: Jim Gaffigan Talks Family, Food and Dad Is Fat," *Chicagoist*, May 10, 2013, http://chicagoist.com/2013/05/10 /interview_jim_gaffigan.php.

69. Michelle Boorstein, "Is Comic Jim Gaffigan the Catholic Church's Newest Evangelizer?," *OnFaith*, June 7, 2013, http://www.faithstreet.com /onfaith/2013/06/07/comic-jim-gaffigan-the-answer-to-the-catholic-churchs -outreach-effort/25450.

70. "Jim Gaffigan on Comedy and His Catholic Faith," *The New Yorker*, October 12, 2015, https://www.youtube.com/watch?v=GCEXcMI99bc.

71. *Beyond the Pale* (New York: Comedy Central Records, 2006).

72. Catholic News Service, *Jim Gaffigan: Being a Catholic Comedian*, 2015, https://www.youtube.com/watch?v=Gy_P3GFhc98.

73. Boorstein, "Is Comic Jim Gaffigan the Catholic Church's Newest Evangelizer?"

74. Maria Macina and John Mulderig, "'Jim Gaffigan Show' Treats Catholicism Seriously, but in a Funny Way | National Catholic Reporter," *National Catholic Reporter*, August 3, 2015, http://ncronline.org/news/art-media/jim -gaffigan-show-treats-catholicism-seriously-funny-way.

75. "Commencement - The Catholic University of America," May 14, 2016, http://commencement.cua.edu/.

76. "Jim Gaffigan on Comedy and His Catholic Faith."

77. "Jim Gaffigan Is Doing Stand-Up for the Pope - CONAN on TBS," *Conan* (TBS, September 15, 2015), https://www.youtube.com/watch?v=LO_xU_IIiR4.

78. Dave Itzkoff, "Jim Gaffigan on Performing Stand-Up for Pope Francis," *New York Times*, September 23, 2015, http://www.nytimes.com/2015/09/23/arts /television/jim-gaffigan-on-performing-stand-up-for-pope-francis.html.

79. Ibid.

80. For more on his orthodoxy, see David O'Reilly, "Chaput: No Communion for Unwed, Gay and Some Divorced Couples," *Philly.com*, July 6, 2016, http://www.philly.com/philly/news/20160706_Chaput__No_Communion_for _unwed__gay_and_some_divorced_couples.html.

81. Sean L. McCarthy, "Jim Gaffigan Live at the Festival of Families in Philadelphia, Warming up the Audience for Pope Francis," *The Comic's Comic*, September 28, 2015, http://thecomicscomic.com/2015/09/28/jim-gaffigan-live -at-the-festival-of-families-in-philadelphia-warming-up-the-audience-for-pope -francis/.

82. "Jim Gaffigan on the 'superhero' Pope," *CBS Sunday Morning*, September 20, 2015, https://www.youtube.com/watch?v=9iaCYldsVJ4.

83. Terry Gross, "Comic Jim Gaffigan on Stand-Up, Faith and Opening for the Pope," *Fresh Air*, September 24, 2015, http://www.npr.org/2015/09/24 /443070367/comic-jim-gaffigan-on-stand-up-faith-and-opening-for-the-pope.

84. Ruth Graham, "America's Top Christian Comedian," *Slate*, September 8, 2015, http://www.slate.com/articles/life/faithbased/2015/09/jim_gaffigan_not _stephen_colbert_is_america_s_top_christian_comedian.html.

85. Catholic News Service, *Jim Gaffigan*.

86. Scott Alessi, "A Catholic Takeover of Late-Night Comedy," Our Sunday Visitor Catholic Publishing Company, April 30, 2014, https://www.osv.com /OSVNewsweekly/National/Article/TabId/717/ArtMID/13622/ArticleID/14609 /A-Catholic-takeover-of-late-night-comedy.aspx.

87. Ibid.

88. Terry Lindvall, *God Mocks a History of Religious Satire from the Hebrew Prophets to Stephen Colbert* (New York: New York University Press, 2015), 264.

89. Matt Emerson, "Colbert's Cloak and Dagger Catechesis," May 27, 2011, http://www.patheos.com/Resources/Additional-Resources/Colberts-Cloak-and -Dagger-Catechesis-Matt-Emerson-05-27-2011.

90. Lindvall, *God Mocks a History of Religious Satire*, 263.

91. Matt Emerson, "Stephen Colbert: Catholicism's Best Pitch Man? - OnFaith," June 2, 2011, http://www.faithstreet.com/onfaith/2011/06/02 /stephen-colbert-catholicisms-best-pitch-man/10756.

92. *The Colbert Report*, "Yahweh or No Way - IHOP & Antonio Federici Ad," Comedy Central, September 27, 2010.

93. Ibid.

94. Lindvall, *God Mocks a History of Religious Satire*, 262.

95. Ibid., 264.

96. Ibid., 265.

97. *The Colbert Report*, "Philip Zimbardo," Comedy Central, February 11, 2008.

98. Kimberly Winston, "Stephen Colbert May Play Religion for Laughs, but His Thoughtful Catholicism Still Shows Through," *Washington Post*, October 15, 2010, sec. Religion, http://www.washingtonpost.com/wp-dyn/content /article/2010/10/15/AR2010101505758.html.

99. Lindvall, *God Mocks a History of Religious Satire*, 265.

100. Terry Gross, "A Fake Newsman's Fake Newsman: Stephen Colbert," *Fresh Air* (NPR, January 24, 2005), http://www.npr.org/templates/story/story .php?storyId=4464017.

5. Colbert Catholicism

1. Jerome P. Baggett, *Sense of the Faithful: How American Catholics Live Their Faith*, Reprint edition (New York: Oxford University Press, 2011), 8.

2. James T. Fisher, *Communion of Immigrants: A History of Catholics in America* (New York: Oxford University Press, 2002); Timothy L. Hall, "John

Carroll," in *American Religious Leaders*, ed. Timothy L. Hall (Infobase Publishing, 2014), 54–55.

3. For more on these examples, see Rebecca A. Fried, "No Irish Need Deny: Evidence for the Historicity of NINA Restrictions in Advertisements and Signs," *Journal of Social History* 49, no. 4 (June 1, 2016): 829–54; Maria Monk et al., *Awful Disclosures* (M. Monk, 1836); "'The American River Ganges'—30 September, 1871 | Illustrating Chinese Exclusion," https://thomasnastcartoons .com/irish-catholic-cartoons/the-american-river-ganges-1871/.

4. Bruce Levine, "Conservatism, Nativism, and Slavery: Thomas R. Whitney and the Origins of the Know-Nothing Party," *Journal of American History* 88, no. 2 (2001): 456.

5. Will Herberg, *Protestant, Catholic, Jew: An Essay in American Religious Sociology* (New York: Doubleday, 1956), 231.

6. Tracy Fessenden, *Culture and Redemption: Religion, the Secular, and American Literature* (Princeton, N.J.: Princeton University Press, 2007).

7. Kevin M. Schultz, *Tri-Faith America: How Catholics and Jews Held Postwar America to Its Protestant Promise* (Oxford: Oxford University Press, 2013).

8. *The Colbert Report*, "William Donohue," Comedy Central, July 25, 2006.

9. Ibid.

10. James P. McCartin, *Prayers of the Faithful: The Shifting Spiritual Life of American Catholics* (Cambridge, Mass.: Harvard University Press, 2010), 8.

11. Jon Butler, "Historical Heresy: Catholicism as a Model for American Religious History," in *Belief in History: Innovative Approaches to European and American Religion*, ed. Thomas Kselman (Notre Dame, Ind.: University of Notre Dame Press, 1991).

12. McCartin, *Prayers of the Faithful*, 104.

13. Ibid., 108.

14. Timothy I. Kelly, *The Transformation of American Catholicism: The Pittsburgh Laity and the Second Vatican Council, 1950–1972* (Notre Dame, Ind.: University of Notre Dame Press, 2009); Colleen McDannell, *The Spirit of Vatican II: A History of Catholic Reform in America* (New York: Basic Books, 2011).

15. Wade Clark Roof, *A Generation of Seekers: The Spiritual Journeys of the Baby Boom Generation* (San Francisco: HarperSanFrancisco, 1993); Robert Wuthnow, *The Restructuring of American Religion* (Princeton, N.J.: Princeton University Press, 1988).

16. I am thinking specifically of nonsanctioned but ever-present lay and ethnic practices. Although there are hundreds of examples, some in particular: Kristy Nabhan-Warren, *The Virgin of El Barrio: Marian Apparitions, Catholic Evangelizing, and Mexican American Activism* (New York: New York University Press, 2005); Robert A. Orsi, "Everyday Miracles: The Study of Lived Religion,"

in *Lived Religion in America: Toward a History of Practice*, ed. David D. Hall (Princeton, N.J.: Princeton University Press, 1997), 3–21; Jennifer Scheper Hughes, *Biography of a Mexican Crucifix: Lived Religion and Local Faith from the Conquest to the Present* (New York: Oxford University Press, USA, 2010).

17. Mary Ellen Konieczny, *The Spirit's Tether: Family, Work, and Religion among American Catholics* (Oxford: Oxford University Press, 2013), 9.

18. Andrew M. Greeley, *The Communal Catholic: A Personal Manifesto* (New York: Seabury Press, 1976).

19. *The Colbert Report*, "Garry Wills," Comedy Central, February 11, 2013.

20. Ibid.

21. The quotation is from Thomas J. Ferraro, "Not-Just-Cultural Catholics," in *Catholic Lives, Contemporary America*, ed. Thomas J. Ferraro (Durham, N.C.: Duke University Press, 1997), 1–18; Ferraro sees a connection between cultural Catholicism and American Catholic intellectualism. For more, see Philip Gleason, "A Look Back at the Catholic Intellectualism Issue," *U.S. Catholic Historian* 13, no. 1 (1995): 19–37; James T. Fisher, "Alternative Sources of Catholic Intellectual Vitality," *U.S. Catholic Historian* 13, no. 1 (1995): 81–94.

22. "Cultural Catholicism" is a term I have researched previously in my 2013 master's thesis at Northwestern University, "Commodified Catholicism: Essentialized Image of Catholic Childhood at *Late Nite Catechism*." As the writers and actresses of *Late Nite Catechism* define them, cultural Catholics were formed by Catholicism in childhood but may not practice to the same extent that they did as children.

23. David Masci, "Who Are 'Cultural Catholics'?," *Pew Research Center*, September 3, 2015, http://www.pewresearch.org/fact-tank/2015/09/03/who-are -cultural-catholics/.

24. John W. Martens, "'Lukewarm' and '100%' Catholics," *America*, October 25, 2010, http://americamagazine.org/content/good-word/lukewarm -and-100-catholics.

25. "Minn. Archbishop: No 'Lukewarm' Catholics Welcome," *USA TODAY*, October 19, 2010, http://usatoday30.usatoday.com/news/religion/2010-10-20 -catholic19_ST_N.htm.

26. Ibid.

27. Martens, "'Lukewarm' and '100%' Catholics."

28. Ibid.

29. Andrew M. Greeley, "Cafeteria Catholicism: Do You Have to Eat Everything on Your Plate," *U.S. Catholic* 50 (January 1985): 18.

30. One example is in the *Fidelity* magazine, where E. Michael Jones critiques Father McBrien's article "Catholicism à la carte has an ever-changing menu." For more, see E. Michael Jones, "Father McBrien and the New Dissent," *Fidelity* 5 (December 1986): 20–33.

31. Rea Nolan Martin, "Proud to Be a Cafeteria Catholic," *The Huffington Post*, January 28, 2014, http://www.huffingtonpost.com/rea-nolan-martin /proud-to-be-a-cafeteria-c_b_4676955.html.

32. Isabella R. Moyer, "Proud to Be a Cafeteria Catholic," USCatholic.org, July 21, 2015, http://www.uscatholic.org/articles/201507/proud-be-cafeteria -catholic-30253.

33. Ibid.

34. Sarah del Rio, "If Cafeteria Catholicism Is a Thing, Then I'm the Head Lunch Lady," *BLUNTmoms*, January 14, 2016, http://www.bluntmoms.com /cafeteria-catholicism-thing-im-head-lunch-lady/.

35. William V. D'Antonio, Michele Dillon, and Mary L. Gautier, CARA (Center for Applied Research in the Apostolate) at Georgetown University, *American Catholics in Transition* (Lanham, Md.: Rowman & Littlefield, 2013).

36. Ibid., 47.

37. Michele Dillon, *Catholic Identity: Balancing Reason, Faith, and Power*, First edition (New York: Cambridge University Press, 1999), 4.

38. Baggett, *Sense of the Faithful*, 5.

39. For the term "thinking Catholics," I look to Father Thomas Reese S.J.'s work while a visiting scholar at Santa Clara University. See "Santa Clara Magazine - Ten Guidelines for Thinking Catholics," September 21, 2006, http://www.scu.edu/scm/fall2006/reese.cfm.

40. *The Colbert Report*, "Stephen's Lenten Sacrifice," Comedy Central, February 22, 2012.

41. "Stephen Colbert Gets Celebrity Faith Right • /R/Christianity," *Reddit*, 2015, https://www.reddit.com/r/Christianity/comments/3icz72/stephen _colbert_gets_celebrity_faith_right/.

42. Ibid.

43. Ibid.

44. Ibid.

45. The website from which this image was initially found is now defunct, and the image has been deleted. "10 Catholic Memes for Your Friday," Catholic Cravings, http://www.lauramcalister.com/2013/11/15/10-catholic-memes-friday/, accessed February 11, 2015.

46. America Media, *Colbert Catechism: Stephen Colbert Professes His Faith to Fr. James Martin*, Filmed March 2, 2015. Youtube video, 6:42. Posted March 2, 2015. https://www.youtube.com/watch?v=o-zxn-YGUI4.

47. Ibid.

48. Joel Lovell, "Stephen Colbert on Making The Late Show His Own," *GQ*, August 17, 2015, http://www.gq.com/story/stephen-colbert-gq-cover-story.

49. Ibid.

50. Melissa Locker, "Stephen Colbert Proves He's Still the Lord of the Rings Trivia King | TIME," August 5, 2016, http://time.com/4440615/stephen-colbert-late-show-lord-of-the-rings/.

51. Lovell, "Stephen Colbert on Making The Late Show His Own."

52. Ibid.

53. Ibid.

54. Ibid.

55. Paul Provenza and Dan Dion, *Satiristas: Comedians, Contrarians, Raconteurs & Vulgarians* (New York: It Books, 2010), 30.

56. Lovell, "Stephen Colbert on Making The Late Show His Own."

57. Laurie Goodstein, "Colbert and Dolan Open Up on Spirituality," *New York Times*, September 15, 2012, http://www.nytimes.com/2012/09/16/nyregion/stephen-colbert-and-cardinal-cardinal-timothy-dolan-at-fordham-university.html.

58. Ibid.

59. John L. Allen Jr., "League's Dark Vision Divides Catholics: Dispute over TV Show Affords New Visibility," *National Catholic Reporter* 34, no. 2 (October 31, 1997): 3–5.

60. *The Colbert Report*, "William Donohue," Comedy Central, July 25, 2006.

61. Ibid.

62. Ibid.

63. For example, Donohue's critiques of *South Park* are illustrated in David Feltmate, "Cowards, Critics, and Catholics: The Catholic League for Religious and Civil Rights, South Park, and the Politics of Religious Humor in the United States," *Bulletin for the Study of Religion* 42, no. 3 (September 2013): 2–11.

64. "About Us: Catholic League," Catholic League for Religious and Civil Rights, n.d., http://www.catholicleague.org/about-us/.

65. Jacob Bernstein, "Bill Donohue: The Catholic League's Attack Dog," *WWD*, February 2, 2007, 17–17.

66. J. Matthew Wilson, "Catholic League for Religious and Civil Rights," in *Encyclopedia of American Religion and Politics*, ed. Paul A. Djupe and Laura R. Olson (New York: Facts on File, 2003).

67. Mary Jo Weaver and R. Scott Appleby, *Being Right: Conservative Catholics in America* (Bloomington: Indiana University Press, 1995), 343.

68. *The Colbert Report*, "William Donohue," Comedy Central, July 25, 2006.

69. Ibid.

70. *The Colbert Report*, "Spider-Pope," Comedy Central, September 29, 2009.

71. BishopAccountability.org is one of the most factual accounts, especially from the victims' perspectives. "Data on the Crisis: The Human Toll," http://www.bishop-accountability.org/AtAGlance/data.htm.

72. Christopher Titus, "Pedophilic Priests," *Christopher Titus: The 5th Annual End of the World Tour* (Comedy Central, March 17, 2007), http://www.cc .com/video-clips/426kni/stand-up-christopher-titus—pedophilic-priests.

73. Robin Williams and Home Box Office (Firme), *Robin Williams Live on Broadway* (New York: Sony Music Entertainment, manufactured by Columbia Music Video, 2002).

74. George Carlin, *When Will Jesus Bring the Pork Chops?* (New York: Hachette Books, 2004), 254.

75. Louis C.K., *Louis C.K. Learns about the Catholic Church*, Short film, Comedy genre, (2007).

76. *The Colbert Report*, "Clergy-Matic Ecclesi-Action Center 3:16," Comedy Central, May 19, 2011.

77. Ibid.

78. Ibid.

79. Ibid.

80. Phil Ferguson, "Clergy-Matic Ecclesi-Action Center 3:16—Colbert," *Skeptic Money*, May 25, 2011, http://www.skepticmoney.com/clergy-matic -ecclesi-action-center-316-colbert/; Richard Tutching, "To Anne Rice: From Stephen Colbert Anne, You'll Get a Good Laugh! . . . - Richard Tutching," *Facebook*, May 21, 2011, https://www.facebook.com/annericefanpage/posts /111328488954669.

81. TV By The Numbers, "'The Daily Show' Tops the Competition in 2Q; 'Chelsea Lately' Surpasses Conan | TV By The Numbers by zap2it.com | Page 97004," June 30, 2011, http://tvbythenumbers.zap2it.com/2011/06/30/the-daily-sh ow-tops-the-competition-in-2q-chelsea-lately-surpasses-conan/97004/.

82. Laurie Goodstein, "In Milwaukee Post, Cardinal Authorized Paying Abusers," *New York Times*, May 30, 2012, http://www.nytimes.com/2012/05/31 /us/cardinal-authorized-payments-to-abusers.html.

83. *The Colbert Report*, "Timothy Dolan Pt. 1," Comedy Central, September 3, 2013.

84. Ibid.

85. Ibid.

86. Ibid.

6. Colbert as Cultural Warrior

1. For more, see Roger Chapman, *Culture Wars: An Encyclopedia of Issues, Viewpoints, and Voices* (Armonk, N.Y.: M. E. Sharpe, 2010), xxvii.

2. James Davison Hunter, *Culture Wars: The Struggle to Define America* (New York: Basic Books, 1991); Andrew Hartman, *A War for the Soul of America* (Chicago: University of Chicago Press, 2015).

3. Susan Friend Harding, *The Book of Jerry Falwell: Fundamentalist Language and Politics* (Princeton, N.J.: Princeton University Press, 2001); William Martin, *With God on Our Side: The Rise of the Religious Right in America* (New York: Broadway Books, 2005).

4. Hunter, *Culture Wars*.

5. Ryan L. Claassen, *Godless Democrats and Pious Republicans? Party Activists, Party Capture, and the "God Gap"* (New York: Cambridge University Press, 2015), 1.

6. Hunter, *Culture Wars*.

7. Chapman, *Culture Wars: An Encyclopedia of Issues, Viewpoints, and Voices*, xxvii.

8. Irene Taviss Thomson, *Culture Wars and Enduring American Dilemmas* (Ann Arbor: University of Michigan Press, 2010).

9. Sylvester A. Johnson, *African American Religions, 1500–2000: Colonialism, Democracy, and Freedom* (New York: Cambridge University Press, 2015).

10. Bruno Latour, *We Have Never Been Modern*, trans. Catherine Porter (Cambridge, Mass.: Harvard University Press, 1993).

11. Charles Taylor, *A Secular Age* (Cambridge, Mass.: Belknap Press of Harvard University Press, 2007).

12. Heather L. LaMarre, Kristen D. Landreville, and Michael A. Beam, "The Irony of Satire: Political Ideology and the Motivation to See What You Want to See in The Colbert Report," *The International Journal of Press/Politics* 14, no. 2 (April 1, 2009): 212–31.

13. Fieldnotes 11.19.2014.

14. Fieldnotes 11.19.2014.

15. Wade Clark Roof, *A Generation of Seekers: The Spiritual Journeys of the Baby Boom Generation* (San Francisco: HarperSanFrancisco, 1993); Peter Steinfels, "Conversations/Wade Clark Roof; Charting the Currents of Belief for the Generation That Rebelled," *New York Times*, May 30, 1993, sec. Week in Review, http://www.nytimes.com/1993/05/30/weekinreview/conversations-wade-clark-roof-charting-currents-belief-for-generation-that.html.

16. Robert C. Fuller, *Spiritual, But Not Religious: Understanding Unchurched America* (Oxford: Oxford University Press, 2001).

17. Fieldnotes 11.19.2014.

18. *The Colbert Report*, "Extreme Measures for Boosting Church Attendance," Comedy Central, April 21, 2014.

19. *The Colbert Report*, "Richard Dawkins," Comedy Central, September 30, 2009.

20. Fieldnotes 11.20.2014.

21. Marvin Kitman, *The Man Who Would Not Shut Up: The Rise of Bill O'Reilly* (New York: Macmillan, 2008).

22. Jonathan Gray, Jeffrey P. Jones, and Ethan Thompson, *Satire TV: Politics and Comedy in the Post-Network Era* (New York: New York University Press, 2009), 128.

23. Ibid., 129.

24. *The O'Reilly Factor*, "The O'Reilly Factor," January 18, 2007.

25. *The Colbert Report*, "Bill O'Reilly Interview," Comedy Central, January 18, 2007.

26. Andrew Gold, "Colbert Assaults Punditocracy," *Glenview Announcements*, October 13, 2005, http://www.highbeam.com/doc/1N1 -110D9D4A42E0FFE0.html.

27. *The Colbert Report*, "Bill O'Reilly Interview," Comedy Central, January 18, 2007.

28. For more, see Emily Steel and Michael S. Schmidt, "Bill O'Reilly Settled New Harassment Claim, Then Fox Renewed His Contract," *New York Times*, October 21, 2017, sec. Media. https://www.nytimes.com/2017/10/21/business /media/bill-oreilly-sexual-harassment.html.

29. Fieldnotes 11.19.14.

30. Sigmund Freud, *Jokes and Their Relation to the Unconscious* (New York: Norton, 1960).

31. Liz Halloran, "Glenn Beck Comes to D.C., Controversy Follows," *NPR .org*, August 27, 2010, http://www.npr.org/templates/story/story.php?storyId =129449408.

32. Meena Hartenstein, "Huge Range in Crowd Estimates at Glenn Beck Rally - NY Daily News," *New York Daily News*, August 29, 2010, http://www .nydailynews.com/news/politics/crowd-estimates-glenn-beck-restoring-honor -rally-depend-dramatically-article-1.200846.

33. Interestingly, Catholic missionaries have also been called "Black Robes"; for more, see Jay P. Dolan, *The American Catholic Experience* (Garden City, N.Y.: Doubleday, 1985).

34. James Hohmann, "Beck Claims King Legacy through God," Politico, August 28, 2010, http://www.politico.com/news/stories/0810/41556.html.

35. For more, see Sarah Posner, "Evangelicals Have 'Deep Concerns' about Beck," *Religion Dispatches*, September 1, 2010, http://religiondispatches.org /evangelicals-have-deep-concerns-about-beck/.

36. *The Daily Show*, "Rally to Restore Sanity Announcement," Comedy Central, September 16, 2010.

37. Stephen C. Webster, "Scientific Estimate: 'Sanity' Rally More than Twice the Size of Beck's August Tea Party," *Rawstory*, October 31, 2010,

http://www.rawstory.com/2010/10/scientific-estimate-sanity-rally-size-becks-tea-party/.

38. "Rally to Restore Sanity - Full" Comedy Central, October 30, 2010.

39. Brian Montopoli, "Jon Stewart Rallies for Sanity—and against Cable News," October 31, 2010, http://www.cbsnews.com/news/jon-stewart-rallies-for-sanity-and-against-cable-news/.

40. Missy Yates, "Father Guido Sarducci: Father Guido Sarducci Gives Benediction at Rally to Restore Sanity," *Long Island Press*, October 30, 2010, http://archive.longislandpress.com/2010/10/30/father-guido-sarducci-father-guido-sarducci-gives-benediction-at-rally-to-restore-sanity/.

41. Ibid.

42. "Rally to Restore Sanity - Full" Comedy Central, October 30, 2010.

43. Ibid.

44. Robert N. Bellah, "Civil Religion in America," *Daedalus* 134, no. 4 (2005): 40–55.

45. "Rally to Restore Sanity - Full" Comedy Central, October 30, 2010.

46. Morning Edition, "Stewart, Colbert Honor 'Greatest, Strongest Country,'" *NPR.org*, November 1, 2010, http://www.npr.org/templates/story/story.php?storyId=130969245.

47. "Rally to Restore Sanity - Full" Comedy Central, October 30, 2010.

48. While the original tweet has been removed, the quote was from a "Sport Report" segment; see *The Colbert Report*, "Sport Report - Professional Soccer Toddler, Golf Innovations & Washington Redskins Charm Offensive," Comedy Central, March 26, 2014.

49. Julia Carrie Wong, "Who's Afraid of Suey Park?," *The Nation*, March 31, 2014, http://www.thenation.com/article/whos-afraid-suey-park/.

50. Elizabeth Bruenig, "Why Won't Twitter Forgive Suey Park?," *New Republic*, May 20, 2015, https://newrepublic.com/article/121861/suey-parkof-cancelcolbert-fame-has-stopped-fighting-twitter.

51. Alex Stedman, "Stephen Colbert Accused of Racism with #Cancel-Colbert Campaign," *Variety*, March 27, 2014, http://variety.com/2014/tv/news/stephen-colbert-accused-of-racism-with-cancelcolbert-campaign-1201149494/.

52. Ibid.

53. Ibid.

54. "#CancelColbert - Twitter Search," n.d., https://twitter.com/search?q=%23CancelColbert.

55. Wong, "Who's Afraid of Suey Park?"

56. Arthur Chu, "Suey Park and Arthur Chu: A Dialogue Between Two Hashtag Warriors," *Thought Catalog* (blog), November 12, 2015, http://

thoughtcatalog.com/arthur-chu/2015/11/suey-park-and-arthur-chu-a-dialogue
-between-two-hashtag-warriors/.

57. Angela Watercutter, "Here's What Happened to the Woman Who
Started #CancelColbert," *Wired*, February 22, 2016, http://www.wired.com
/2016/02/cancelcolbert-what-happened/.

58. Chu, "Suey Park And Arthur Chu."

59. Bruenig, "Why Won't Twitter Forgive Suey Park?"

60. Ibid.

61. "Killjoy Prophets - GoGetFunding | GoGetFunding," http://
gogetfunding.com/killjoy-prophets-1/.

62. Mary Elizabeth Williams, "The Redemption of #CancelColbert's Suey
Park: Can Twitter Forgive and Forget?," *Salon*, May 22, 2015, http://www.salon
.com/2015/05/22/the_redemption_of_cancelcolberts_suey_park_can_twitter
_forgive_and_forget/.

7. Colbert's Continued Presence

1. Bill Carter, "Colbert Will Host 'Late Show,' Playing Himself for a
Change," *New York Times*, April 10, 2014, http://www.nytimes.com/2014/04/11
/business/media/stephen-colbert-to-succeed-letterman-on-late-show.html.

2. *The Colbert Report*, "December 18, 2014 - Grimmy," Comedy Central,
December 18, 2014.

3. Terry Gross, "'Late Show' Host Says He Has Finally Found His Post–
'Colbert Report' Voice," *Fresh Air* (NPR), November 2, 2016, http://www.npr
.org/2016/11/02/500303201/late-show-host-stephen-colbert-says-hes-finally
-found-his-post-report-voice.

4. *Vanity Fair* and The Scene, "Conan O'Brien, Stephen Colbert, and Other
Late Night Hosts Describe Each Other with One Word," Vanity Fair Videos,
September 16, 2015, https://thescene.com/watch/vanityfair/conan-o-brien
-stephen-colbert-and-other-late-night-hosts-describe-each-other-with-one
-word.

5. Scott Alessi, "A Catholic Takeover of Late-Night Comedy," Our Sunday
Visitor Catholic Publishing Company, April 30, 2014, https://www.osv.com
/OSVNewsweekly/National/Article/TabId/717/ArtMID/13622/ArticleID/14609
/A-Catholic-takeover-of-late-night-comedy.aspx.

6. Ibid.

7. Samantha Bee, *I Know I Am, but What Are You?* (New York: Gallery
Books, 2010).

8. Paul Provenza and Dan Dion, *Satiristas: Comedians, Contrarians,
Raconteurs & Vulgarians*, First edition (New York: It Books, 2010), 56.

9. Terry Gross, "Late Night 'Thank You Notes' from Jimmy Fallon," *NPR .org*, May 23, 2011, http://www.npr.org/2011/05/23/136462013/late-night-thank -you-notes-from-jimmy-fallon.

10. Gross, "'Late Show' Host Says He Has Finally Found His Post–'Colbert Report' Voice."

11. Alison Lesley, "Stephen Colbert - Comedian, TV Host . . . Catholic?," *World Religion News*, September 12, 2015, http://www.worldreligionnews.com /religion-news/christianity/stephen-colbert-comedian-tv-host-catholic.

12. "The Late Show with Stephen Colbert Cathedral Mug | CBS Store," http://www.cbsstore.com/the-late-show-with-stephen-colbert-cathedral-mug /detail.php?p=1452895.

13. *The Late Show with Stephen Colbert*, "Stephen & Patricia Heaton Have a Catholic Throwdown," CBS, January 18, 2016.

14. *The Late Show with Stephen Colbert*, Episode 3. CBS, September 10, 2015.

15. Ibid.

16. Ibid.

17. Ibid.

18. *The Late Show with Stephen Colbert*, "Stephen Colbert's Midnight Confessions," CBS, November 10, 2015.

19. Ibid.

20. *The Late Show with Stephen Colbert*, "Stephen Colbert's Midnight Confessions," CBS, November 10, 2015; *The Late Show with Stephen Colbert*, "Stephen Colbert's Midnight Confessions VI," CBS, April 6, 2016.

21. *The Late Show with Stephen Colbert*, "Stephen Colbert's Midnight Confessions VI," CBS, April 6, 2016.

22. *The Late Show with Stephen Colbert*, "Stephen Colbert's Midnight Confessions XXXVI," CBS, January 12, 2018.

23. Stephen Colbert and Sean Kelly, *Stephen Colbert's Midnight Confessions* (New York: Simon & Schuster), 2017.

24. *The Late Show with Stephen Colbert*, "Mark Ruffalo Talks 2016, His New Film and the Catholic Church," CBS, November 13, 2015.

25. *The Late Show with Stephen Colbert*, "The Late Show with Stephen Colbert (Andrew Sullivan, Maria Shriver, Jim Gaffigan, Archbishop Thomas Wenski)," CBS, September 24, 2015.

26. Ibid.

27. Ibid.

28. Gross, "'Late Show' Host Says He Has Finally Found His Post–'Colbert Report' Voice."

29. For more, see Josh Hill, "Stephen Colbert Has Been Fighting Alternative Facts since 2003," Last Night On, January 25, 2017, https://lastnighton.com /2017/01/25/colbert-report-alternative-facts/; Megh Wright, "Stephen Colbert

vs. 'Alternative Facts': A Lifelong Rivalry," Splitsider, January 24, 2017, http://splitsider.com/2017/01/stephen-colbert-vs-alternative-facts-a-lifelong -rivalry/.

30. Gross, "'Late Show' Host Says He Has Finally Found His Post–'Colbert Report' Voice."

31. Lisa Rogak, *And Nothing But the Truthiness: The Rise (and Further Rise) of Stephen Colbert* (New York: Thomas Dunne Books, 2011), 127.

32. Jim Hoskinson, "Stephen Colbert's Live Election Night Democracy's Series Finale: Who's Going to Clean Up This Sh*t?," November 8, 2016.

Selected Bibliography

10 Catholic Memes for Your Friday. Digital image. Catholic Cravings. Nov. 11, 2013. http://www.lauramcalister.com/2013/11/15/10-catholic-memes-friday/, accessed February 11, 2015.

Alessi, Scott. "A Catholic Takeover of Late-Night Comedy." *Our Sunday Visitor Catholic Publishing Company*, April 30, 2014, https://www.osv.com /OSVNewsweekly/National/Article/TabId/717/ArtMID/13622/ArticleID /14609/A-Catholic-takeover-of-late-night-comedy.aspx.

Altschuler, Glenn C., and Patrick M. Burns. "Snarlin' Carlin: The Odyssey of a Libertarian." *Studies in American Humor*, no. 20 (2009): 42–57.

Amarasingam, Amarnath. *The Stewart/Colbert Effect: Essays on the Real Impacts of Fake News* (Jefferson, N.C.: McFarland, 2011).

America Media. "Colbert Catechism: Stephen Colbert Professes His Faith to Fr. James Martin," Filmed March 2, 2015. Youtube video, 6:42. Posted [March 2, 2015]. https://www.youtube.com/watch?v=o-zxn-YGUI4.

Appleby, R. Scott, and Kathleen Sprows Cummings. *Catholics in the American Century: Recasting Narratives of U.S. History* (Ithaca, N.Y.: Cornell University Press, 2012).

Apte, Mahadev L. *Humor and Laughter: An Anthropological Approach* (Ithaca, N.Y.: Cornell University Press, 1985).

Arbuckle, Gerald A. *Laughing with God: Humor, Culture, and Transformation* (Collegeville, Minn.: Liturgical Press, 2008).

Askew, Kelly, and Richard R. Wilk. *The Anthropology of Media: A Reader* (Malden, Mass.: Blackwell, 2002).

Baggett, Jerome P. *Sense of the Faithful: How American Catholics Live Their Faith* (New York: Oxford University Press, 2011).

Baker, Kelly J. "When Is a Laugh Just a Laugh? Never." *Bulletin for the Study of Religion* 42, no. 3 (August 19, 2013): 1.

Baym, Geoffrey. "The Daily Show: Discursive Integration and the Reinvention of Political Journalism." *Political Communication* 22, no. 3 (2005): 259–76.

———. *From Cronkite to Colbert: The Evolution of Broadcast News* (Boulder, Colo.: Paradigm, 2009).

Beale, Stephen. "Stephen Colbert and America's Catholic Comic Moment." *National Catholic Register*, June 3, 2016. http://www.ncregister.com/daily -news/stephen-colbert-and-americas-catholic-comic-moment/.

Bell, Nancy D., Scott Crossley, and Christian F. Hempelmann. "Wordplay in Church Marquees." *Humor: International Journal of Humor Research* 24, no. 2 (May 2011): 187–202.

Ben-Amos, Dan. "The 'Myth' of Jewish Humor." *Western Folklore* 32, no. 2 (1973): 112–31.

Benacka, Elizabeth. *Rhetoric, Humor, and the Public Sphere: From Socrates to Stephen Colbert* (Lanham, Md.: Rowman & Littlefield, 2016).

Bendyna, Mary E., R.S.M., John C. Green, Mark J. Rozell, and Clyde Wilcox. "Uneasy Alliance: Conservative Catholics and the Christian Right." *Sociology of Religion* 62, no. 1 (2001): 51–64.

Berger, Peter L. *Redeeming Laughter: The Comic Dimension of Human Experience* (Boston: de Gruyter, 1997).

Bergson, Henri. *Laughter: An Essay on the Meaning of the Comic*, trans. Cloudesley Brereton (London: Macmillan, 1911).

Biema, David Van. "Father Martin: The Priest Who Prays for Stephen Colbert." *Time*, March 7, 2010.

Black, Gregory D. *Hollywood Censored: Morality Codes, Catholics, and the Movies* (New York: Cambridge University Press, 1996).

———. *The Catholic Crusade against the Movies, 1940–1975* (New York: Cambridge University Press, 1998).

Booth, Wayne C. *A Rhetoric of Irony* (Chicago: University of Chicago Press, 1975).

Borer, Michael Ian, and Adam Murphree. "Framing Catholicism: Jack Chick's Anti-Catholic Cartoons and the Flexible Boundaries of the Culture Wars." *Religion and American Culture* 18, no. 1 (2008): 95–112.

Boskin, Joseph. *Rebellious Laughter: People's Humor in American Culture* (Syracuse, N.Y.: Syracuse University Press, 1997).

Boskin, Joseph, ed. *The Humor Prism in 20th Century American Society* (Detroit: Wayne State University Press, 1997).

Boyea, Earl. "The Reverend Charles Coughlin and the Church: The Gallagher Years, 1930–1937." *Catholic Historical Review* 81, no. 2 (April 1, 1995): 211–25.

Brants, Kees. "Who's Afraid of Infotainment?" *European Journal of Communication* 13, no. 3 (September 1, 1998): 315–35.

Brinkley, Alan. *Voices of Protest: Huey Long, Father Coughlin, and the Great Depression* (New York: Knopf, 1982).

Brodie, Ian. "Stand-up Comedy as a Genre of Intimacy." *Ethnologies* 30, no. 2 (2008): 153–80.

Bruenig, Elizabeth. "Why Won't Twitter Forgive Suey Park?" *New Republic*, May 20, 2015. https://newrepublic.com/article/121861/suey-parkof -cancelcolbert-fame-has-stopped-fighting-twitter.

Cadegan, Una M. "Guardians of Democracy or Cultural Storm Troopers?: American Catholics and the Control of Popular Media, 1934–1966." *The Catholic Historical Review* 87, no. 2

Callaghan, Jennifer A. "'Not a Fully Homogeneous Grouping': Forming an Office of Worship in the Archdiocese of Seattle." *U.S. Catholic Historian* 33, no. 2 (2015): 25–48.

Campbell, Heidi A. *When Religion Meets New Media* (New York: Routledge, 2010).

———. *Digital Religion: Understanding Religious Practice in New Media Worlds* (New York: Routledge, 2012).

Campbell, Heidi A., and Gregory P. Grieve. *Playing with Religion in Digital Games* (Bloomington: Indiana University Press, 2014).

Capps, Donald. "Religion and Humor: Estranged Bedfellows." *Pastoral Psychology* 54, no. 5 (May 2006): 413–38.

Carpenter, Ronald H. *Father Charles E. Coughlin: Surrogate Spokesman for the Disaffected* (Westport, Conn.: Greenwood Press, 1998).

Carter, Bill. "Colbert Will Host 'Late Show,' Playing Himself for a Change." *New York Times*, April 10, 2014. http://www.nytimes.com/2014/04/11 /business/media/stephen-colbert-to-succeed-letterman-on-late-show.html.

Chapman, Roger. *Culture Wars: An Encyclopedia of Issues, Viewpoints, and Voices* (Armonk, N.Y.: M. E. Sharpe, 2010).

Chase, Jefferson S. *Inciting Laughter: The Development of "Jewish Humor" in 19th Century German Culture* (Boston: de Gruyter, 1999).

Cheong, Pauline Hope. *Digital Religion, Social Media, and Culture: Perspectives, Practices, and Futures* (New York: Lang, 2012).

Chinnici, Joseph P. *When Values Collide: The Catholic Church, Sexual Abuse, and the Challenges of Leadership* (Maryknoll, N.Y.: Orbis, 2010).

Claassen, Ryan L. *Godless Democrats and Pious Republicans? Party Activists, Party Capture, and the "God Gap"* (New York: Cambridge University Press, 2015).

Cowan, Douglas E. "'And Take Your Invisible Friends with You': Atheist Comedy and Religious Conversation (May Contain Offensive Language)." *Bulletin for the Study of Religion* 42, no. 3 (August 3, 2013): 32–36.

Cox, Harvey G. *Feast of Fools: Theological Essay on Festivity and Fantasy* (Cambridge, Mass.: Harvard University Press, 2013).

Cressler, Matthew J. *Authentically Black and Truly Catholic: The Rise of Black Catholicism in the Great Migration* (New York: New York University Press, 2017).

Cummings, Kathleen Sprows. *New Women of the Old Faith: Gender and American Catholicism in the Progressive Era* (Chapel Hill: University of North Carolina Press, 2009).

D'Antonio, William V., Michele Dillon, and Mary L. Gautier. *American Catholics in Transition* (Lanham, Md.: Rowman & Littlefield, 2013).

Davies, Christie. *Ethnic Humor around the World: A Comparative Analysis* (Bloomington: Indiana University Press, 1990).

———. *The Mirth of Nations* (New Brunswick, N.J.: Transaction, 2002).

Day, Amber. *Satire and Dissent: Interventions in Contemporary Political Debate* (Bloomington: Indiana University Press, 2011).

Derry, Ken. "A Buddhist, a Christian, and an Atheist Walk into a Classroom: Pedagogical Reflections on Religion and Humor." *Bulletin for the Study of Religion* 42, no. 3 (August 23, 2013): 37–42.

DesRochers, Rick. *The Comic Offense from Vaudeville to Contemporary Comedy: Larry David, Tina Fey, Stephen Colbert, and Dave Chappelle* (New York: Bloomsbury, 2014).

Dierberg, Jill E. "Searching for Truth(iness): Mapping the Religio-Political Landscape and Identity of Christian Emerging Adults through a Reception Study of 'The Colbert Report.'" Ph.D. dissertation, University of Denver, 2012.

Dix, Tara. "Catholic Humor Painfully Un-Funny." *U.S. Catholic* 69, no. 1 (January 2004).

Dokecki, Paul R. *The Clergy Sexual Abuse Crisis: Reform and Renewal in the Catholic Community* (Washington: Georgetown University Press, 2004).

Dolan, Jay P. *The Immigrant Church: New York's Irish and German Catholics, 1815–1865* Notre Dame, Ind.: University of Notre Dame Press, 1983).

———. *The American Catholic Experience* (Garden City, N.Y.: Doubleday, 1985).

———. *In Search of an American Catholicism: A History of Religion and Culture in Tension* (New York: Oxford University Press, 2003).

Douglas, Mary. "The Social Control of Cognition: Some Factors in Joke Perception." *Man* 3, no. 3 (September 1, 1968): 361–76.

Eckardt, A. Roy. *How to Tell God from the Devil: On the Way to Comedy* (New Brunswick, N.J.: Transaction, 1995).

Elliott, Robert C. *Power of Satire: Magic, Ritual, Art* (Princeton, N.J.: Princeton University Press, 1960).

Emerson, Matt. "Colbert's Cloak and Dagger Catechesis." *Pathos*, May 27, 2011. http://www.patheos.com/Resources/Additional-Resources/Colberts-Cloak -and-Dagger-Catechesis-Matt-Emerson-05-27-2011.

———. "Stephen Colbert: Catholicism's Best Pitch Man?" *OnFaith*, June 2, 2011. http://www.faithstreet.com/onfaith/2011/06/02/stephen-colbert -catholicisms-best-pitch-man/10756.

Farhi, Paul. "Truthinessology: The Stephen Colbert Effect Becomes an Obsession in Academia." *Washington Post*, July 9, 2012. https://www .washingtonpost.com/lifestyle/style/truthinessology-the-stephen-colbert -effect-becomes-an-obsession-in-academia/2012/07/09/gJQAYgiHZW_story .html.

Feltmate, David. "Cowards, Critics, and Catholics: The Catholic League for Religious and Civil Rights, South Park and the Politics of Religious Humor in the United States." *Bulletin for the Study of Religion* 42, no. 3 (June 7, 2013): 2–11.

———. "It's Funny Because It's True? The Simpsons, Satire, and the Significance of Religious Humor in Popular Culture." *Journal of the American Academy of Religion* 81, no. 1 (March 1, 2013): 222–48.

———. "Religion and Humor: A Bibliography." *Bulletin for the Study of Religion* 42, no. 3 (August 19, 2013): 47–48.

Ferguson, Phil. "Clergy-Matic Ecclesi-Action Center 3:16—Colbert." *Skeptic Money*, May 25, 2011. http://www.skepticmoney.com/clergy-matic-ecclesi -action-center-316-colbert/.

Ferraro, Thomas, ed. *Catholic Lives, Contemporary America* (Durham, N.C.: Duke University Press, 1997).

Fields, Kathleen Riley. *Bishop Fulton J. Sheen: An American Catholic Response to the Twentieth Century* (Notre Dame, Ind.: University of Notre Dame Press, 1988).

———. "'A Life of Mystery and Adventure': Fulton Sheen's Reflections on the Priesthood." *U.S. Catholic Historian* 11, no. 1 (1993): 63–82.

Fisher, James T. "Alternative Sources of Catholic Intellectual Vitality." *U.S. Catholic Historian* 13, no. 1 (1995): 81–94.

———. *Communion of Immigrants: A History of Catholics in America* (New York: Oxford University Press, 2002).

Freud, Sigmund. *Jokes and Their Relation to the Unconscious*, trans. James Strachey (New York: Norton, 1889).

Fuller, Robert C. *Spiritual, But Not Religious: Understanding Unchurched America* (New York: Oxford University Press, 2001).

Gibson, David. "Colbert the Catechist." *Sacred and Profane*, February 13, 2013. http://davidgibson.religionnews.com/2013/02/13/colbert-the -catechist/.

Gilbert, Joanne R. *Performing Marginality: Humor, Gender, and Cultural Critique.* Humor in Life and Letters Series (Detroit: Wayne State University Press, 2004).

Giles, Paul. *American Catholic Arts and Fictions: Culture, Ideology, Aesthetics* (New York: Cambridge University Press, 1992).

Goodstein, Laurie. "Christians Urged to Boycott Glenn Beck." *The Caucus: The Politics and Government Blog of the New York Times*, March 11, 2010. http://thecaucus.blogs.nytimes.com/2010/03/11/christians-urged-to-boycott-glenn-beck/.

———. "In Milwaukee Post, Cardinal Authorized Paying Abusers." *New York Times*, May 30, 2012. http://www.nytimes.com/2012/05/31/us/cardinal-authorized-payments-to-abusers.html.

Graham, Ruth. "America's Top Christian Comedian." *Slate*, September 8, 2015. http://www.slate.com/articles/life/faithbased/2015/09/jim_gaffigan_not_stephen_colbert_is_america_s_top_christian_comedian.html.

Gray, Jonathan, Jeffrey P. Jones, and Ethan Thompson. *Satire TV: Politics and Comedy in the Post-Network Era* (New York: New York University Press, 2009).

Greeley, Andrew M. "Cafeteria Catholicism: Do You Have to Eat Everything on Your Plate." *U.S. Catholic* 50 (January 1985): 18–25.

———. *The Catholic Imagination* (Berkeley: University of California Press, 2001).

Griffin, Dustin. *Satire: A Critical Reintroduction* (Lexington: University Press of Kentucky, 1994).

Grondin, David. "Understanding Culture Wars through Satirical/Political Infotainment TV: Jon Stewart and The Daily Show's Critique as Mediated Re-Enactement of the Culture War." *Canadian Review of American Studies* 42, no. 3 (January 1, 2012): 347–70.

Hangen, Tona J. *Redeeming the Dial: Radio, Religion, and Popular Culture in America* (Chapel Hill: University of North Carolina Press, 2002).

Hariman, Robert. "Political Parody and Public Culture." *Quarterly Journal of Speech* 94, no. 3 (2008): 247–72.

Hempelmann, Christian F. "'99 Nuns Giggle, 1 Nun Gasps': The Not-All-That-Christian Natural Class of Christian Jokes." *Humor: International Journal of Humor Research* 16, no. 1 (January 2003): 1.

Hengen, Shannon, ed. *Performing Gender and Comedy: Theories, Texts and Contexts* (Amsterdam: Gordon and Breach, 1998).

Hiatt, Brian. "Stephen Colbert: Rolling Stone Interview on Trump, Late Night Journey." *Rolling Stone*, August 29, 2018. https://www.rollingstone.com/tv/tv-features/stephen-colbert-late-show-rolling-stone-interview-716439/.

Hill, Josh. "Stephen Colbert Has Been Fighting Alternative Facts since 2003." *Last Night On*, January 25, 2017. https://lastnighton.com/2017/01/25/colbert-report-alternative-facts/.

Hmielowski, Jay D., R. Lance Holbert, and Jayeon Lee. "Predicting the Consumption of Political TV Satire: Affinity for Political Humor, The Daily Show, and the Colbert Report." *Communication Monographs* 78, no. 1 (2011): 96.

Hokenson, Jan. *The Idea of Comedy: History, Theory, Critique* (Madison, N.J.: Fairleigh Dickinson University Press, 2006).

Holland, Norman Norwood. *Laughing, a Psychology of Humor* (Ithaca, N.Y.: Cornell University Press, 1982).

Hoover, Stewart M. *Religion in the Media Age (Media, Religion and Culture)*. First edition (New York: Routledge, 2006).

———. *The Media and Religious Authority* (University Park: Pennsylvania State University Press, 2016).

———. "Religious Authority in the Media Age," in *The Media and Religious Authority*, ed. Stewart M. Hoover (University Park: Pennsylvania State University Press, 2016), 15–36.

Hoover, Stewart M., and Lynn Schofield Clark, eds. *Practicing Religion in the Age of the Media: Explorations in Media, Religion, and Culture* (New York: Columbia University Press, 2002).

Horsfield, Peter. "The Media and Religious Authority from Ancient to Modern," in *The Media and Religious Authority*, ed. Stewart M. Hoover (University Park: Pennsylvania State University Press, 2016), 37–66.

Horton, Shaun. "Of Pastors and Petticoats: Humor and Authority in Puritan New England." *The New England Quarterly* 82, no. 4 (2009): 608–36.

Howard, Robert Glenn. *Digital Jesus: The Making of a New Christian Fundamentalist Community on the Internet* (New York: New York University Press, 2011).

Huddleston, Tom, Jr. "'Stephen Colbert' No Longer Can Appear on 'The Late Show.'" *Fortune*, July 28, 2016. http://fortune.com/2016/07/28/stephen-colbert-late-show-lawyers/.

Hughes, Jennifer Scheper. *Biography of a Mexican Crucifix: Lived Religion and Local Faith from the Conquest to the Present* (New York: Oxford University Press, 2010).

Hunter, James Davison. *Culture Wars: The Struggle to Define America* (New York: Basic Books, 1991).

Hyers, Conrad. *And God Created Laughter: The Bible as Divine Comedy* (Atlanta: Westminster John Knox Press, 1988).

Hyers, M. Conrad, ed. *Holy Laughter: Essays on Religion in the Comic Perspective* (New York: The Seabury Press, 1969).

Itzkoff, Dave. "Jim Gaffigan on Performing Stand-Up for Pope Francis." *New York Times*, September 23, 2015. http://www.nytimes.com/2015/09/23/arts/television/jim-gaffigan-on-performing-stand-up-for-pope-francis.html.

Jenkins, Henry. *Convergence Culture: Where Old and New Media Collide* (New York: New York University Press, 2006).

Jenkins, Henry, Sam Ford, and Joshua Green. *Spreadable Media: Creating Value and Meaning in a Networked Culture* (New York: New York University Press, 2013).

Joeckel, Samuel. "Funny as Hell: Christianity and Humor Reconsidered." *Humor: International Journal of Humor Research* 21, no. 4 (October 2008): 415–33.

Jones, Jeffrey P. *Entertaining Politics: Satiric Television and Political Engagement* (Lanham, Md.: Rowman & Littlefield, 2009).

Jordan, Paul Neal. "Religious Satire in Hollywood: How Borat and Saved! Utilize the Offensive Art to Foster Interreligious Dialogue." *Religion* 1, no. 3 (2009): 85.

Kercher, Stephen E. *Revel with a Cause: Liberal Satire in Postwar America* (Chicago: University of Chicago Press, 2006).

Kesterson, David B. "Reflections and Confessions of a Humor Scholar." *Studies in American Humor* 3, no. 13 (2006): 71.

Koehlinger, Amy. "Catholic Distinctiveness and the Challenge of American Denominationalism." In *American Denominational History: Perspectives on the Past, Prospects for the Future*, ed. Keith Harper (Tuscaloosa: University of Alabama Press, 2008), 7–30.

Koehlinger, Amy, and Jeannine Hill Fletcher. "Pursuing a Field of Critical Catholic Studies." *American Catholic Studies* 125, no. 3 (2014): 5–7.

Kohut, Andrew, Carroll Doherty, Michael Dimock, and Scott Keeter. "Trends in News Consumption, 1991–2012: In Changing News Landscape, Even Television Is Vulnerable." *The Pew Research Center for The People and The Press*, September 27, 2012. http://www.people-press.org/files/legacy-pdf /2012%20News%20Consumption%20Report.pdf.

Konieczny, Mary Ellen. *The Spirit's Tether: Family, Work, and Religion among American Catholics* (New York: Oxford University Press, 2013).

Laderman, Gary. *Sacred Matters: Celebrity Worship, Sexual Ecstasies, the Living Dead, and Other Signs of Religious Life in the United States* (New York: The New Press, 2010).

LaMarre, Heather L., Kristen D. Landreville, and Michael A. Beam. "The Irony of Satire: Political Ideology and the Motivation to See What You Want to See in The Colbert Report." *The International Journal of Press/Politics* 14, no. 2 (April 1, 2009): 212–31.

Lamm, R. "Can We Laugh at God?" *Journal of Popular Film & Television* 19, no. 2 (Summer 1991): 81.

LaPlante, Joseph R. "Comedy Ties Faith, Family." *Our Sunday Visitor Catholic Publishing Company*, June 24, 2015. https://www.osv.com/Article/TabId/493 /ArtMID/13569/ArticleID/17719/Comedy-ties-faith-family.aspx.

The Late Show with Stephen Colbert, "The Late Show with Stephen Colbert: (Andrew Sullivan, Maria Shriver, Jim Gaffigan, Archbishop Thomas Wenski)." CBS, September 24, 2015.

Laude, Patrick. *Divine Play, Sacred Laughter, and Spiritual Understanding* (London: Palgrave Macmillan, 2005).

Laycock, Joseph P. "Laughing Matters: 'Parody Religions' and the Command to Compare." *Bulletin for the Study of Religion* 42, no. 3 (June 7, 2013): 19–26.

Lesley, Alison. "Stephen Colbert - Comedian, TV Host . . . Catholic?" *World Religion News*, September 12, 2015. http://www.worldreligionnews.com /religion-news/christianity/stephen-colbert-comedian-tv-host-catholic.

Lewis, Paul. *Cracking Up: American Humor in a Time of Conflict* (Chicago: University of Chicago Press, 2006).

Lewis, Todd V. "Religious Rhetoric and the Comic Frame in The Simpsons." *Journal of Media & Religion* 1, no. 3 (July 2002): 153.

Linderman, Alf. "Media and (Vicarious) Religion: Two Levels of Religious Authority." In *The Media and Religious Authority*, ed. Stewart M. Hoover (University Park: Pennsylvania State University Press, 2016), 67–80.

Lindvall, Terry. *God Mocks: A History of Religious Satire from the Hebrew Prophets to Stephen Colbert* (New York: New York University Press, 2015).

Lofton, Kathryn. "The Theodicy of George Carlin." *Religion Dispatches*, January 14, 2010. http://religiondispatches.org/the-theodicy-of-george-carlin/.

———. *Oprah: The Gospel of an Icon* (Berkeley: University of California Press, 2011).

———. *Consuming Religion* (Chicago: University of Chicago Press, 2017).

Longenecker, Fr. Dwight. "Comedians Need to Stop Taking Everything So Seriously." *National Catholic Register*, April 5, 2016. http://www.ncregister .com/blog/longenecker/comedians-need-to-stop-taking-everything-so -seriously/.

Lynch, Christopher Owen. *Selling Catholicism: Bishop Sheen and the Power of Television* (Lexington: University Press of Kentucky, 1998).

Macina, Maria, and John Mulderig. "'Jim Gaffigan Show' Treats Catholicism Seriously, but in a Funny Way." *National Catholic Reporter*, August 3, 2015. http://ncronline.org/news/art-media/jim-gaffigan-show-treats-catholicism -seriously-funny-way.

Macke, Matthew. "Reading Catholicism in Late-Night TV." *The Observer*, March 20, 2016. http://ndsmcobserver.com/2016/03/what-late-night-can-tell -us-about-catholicism-in-america/.

Manning, Patrick R. "Truth and Truthiness." *America* magazine, January 22, 2014. http://americamagazine.org/issue/truth-and-truthiness.

Marc, David. *Comic Visions: Television Comedy and American Culture* (Malden, Mass.: Wiley-Blackwell, 1997).

Marcus, Sheldon. *Father Coughlin: The Tumultuous Life of the Priest of the Little Flower* (Boston: Little, Brown, 1973).

Marshall, Kelli. "Louie's 'God' as Cathartic Television." In *Media Res: A Media Commons Project*, March 22, 2012. http://www.criticalcommons.org /Members/kellimarshall/clips/louie_god.mp4/embed_view.

Marshall, P. David. *Celebrity and Power: Fame in Contemporary Culture* (Minneapolis: University of Minnesota Press, 2014).

Martens, John W. "'Lukewarm' and '100%' Catholics." *America* magazine, October 25, 2010. http://americamagazine.org/content/good-word /lukewarm-and-100-catholics.

Martin, James. *Between Heaven and Mirth: Why Joy, Humor, and Laughter Are at the Heart of the Spiritual Life* (New York: HarperOne, 2012).

Martin, Rea Nolan. "Proud to Be a Cafeteria Catholic." *The Huffington Post*, January 28, 2014. http://www.huffingtonpost.com/rea-nolan-martin/proud -to-be-a-cafeteria-c_b_4676955.html.

Masci, David. "Who Are 'Cultural Catholics'?" *Pew Research Center*, September 3, 2015. http://www.pewresearch.org/fact-tank/2015/09/03/who-are -cultural-catholics/.

Massa, Mark S. *Catholics and American Culture: Fulton Sheen, Dorothy Day, and the Notre Dame Football Team* (New York: Crossroad, 1999).

Massa, Mark, and Catherine Osborne. *American Catholic History: A Documentary Reader* (New York: New York University Press, 2008).

Matovina, Timothy M. *Latino Catholicism: Transformation in America's Largest Church* (Princeton, N.J.: Princeton University Press, 2012).

McCartin, James P. *Prayers of the Faithful: The Shifting Spiritual Life of American Catholics* (Cambridge, Mass.: Harvard University Press, 2010).

McClennen, Sophia A. *America According to Colbert: Satire as Public Pedagogy* (New York: Palgrave Macmillan, 2011).

McCormick, Patrick. "This Jest in." *U.S. Catholic* 74, no. 6 (June 2009): 42–43.

McGrath, Charles. "How Many Stephen Colberts Are There? - NYTimes.com," *New York Times*, January 4, 2012. http://www.nytimes.com/2012/01/08 /magazine/stephen-colbert.html?pagewanted=all.

McGreevy, John T. *Parish Boundaries: The Catholic Encounter with Race in the Twentieth-Century Urban North* (Chicago: University of Chicago Press, 1998).

———. *Catholicism and American Freedom: A History* (New York: Norton, 2003).

McGuinness, Margaret M. *Called to Serve: A History of Nuns in America* (New York: New York University Press, 2013).

McIntyre, Elisha. "Knock Knocking on Heaven's Door: Humour and Religion in Mormon Comedy." In *Handbook of New Religions and Cultural Production*, ed. Carole Cusack and Alex Norman (Boston: Brill, 2012).

Meddaugh, Priscilla. "Bakhtin, Colbert, and the Center of Discourse: Is There No 'Truthiness' in Humor?" *Critical Studies in Media Communication* 27, no. 4 (2010): 376–90.

Meyer, John C. "Humor as a Double-Edged Sword: Four Functions of Humor in Communication." *Communication Theory* 10, no. 3 (August 1, 2000): 310–31.

Miller, Emily McFarlan. "A Funny Thing Happened in That Joke with the Pope Contest . . ." *Religion News Service*, October 8, 2015. http://religionnews.com /2015/10/08/funny-thing-happened-joke-pope-contest/.

Morreall, John. *Comedy, Tragedy, and Religion* (Albany: State University of New York Press, 1999).

———. *Comic Relief: A Comprehensive Philosophy of Humor* (Malden, Mass.: Wiley-Blackwell, 2009).

Morris, Charles R. *American Catholic: The Saints and Sinners Who Built America's Most Powerful Church* (New York: Vintage, 1998).

Moyer, Isabella R. "Proud to Be a Cafeteria Catholic." *USCatholic.org*, July 21, 2015. http://www.uscatholic.org/articles/201507/proud-be-cafeteria-catholic -30253.

Mullen, Lincoln. "Catholics Who Aren't Catholic." *The Atlantic*, September 8, 2015. http://www.theatlantic.com/politics/archive/2015/09/catholics-who -arent-catholic/404113/.

Nabhan-Warren, Kristy. *The Virgin of El Barrio: Marian Apparitions, Catholic Evangelizing, and Mexican American Activism* (New York: New York University Press, 2005).

———. *The Cursillo Movement in America: Catholics, Protestants, and Fourth-Day Spirituality* (Durham: University of North Carolina Press, 2013).

Oring, Elliott. *Engaging Humor* (Urbana: University of Illinois Press, 2008).

Orsi, Robert A. *Thank You, St. Jude: Women's Devotion to the Patron Saint of Hopeless Causes* (New Haven, Conn.: Yale University Press, 1998).

———. *Between Heaven and Earth: The Religious Worlds People Make and the Scholars Who Study Them* (Princeton, N.J.: Princeton University Press, 2006).

———. *The Madonna of 115th Street: Faith and Community in Italian Harlem, 1880–1950*, Third edition (New Haven, Conn.: Yale University Press, 2010).

Palmer, James C. "An Analysis of the Themes of Bishop Fulton J. Sheen's TV Talks." *The Southern Speech Journal* 30, no. 3 (March 1, 1965): 223–30.

Polhemus, Robert M. *Comic Faith: The Great Tradition from Austen to Joyce* (Chicago: University of Chicago Press, 1982).

Pritchard, Elizabeth A. "Seriously, What Does 'Taking Religion Seriously' Mean?" *Journal of the American Academy of Religion* 78, no. 4 (December 1, 2010): 1087–111.

Provenza, Paul, and Dan Dion. *Satiristas: Comedians, Contrarians, Raconteurs & Vulgarians* (New York: It Books, 2010).

Rabin, Nathan. "Louie: 'God,'" *AV Club*, August 31, 2010. http://www.avclub .com/tvclub/louie-god-44549.

Rezac, Mary. "Meet the Man behind the Mysterious Eye of the Tiber." *Catholic News Agency*, January 2, 2016. http://www.catholicnewsagency.com/news /whos-behind-the-mysterious-eye-of-the-tiber-70906/.

Robinson, Kara Mayer. "Comedian Jim Gaffigan Takes Sundays off from Stand-Up." *New York Times*, May 10, 2013. http://www.nytimes.com/2013/05 /12/nyregion/comedian-jim-gaffigan-takes-sundays-off-from-stand-up.html.

Roof, Wade Clark. *A Generation of Seekers: The Spiritual Journeys of the Baby Boom Generation* (San Francisco: Harper, 1993).

———. *Spiritual Marketplace: Baby Boomers and the Remaking of American Religion* (Princeton, N.J.: Princeton University Press, 2001).

Rogak, Lisa. *And Nothing But the Truthiness: The Rise (and Further Rise) of Stephen Colbert* (New York: Thomas Dunne, 2011).

Schofield Clark, Lynn. "Religion and Authority in a Remix Culture: How a Late Night TV Host Became an Authority on Religion." In *Religion, Media and Culture: A Reader*, ed. Gordon Lynch, Jolyon P Mitchell, and Anna Strhan (New York: Routledge, 2012).

———. "Afterword: The Media and Religious Authority." In *The Media and Religious Authority*, ed. Stewart M. Hoover (University Park: Pennsylvania State University Press, 2016), 253–67.

Shafer, Ingrid. "Introduction: The Catholic Imagination in Popular Film and Television." *Journal of Popular Film and Television* 19, no. 2 (Summer 1991): 50–57.

Sheedy, Matt K., and David Feltmate. "Humor and Religion: An Interview with David Feltmate." *Bulletin for the Study of Religion* 42, no. 3 (August 3, 2013): 43–46.

Shouse, Eric, and Bernard Timberg. "A Festivus for the Restivus: Jewish-American Comedians Respond to Christmas as the National American Holiday." *Humor: International Journal of Humor Research* 25, no. 2 (April 2012): 133–53.

Smith, Anthony Burke. *The Look of Catholics: Portrayals in Popular Culture from the Great Depression to the Cold War* (Lawrence: University Press of Kansas, 2010).

Stever, Gayle S. "Celebrity Worship: Critiquing a Construct." *Journal of Applied Social Psychology* 41, no. 6 (June 1, 2011): 1356–70.

Strauss, Neil. "Stephen Colbert on Deconstructing the Colbert Nation." *Rolling Stone*, September 2, 2009. http://www.rollingstone.com/culture/news /stephen-colbert-on-deconstructing-the-news-religion-and-the-colbert -nation-20090902.

———. "The Subversive Joy of Stephen Colbert." *Rolling Stone*, September 17, 2009. http://www.rollingstone.com/movies/news/the-subversive-joy-of -stephen-colbert-20090917.

Sullivan, James. *Seven Dirty Words: The Life and Crimes of George Carlin* (New York: Da Capo, 2011).

Swartz, David R. *Moral Minority: The Evangelical Left in an Age of Conservatism* (Philadelphia: University of Pennsylvania Press, 2012).

Tanny, Jarrod. "The Anti-Gospel of Lenny, Larry and Sarah: Jewish Humor and the Desecration of Christendom." *American Jewish History* 99, no. 2 (2015): 167–93.

Taylor, Sarah McFarland. *Green Sisters: A Spiritual Ecology* (Cambridge, Mass.: Harvard University Press, 2007).

Thussu, Daya Kishan. *News as Entertainment: The Rise of Global Infotainment* (London: SAGE, 2008).

Tracy, David. *The Analogical Imagination: Christian Theology and the Culture of Pluralism* (New York: Crossroad, 1981).

Vanity Fair, and The Scene. "Conan O'Brien, Stephen Colbert, and Other Late Night Hosts Describe Each Other With One Word." *Vanity Fair Videos,* September 16, 2015. https://thescene.com/watch/vanityfair/conan-o-brien -stephen-colbert-and-other-late-night-hosts-describe-each-other-with-one -word.

Veale, Tony. "Incongruity in Humor: Root Cause or Epiphenomenon?" *Humor: International Journal of Humor Research* 17, no. 4 (October 2004): 419–28.

Wagner, Rachel. *Godwired: Religion, Ritual, and Virtual Reality* (New York: Routledge, 2012).

Waisanen, Don J. "A Citizen's Guide to Democracy Inaction: Jon Stewart and Stephen Colbert's Comic Rhetorical Criticism." *Southern Communication Journal* 74, no. 2 (April 28, 2009): 119–40.

Walker, Nancy A. *A Very Serious Thing: Women's Humor and American Culture* (Minneapolis: University of Minnesota Press, 1988).

Walker, Nancy A., ed. *What's So Funny? Humor in American Culture* (Wilmington, Del.: Rowman & Littlefield, 1998).

Walton, Jonathan L. *Watch This! The Ethics and Aesthetics of Black Televangelism* (New York: New York University Press, 2009).

Ward, Louis B. *Father Charles E. Coughlin: An Authorized Biography.* Detroit: Tower, 1933.

Warren, Donald. *Radio Priest: Charles Coughlin, the Father of Hate Radio* (New York: Free Press, 1996).

Watkins, Mel. *On the Real Side: A History of African American Comedy* (Chicago: Lawrence Hill, 1999).

Weaver, Mary Jo. *What's Left? Liberal American Catholics* (Bloomington: Indiana University Press, 1999).

Weaver, Mary Jo, and R. Scott Appleby. *Being Right: Conservative Catholics in America* (Bloomington: Indiana University Press, 1995).

Weaver, Simon. "The 'Other' Laughs Back: Humour and Resistance in Anti-Racist Comedy." *Sociology* 44, no. 1 (2010): 31–48.

Weinstein, David. *The Forgotten Network: DuMont and the Birth of American Television* (Philadelphia: Temple University Press, 2006).

Weisenfeld, Judith. *Hollywood Be Thy Name: African American Religion in American Film, 1929–1949* (Berkeley: University of California Press, 2007).

Welch, Derek. "'Eye of the Tiber' - The Catholic Answer to 'The Onion,'" *World Religion News*, January 11, 2016. http://www.worldreligionnews.com/religion-news/christianity/eye-of-the-tiber-the-catholic-answer-to-the-onion.

Williams, Peter W. *America's Religions: From Their Origins to the Twenty-First Century*, Fourth edition (Urbana: University of Illinois Press, 2015).

Winston, Diane. *Small Screen, Big Picture: Television and Lived Religion* (Waco, Tex.: Baylor University Press, 2009).

———. *The Oxford Handbook of Religion and the American News Media* (New York: Oxford University Press, 2012).

Winston, Kimberly. "Stephen Colbert May Play Religion for Laughs, but His Thoughtful Catholicism Still Shows Through." *Washington Post*, October 15, 2010, sec. Religion. http://www.washingtonpost.com/wp-dyn/content/article/2010/10/15/AR2010101505758.html.

Wisse, Ruth R. *No Joke: Making Jewish Humor* (Princeton, N.J.: Princeton University Press, 2013).

Wong, Julia Carrie. "Who's Afraid of Suey Park?" *The Nation*, March 31, 2014. http://www.thenation.com/article/whos-afraid-suey-park/.

Wuthnow, Robert. *The Restructuring of American Religion* (Princeton, N.J.: Princeton University Press, 1988).

———. *After the Baby Boomers: How Twenty- and Thirty-Somethings Are Shaping the Future of American Religion* (Princeton, N.J.: Princeton University Press, 2010).

Young, Dannagal G., and Russell M. Tisinger. "Dispelling Late-Night Myths." *The Harvard International Journal of Press/Politics* 11, no. 3 (Summer 2006): 113–34.

Zimmer, Ben. "Truthiness." *New York Times*, October 13, 2010. http://www.nytimes.com/2010/10/17/magazine/17FOB-onlanguage-t.html.

Index

Stephen Colbert in small caps refers to the character played by Stephen Colbert.

African American humor, 78
aggiornamento, 103
Ailes, Roger, 139
à la carte (cafeteria) Catholics, 7–8, 104, 108–12, 194n30
Aleichem, Sholem, 188n17
Alfred E. Smith Memorial Foundation dinner, 69–70
Allen, John L., Jr., 120
Alper, Bob, 84
America (Jesuit magazine): about, 64–65; on Catholic League's censorship, 121; on Colbert's evangelizing style, 2; on lukewarm Catholics, 107
American Catholics in Transition (D'Antonio, Dillon, and Gautier), 110
American Civil Liberties Union, 120
American Dialect Society, 13
"The American River Ganges" (cartoon), 101
Angelica, Mother, 24
Annenberg Public Policy Center study, on *The Colbert Report's* news reporting, 6
anti-Catholicism, 6–7, 29, 34–35, 102, 120–23, 180n19
Antonio Federrici ice cream, 96–97
Arrupe, Pedro, 67
Avenue Q (musical), 77
The Awful Disclosures of Maria Monk (Monk), 101

Baby Boomer generation, 87, 136
Baggett, Jerome, 110
Bakhtin, Mikhail, 78
Baym, Geoffrey, 139

Beale, Stephen, 84
Beck, Glenn, 65–66, 142–43
Bee, Samantha, 153–54
Beecher, Lyman, 35
The Bells of St. Mary's (film), 24
benediction, 144–45
Benedict XVI (pope), 10, 62, 68, 130
Berger, Arthur Asa, 12, 55
Berle, Milton, 32–33
Between Heaven and Mirth (Martin), 69
Biden, Beau, 155–56
Biden, Joe, 21, 155–56
bin Laden, Osama, 45
BishopAccountability.org, 124, 196n71
Bismarck, Otto von, 132
Boorstein, Michelle, 92
"born again," 73–74
Boskin, Joseph, 12
Boston Globe, clerical sexual abuse scandal, 158–59
Brown, Dan, 126
Bruce, Lenny, 87, 89
Bush, George W., 4, 45
Busted Halo (media site), 72

cafeteria (à la carte) Catholics, 7–8, 104, 108–12, 194n30
Canadian Salt and Light Catholic Media Foundation, 73–74
#cancelcolbert, 21, 148–51
Captain Catholicism, 2, 48, 57–63, 70, 75
Carbone, Christopher, 149
"The Cardinal and Colbert" debate event, 70–72, 118
Carlin, George, 76–77, 87–90, 96, 98, 125

Carlin, Mary, 89
Carson, Johnny, 1, 48
catechism humor: of Colbert, 2, 20–21, 48–57, 63–75, 117–18; COLBERT as Captain Catholicism, 2, 48, 57–63, 70, 75; of institutional authority, 32–34
Catholic Bishops of Latin America (CELAM), 67
Catholic exceptionalism, 104, 116–17
Catholic guilt, 106, 157
Catholic Hour (radio broadcast), 33
Catholic humor: categories of, 76–85, 98; catharsis of, 90–91; Catholic identity and, 20, 25, 46, 69–71, 76–77, 95–98, 153–54; in culture wars, 134–39; defined, 76–77; overview, 3, 12–13; patron saint of comedians, 161; religious authorities use of, 36–47; religious authority confrontations as, 87–90; religious authority parodies, 85–86; sacred and profane distinction in, 54–55; sanctioned comedy, 91–95; stereotypes and, 49, 51–57, 80–85, 158. *See also* catechism humor; *specific comedians*
Catholic Identity (Dillon), 110
Catholic imagination, 32, 181–82n43
Catholic League for Religious and Civil Rights, 120, 121–23
Catholics and Catholicism: anti-Catholicism and, 6–7, 29, 34–35, 102, 120–23, 180n19; Colbert's influence on, 2–3, 7–8 (*see also* Colbert Catholicism); defined, 6, 8–9; historical context, 6–7, 9, 100–2; influence on Colbert, 2–3, 6–10, 23, 25, 70–75, 154–57; multiplicity of, 7–9, 13, 21, 57–63, 98, 102–12 (*see also specific types of Catholics*); paradox of, 8–10; patriotism and, 31, 35, 39–40; sex abuse scandal, 21, 94, 97–98, 123–30, 158–59. *See also* catechism humor; Catholic humor; culture wars; identity (religious); religious authorities
Catholics-in-name-only (CINOs), 109
Catholic University of America, 92–93

Catholic Worker movement, 66, 101
CBS Sunday Morning, 38, 94–95
Chaplain of Colbert Nation. *See* Martin, Father James
Chapman, Roger, 133
Chaput, Charles J., 94
Christian Century (magazine), on Sheen, 34–35
Chu, Arthur, 150
Church of the Little Flower (Detroit), 29–30
CINOs (Catholics-in-name-only), 109
C.K., Louis, 76–77, 90–91, 96, 98, 125–26
Claassen, Ryan L., 133
Clark, Lynn Schofield, 11, 17, 27
clergy sex abuse scandal, 21, 94, 97–98, 123–30, 158–59
Cohen, Sacha Baron, 86
Colbert, Stephen: as America's most famous Catholic, 7 (*see also* STEPHEN COLBERT); analysis of, 17–20; as cafeteria Catholic, 8, 110–12; catechism of, 2, 20–21, 48–57, 63–75, 117–18; as Catholic comedian, 20, 25, 46, 69–71, 76–77, 95–98; Catholic humor of, 76–80; Catholic identity of, 2–3, 6–10, 23, 25, 70–75, 148–51, 154–57; on COLBERT character development, 1–2, 4, 21, 48, 139–42; on coping with tragedy, 21, 114–17, 155–56; on difficulty of maintaining COLBERT persona, 71, 73–74, 161–62; early life, 38, 115; multiplicity of, 7, 13, 16–17, 21, 59–63, 73–75, 98, 110–12, 131; on Novello, 85–90; on O'Reilly, 140; post-COLBERT, 153–61, 163–64; priest fandom of, 63–65, 69; "Rally to Restore Sanity and/or Fear" (2010), 11, 21, 86, 142–47; as reflection of contemporary American Catholicism, 2–3, 7–9 (*see also* Colbert Catholicism); as religious authority, 25–28, 39–40, 42, 46–47, 63–65, 69, 72–73, 97–98, 129–30, 159–61; transmediation of, 10–11, 16–17, 27–28, 148–49; on truthiness, 15.

See also Colbert Catholicism; *The Colbert Report*

Colbert Catholicism: basis for, 113–14; on conflict within the Catholic Church, 123–31; context of, 100–4; defined, 99–100, 112–13, 156; overview, 2–3, 7–9, 21; response to anti-Catholicism by, 102, 120–23; tenets of, 114–20, 155–58

Colbert Nation: chaplain of, 18, 25, 46, 64–65 (*see also* Martin, Father James); demographics, 49–50, 136–39; #IStandWithColbert, 150; transmediation of Colbert and COLBERT by, 5, 10–11, 25

ColbertNation.com, 5

Colbert-NewsHub.com, 11

The Colbert Report: "2011–A Rock Odyssey featuring Jack White—Catholic Throwdown" episode, 20, 51–54, 55–57; analysis of, 13–19, 42–43, 45–46, 165–71; Brown as guest on, 126–29; #cancelcolbert culture war, 148–51; on clergy sex abuse scandal, 123–29; conclusion of, 21, 152–53; as *Daily Show* spin off, 38; debut, 2, 4, 13; Donohue as guest on, 120–23; as infotainment parody, 4–6, 12, 32, 46; as news source, 6; O'Reilly as guest on, 139–41; "Paul Ryan's Christian Budget Cuts," 60–61; popularity of, 4–5 (*see also* Colbert Nation); priest fandom on, 63–69, 129–31; "Rally to Restore Sanity and/or Fear" (2010), 11, 21, 86, 142–47; transmediation of, 138–39; Wills as guest on, 105–6; "The Wørd," 13; "Yahweh or No Way," 20, 23–24, 25, 38–43, 45, 46. *See also* STEPHEN COLBERT

comedians, patron saint of, 161

comedy-religion intersection. *See* catechism humor; Catholic humor; satirical commentary

communal Catholics, 105

Conan (television program), 93–94

Conservapedia.com, 8, 110

Consuming Religion (Lofton), 16–17

Corden, James, 153

Corpus Christi Grammar School (New York City), 88, 89

Coughlin, Father Charles, 24, 28, 29–32, 46

Crosby, Bing, 24

cultural Catholics, 105, 106–7, 157, 194nn21–22

cultural narcissism, 10

culture wars: #cancelcolbert as, 148–51; of Catholic identity, 59–60; Colbert's influence on, 2–3; Coughlin and, 29–32; defined, 132; overview, 21, 132–33; political polarization and, 11, 12–13, 21, 86, 134, 142–47; religious context of, 132–39; stereotypes and, 134–35, 139–47

Culture Wars: The Struggle to Define America (Hunter), 132–33

Cushing, Richard Cardinal, 88

Cutié, Alberto R., 63

The Daily Show (television program), 4, 5, 38, 41, 79, 143, 154. *See also* Stewart, Jon

Dante Alighieri, 82

D'Antonio, William, 110

Davies, Christie, 77, 80

Dawkins, Richard, 118, 138

Day, Amber, 14

Day, Dorothy, 66, 101

de Chardin, Pierre Teilhard, 69

del Rio, Sarah, 109–10

Deresiewicz, William, 10

Dierberg, Jill, 17

digital age: defined, 19; political polarization and, 12–13; religious authority decentralization in, 20, 23–28

Dillon, Michele, 110

Dionne, E. J., 132

The Divine Comedy (Dante), 82

Dix, Tara, 82

Dogma (film), 87

Dolan, Cardinal Timothy, 69–71, 118, 129–31

Dolan, Jay P., 24, 59–60, 180n19

Dolan, Timothy, 10, 25

Donohue, William, 120–22

DuMont Television Network, 32

Durkheim, Émile, 54

Ebersol, Dick, 89
Eisenhower, Dwight, 127
Emanuel AME Church shootings (2015), 115
Emerson, Matt, 96
Encyclopedia of Humor Studies, 78
Eternal Word Television Net-work (EWTN), 24
ex-Catholics (lapsed Catholics), 102, 108, 122–23, 157
Eye of the Tiber (fake news website), 83

Fallon, Jimmy, 20, 84, 154
Falwell, Jerry, 119, 132
fans of Colbert. *See* Colbert Nation
F.C.C. v. Pacifica Foundation (1978), 87, 89
Federal Communications Commission, 87, 88, 89
Ferraro, Thomas J., 106, 194n21
Festival of Families (2015), 94
Fidelity (magazine), on à la carte Catholicism, 194n30
Fordham University, 70–72, 113, 118
Forerunners of American Fascism (Swing), 30
Foxworthy, Jeff, 77
Francis (pope), 2, 21, 62–63, 84, 93–95, 129–30, 159–61
Frandzone, Jonathan, 149
Fresh Air (radio show), 90, 152–53
Freud, Sigmund, 12, 55, 77–78, 80, 141
Fuller, Robert C., 136

Gaffigan, Jeanne, 92–93
Gaffigan, Jim, 76–77, 91–95, 96, 98, 159–60
Gallagher, Michael J., 29, 31
García, Alan, 45
Gates, Henry Louis, Jr., 57–58
Gautier, Mary, 110
Genesius (saint), 161
Giddens, Anthony, 26–27, 179n9
Gilbert, Joanne, 79
The Glenn Beck Program (radio and streaming program), 66
Glenview Announcements (newspaper), Colbert on O'Reilly in, 140
Goodstein, Laurie, 118
GQ (magazine), on Colbert's religious conceptions, 114–17

Graham, Ruth, 95
Gray, Jonathan, 13–14
Greeley, Andrew, 104–5, 108, 181–82n43
Gross, Terry, 90, 152–53, 154, 161

Hall, David, 175n3
Hangen, Tona, 28–29
Hannity, Sean, 37
Hannity & Colmes, 5
Hardy, Bruce W., 6, 13
Hariman, Robert, 14–15
Heaton, Patricia, 155
Heine, Heinrich, 188n17
Herberg, Will, 101
Heritage Foundation, 120
Hervieu-Leger, Danièle, 175n3
high modernity, 26, 179n9
Hitchens, Christopher, 65, 118
Hitler, Adolf, 31
Hoover, Stewart, 11, 27
Houdek, Diane, 98
Hunter, James Davison, 132–33

identity (religious): catechism of, 57–63, 70; Colbert as Catholic comedian, 20, 25, 46, 69–71, 76–77, 95–98, 153–54; of COLBERT, 2, 48, 57–63, 70, 75; of Colbert Nation, 49–50, 136–39; methodology for analysis of, 3–4
Idle, Eric, 12
incongruity theory, 77–78
infotainment: catechism of, 20, 48–57; Catholic identity and, 57–63, 70; consequences of, 6; by institutional authorities, 29–32; parody of, 4–5, 13–17 (*see also* "truthiness")
institutional authorities. *See* religious authorities
institutional Catholics, 105
International Organization of Marianist Lay Communities, 109
irony. *See* satirical commentary
Isom, Jacob, 144
#IStandWithColbert, 150

Jacobs, Lawrence R., 12
Jamieson, Kathleen Hall, 13
Jesuits of Latin America, 67

Jewish humor, 79–80, 188n17
The Jim Gaffigan Show (television program), 91–92, 94
Joel, Billy, 44
John Paul II (pope), 45, 67
Johnson, Sylvester, 133
Jokes and Their Relation to the Unconscious (Freud), 80
JokeWiththePope.org, 84
Jones, E. Michael, 194n30
Jones, Jeffrey P., 13–14, 39
Jones, Terry, 144
Joyce, James, 82

Kaell, Hillary, 62
Kandra, Greg, 153
Kelly, John, 95
Kennedy, John F., 102
Killing Jesus (O'Reilly), 141
Kimmel, Jimmy, 154
King, Alveda, 142
King, Martin Luther, Jr., 142
KKK (Ku Klux Klan), 29, 78, 102
Know-Nothing Party, 101
Knox College, 16
Konieczny, Mary Ellen, 104
Ku Klux Klan (KKK), 29, 78, 102
Kulturkampf, 132

Laderman, Gary, 17
lapsed Catholics (ex-Catholics), 102, 108, 122–23, 157
The Late Show (television program), 5, 152, 153–61
The Late Show with Stephen Colbert: analysis of, 19; announcement of, 18; Biden interview on, 155–56; catechizing on, 21–22; Colbert's Catholic identity on, 154–57; "Stephen Colbert's Midnight Confessions," 156–58; support for the institutional Catholic Church on, 158–61; "Tour De Francis," 159–60
Latour, Bruno, 133
The Lazlo Letters (Novello), 85–86
Lesley, Alison, 154
Letterman, David, 1, 48, 152
Liebling, Deborah, 78–79
Life Is Worth Living (television program), 32–35

Lincoln, Bruce, 27
Lindvall, Terry, 96
lived religion, 3–4, 11–12, 19–20, 63–64, 175n3
Live on Broadway (HBO special), 125
Lofton, Kathryn, 16–17
Louie (television program), 90–91
Lovell, Joel, 114–17, 118
Lucky Louie (television program), 90
lukewarm Catholics, 104, 107–8
Lynch, Christopher Owen, 34

Madea films, 78
Maher, Bill, 118, 153, 154
Malkin, Michelle, 148
Marcus, Sheldon, 31
marginalization: defined, 77; humor of the marginalized, 76, 77–81, 92–93; as identity maker, 44–45, 77; stereotypes of, 9, 76–81, 99–100, 102
Marianist Lay Communities, 109
Martens, John W., 107
Martin, Father James, 10, 18, 25–26, 46, 50, 64–70, 96, 108, 114
Martin, Rea Nolan, 108–9
Marx, Karl, 31
Massa, Mark, 34, 121
mass media religious authority figures. *See* Colbert, Stephen; Coughlin, Father Charles; Martin, Father James; Sheen, Bishop Fulton J.; STEPHEN COLBERT
McBrien, Father, 194n30
McCartin, James P., 102–3
McGrath, Charles, 16
media age. *See* digital age
media ethnography, 19
Merton, Thomas, 64, 88
Meyers, Seth, 153
Michaels, Lorne, 89
millennials, 136–37
modernity, 26–27, 133–34, 179n9
Modernity and Self-Identity (Giddens), 26
Modernity's Wager (Seligman), 26
Monty Python, 12
Morality in Media, 89
Moral Majority, 132
Moyer, Isabella, 109

Murray, Bill, 84
Mussolini, Benito, 31

Naoum, SC, 83
Nast, Thomas, 101
National Catholic Reporter: named Colbert as "Runner-up to Person on the Year," 2; on Gaffigan, 92
National Union for Social Justice, 30
NBC's Saturday Night (television program), 87. See also *Saturday Night Live*
Newman, Randy, 152
"new voluntarism," 104
New York Times: on Colbert's religious humor, 118; on Mother Teresa's letters, 64–65; on O'Reilly's sexual harassment settlements, 140; on sexual misconduct accusations against C.K., 91
New York Times Magazine: on Dolan's involvement in priest sex abuse scandal, 129; on Novello, 86
Nienstedt, John, 107
Nixon, Richard, 127, 132
Noah, Trevor, 154
nofactzone.net, 11
Nostrae Aetate (Declaration on the Relation of the Church with Non-Christian Religions), 103
Novello, Antonia, 86
Novello, Don, 76–77, 85–86, 98, 145

Obama, Barack, 45, 60–61, 62–63
O'Brien, Conan, 1, 20, 48, 93–94, 154
The Onion, 83
The Oprah Winfrey Show, 5
O'Reilly, Bill, 4, 37, 139–42
The O'Reilly Factor (television program), 4, 139–40
Oring, Elliott, 80
Orsi, Robert A., 175n3
Our Father prayer, 44, 57

Palin, Sarah, 62, 142
Park, Suey, 148–51
parody. *See The Colbert Report*; satirical commentary; STEPHEN COLBERT; "truthiness"
patriotism, 31, 35, 39–40

Perry, Tyler, 78
Pew Research Center: on cultural Catholicism, 106–7; on religious service attendance, 137
Plea for the West (Beecher), 35
Polish Americans, 77
political humor, 40–41, 43, 60–62
Pontifical Mission Societies, 84
presidential election (1928), 29
presidential election (1932), 30
presidential election (2016), 22, 134, 155, 161–63
priest sex abuse scandal, 21, 94, 97–98, 123–30, 158–59
profane, defined, 54–55
Protestant, Catholic, Jew (Herberg), 101
Protestant imagination, 181–82n43
Protestants and Protestantism: COLBERT on, 63, 97, 122; culture wars and, 9, 31, 34–35, 80, 101–2, 134–37, 141–42; demographics, 6; mass media use by, 24
"The Protocols of the Elders of Zion," 31
Provenza, Paul, 117
Psychology Today (magazine), on Jewish humor, 79

Rabin, Nathan, 39–40
"Radio Priest." *See* Coughlin, Father Charles
Radio Priest (Warren), 30
"Rally to Restore Sanity and/or Fear" (2010), 11, 21, 86, 142–47
Reddit (online discussion forum), 111–12
Redeeming the Dial (Hangen), 28–29
relief theory, 78
religion-humor intersection. *See* Catholic humor; satirical commentary
religious authorities: Colbert as, 25–28, 39–40, 42, 46–47, 63–65, 69, 72–73, 97–98, 129–30, 159–61; COLBERT as, 20, 23–28, 37–47; COLBERT on, 97–98; comedic confrontations of, 87–89, 97–98; institutional authority overview, 3–4, 6–7, 9–10, 12, 19–20; parodies of, 85–86; roles of, 70–72

religious identity. *See* identity (religious)

"Restoring Honor" rally (2010), 142–43

Robertson, Pat, 61

Rocca, Mo, 38

Rolling Stone (magazine): on Colbert as a religious teacher, 50; on truthiness, 15; on "Yahweh or No Way" segments, 38–39

Roman, Rachel, 72

Roman Catholic Church. *See* Catholics and Catholicism

Roof, Wade Clark, 136

Roosevelt, Franklin D., 30

Rosica, Thomas, 73–75

Roth, Philip, 80

Ruffalo, Mark, 158–59

Rulli, Lino, 84

Ryan, Paul, 60–61

sacrality, of celebrities, 17

sacredness, 54–55, 115

sanctioned Catholic comedy, 91–95

Satire TV (Gray, Thompson, and Jones), 13–14

satirical commentary, 2–6, 7, 9–10, 12–15, 20–21, 32, 46. See also *The Colbert Report*; STEPHEN COLBERT; "truthiness"

Saturday Night Live (television program), 86, 88–89

Savage, Dan, 123

Schlafly, Andrew, 8

Schultz, Kevin, 102

Second Vatican Council, 9, 103–5

"seeker-centered" generation, 8, 26–27, 104, 136

Seligman, Adam, 26

The Seven Storey Mountain (Merton), 64

sex abuse clergy scandal, 21, 94, 97–98, 123–30, 158–59

Shafer, Ingrid, 181–82n43

Sheen, Bishop Fulton J., 24–25, 28, 32–37, 46

Shriver, Maria, 159

Siegler, Elijah, 11–12

Silent Majority, 132

Silk, Mark, 121

Smith, Alfred E., 29, 101, 180n19

Smith, Anthony Burke, 33

The Smothers Brothers Show (television program), 86

Sobrado, Carl, 72

Social Justice (periodical), 30

Society of Jesus (Jesuits), 67

Spiritual, but Not Religious: Understanding Unchurched America (Fuller), 136

spiritual but not religious (SBNRs), 3, 136–38

Spotlight (film), 124, 158–59

Stegner, Wallace, 30

STEPHEN COLBERT: analysis of, 17–19; anti-Catholicism response by, 102, 120–23; as Captain Catholicism, 2, 48, 57–63, 70, 75; catechism of identity and, 57–63, 117–18; Catholic identity of, 95–98; on celibacy, 63; character development of, 1–2, 4, 21, 48, 139–42; Colbert's difficulty on maintaining persona, 161–62; on conflict within the Catholic Church, 123–31; infotainment-catechism of, 48–57; irony and, 12–13; on popes, 62–63; post–*Colbert Report*, 22; on Protestantism, 63, 97, 122; as reflection of contemporary American Catholicism, 2–3, 7–10, 21; as religious authority, 20, 23–28, 37–47; on religious authority, 97–98; as television's foremost Catholic, 2, 7; transmediation of, 10–11, 16–17, 25; truthiness and, 13–17, 140–42

@Stephenathome, 5, 148–49

stereotypes: culture wars and, 134–35, 138, 139–47; humor and, 49, 51–57, 78–85, 158; of marginalized groups, 9, 76–81, 99–100, 102; sociological categories of, 102–12

Stewart, Jon, 11, 21, 79, 86, 142–47, 152

Stewart, Martha, 58

Strauss, Neil, 50

Sullivan, Andrew, 159–60

Sullivan, James, 87

superiority theory, 77

Survivors Network of those Abused by Priests (SNAP), 129

Swing, Raymond, 29–30

Székely, Louis. *See* C.K., Louis

Taves, Ann, 55
Taylor, Charles, 133–34
televangelism, 46–47
Thomas Ferraro, 106
Thompson, Ethan, 13–14
Thomson, Irene Taviss, 133
Time (magazine), cover story on Sheen, 33
Titus, Christopher, 125
Tolkien, J. R. R., 115
The Tonight Show (television program), 87
Toth, Lazlo, 85
Tracy, David, 181–82n43
tragedy, coping with, 21, 114–17, 155–56
Trump, Donald J., 84, 161–63
"truthiness": defined, 16, 69; of institutional authority, 38, 46; presidential election (2016) and, 22, 134, 161–63; as satirical commentary, 13–17, 69–70, 140–42
Tueth, Michael, 153

unchurched, 136–38
USCatholic blog, 109
U.S. Catholic Magazine: on cafeteria Catholics, 108–9; on Catholic humor, 82

van Elteren, Mel, 10
Vatican II. *See* Second Vatican Council

Wahlberg, Mark, 94
Warren, Donald, 29, 30, 32
Washington Post, on culture wars, 132
"We Didn't Start the Fire" (Joel), 44
We Have Never Been Modern (Latour), 133
Wenski, Thomas, 161
When Will Jesus Bring the Pork Chops (Carlin), 87, 125
White, Jack, 20, 51–54, 55–57
Why Priests? A Failed Tradition (Wills), 105–6
Williams, Robin, 125
Wills, Garry, 105–6
Wilmore, Larry, 154
Winfrey, Oprah, 5
Winston, Diane, 11
Wisse, Ruth R., 188n17
The Witness (television show), 73–75
The Wizard of Oz (film), 42
Wong, Julia Carrie, 150
World Religion News, on Colbert's religion, 154

Zimbardo, Philip, 97

STEPHANIE N. BREHM holds a PhD in religious studies and is an administrator-scholar at Northwestern University.

CATHOLIC PRACTICE IN NORTH AMERICA

JOHN C. SEITZ, SERIES EDITOR

James T. Fisher and Margaret M. McGuinness (eds.), *The Catholic Studies Reader*

Jeremy Bonner, Christopher D. Denny, and Mary Beth Fraser Connolly (eds.), *Empowering the People of God: Catholic Action before and after Vatican II*

Christine Firer Hinze and J. Patrick Hornbeck II (eds.), *More than a Monologue: Sexual Diversity and the Catholic Church. Volume I: Voices of Our Times*

J. Patrick Hornbeck II and Michael A. Norko (eds.), *More than a Monologue: Sexual Diversity and the Catholic Church. Volume II: Inquiry, Thought, and Expression*

Jack Lee Downey, *The Bread of the Strong:* Lacouturisme *and the Folly of the Cross, 1910–1985*

Michael McGregor, *Pure Act: The Uncommon Life of Robert Lax*

Mary Dunn, *The Cruelest of All Mothers: Marie de l'Incarnation, Motherhood, and Christian Tradition*

Dorothy Day and the Catholic Worker: The Miracle of Our Continuance. Photographs by Vivian Cherry, Text by Dorothy Day, Edited with an Introduction and Additional Text by Kate Hennessy

Nicholas K. Rademacher, *Paul Hanly Furfey: Priest, Scientist, Social Reformer*

Margaret M. McGuinness and James T. Fisher (eds.), *Roman Catholicism in the United States: A Thematic History*

Gary J. Adler Jr., Tricia C. Bruce, and Brian Starks (eds.), *American Parishes: Remaking Local Catholicism*

Stephanie N. Brehm, *America's Most Famous Catholic (According to Himself): Stephen Colbert and American Religion in the Twenty-First Century*